Using French
(le français en pratiqu

Day by day method
ASSiMiL

Using French
(le français en pratique)

by

Anthony BULGER

with the editorial assistance of
Jean-Loup CHEREL

illustrations by J.-L. Goussé

B.P. 25
94431 Chennevières-sur-Marne Cedex
FRANCE

ISBN : 2.7005.0109-8

METHOD BOOKS

Bound books, lavishly illustrated, containing lessons and
exercises recorded on cassettes and CDs

Arabic with ease
Dutch with ease
New French with ease
Using French
Business French
German with ease
Hungarian with ease
Italian with ease
Spanish with ease
Using Spanish

INTRODUCTION

This companion volume to our **French with Ease** takes you further into the study of the languge - and more. We give you some of the keys to unlock the mysteries contained in the language. Not just its grammar but how it influences, and is influenced by the people who speak it.

The first volume considered language as behaviour; this book looks at it as a reflection of its environment.

Who is this book for?

If you have finished **French with Ease,** or if you have a **good intermediate knowledge,** which covers the major tenses and their aspects (present, future, *passé composé,* conditional and a basic grounding in the present subjunctive), the formation and position of adjectives and adverbs and a vocabulary of some 500 words, then you are ready.

What will you learn?

That depends on you! What this book contains is an elaboration of the points already mentioned, the introduction of other more literary verb tenses and the development and exploration of all those little details which make the difference between speaking French and having an instinctive feeling for the language.

We also cover questions of register - which words and expressions are appropriate to which circumstances, official language, the media, some literature, and we also take you on a brief tour around the regions of France to give you a broader idea of the country.

Naturally, we do not have the pretension to present the whole French language - this is a practical method, not a reference book - but we hope that, by the end of the seventy lessons, both your active and passive knowledge will have increased at the same rate as your awareness of its origins, developments and particularities and your feeling for the country and its culture.

How is all this presented?

This is an ASSIMIL method with all the traditional ingredients: **daily lessons** broken down into separate parts with notes, explanations and exercices. The situations chosen are functional, notional and humorous and there are suggestions for further study.

How do you approach the method?

Rule One is relax and enjoy it. Especially at an intermediate level, the learner has the impression that further progress is terribly difficult since he tends to see progress in terms of piling bits of information on top of each other. How high can you build a castle of playing cards? Real progress at this stage is made by broadening one's previous knowledge and by making it more flexible (horizontal progress as against vertical progress).

Rule Two is to do something each day. Even if you do not have time to complete a whole lesson, take the book and re-read something you have already seen. Listen to a recording. Try and translate back into French from the English text. Do a set of exercises. Remember, it is counter-productive to do a two-hour session once a week instead of a ten-minute session every day.

Rule Three is don't expect to have an immediate explanation for everything. In a natural learning situation, you would hear a piece of language a few times, getting a better and better idea of what it does or where it fits before finally looking for an explanation. And this is how the method works. This is especially the case with vocabulary. If you spend time worrying about each word you do not know, you will never even get to the end of a text! Our English translations will help you; where a word is particularly common, awkward to place or has many derivatives, we make an immediate note but, as the book progresses, we leave more to your initiative.

It is the same with the grammar. Much can be assimilated by exposure and example; other points need development. Each seventh lesson is devoted to Revision and Notes and it is in these sections that the more difficult points are explained.

It must be remembered that, although French is a more grammatically 'strict' language than English, grammar is still only a way of ordering one's knowledge 'after the fact'.

A note on the English translations

Obviously, French is our target language. The English used in the translation of the texts is a rendition of the sense, not a real translation per se. It is there only as a support and, because of the differences in construction between the two languages, may sometimes sound like 'English as she is spoke'! Pay no attention. It is there to help you, not to hinder your progress by constantly contrasting sentence-structure.

As we progress, the French becomes more idiomatic. The definition of an idiom is a piece of language whose meaning is not clear from its component parts. We try to give you equivalents where they exist. If there are several, you may find one alternative in the translation of the texts and the other in the translation of the exercises. We are trying to displace your dependence on English and to broaden your perception of French. Where a literary form is used in the main French text, a more familiar, spoken equivalent is generally used in the EXERCICES.

A note on liaisons

The liaison - the running-on of the final consonant of one word to an initial vowel of the following word - is a sign of educated speech. It is a sign that the person is aware of the word values of the language. In everyday speech it is fairly rare but when read by an 'educated' speaker or a person delivering a piece of prose for public consumption - a politician or a newsreader - the liaison tends to appear rather too often! In our book, we allow liaisons to appear in everything but everyday speech i.e. where one would hear them if one were living in France. Don't be surprised then if you hear a liaison in a text where the style is very formal and not in an exercise where the same sentence may appear in a more relaxed register.

Finally, we hope you will have as much fun using this book as we had in writing it.

Bon courage !

PREMIERE (1ʳᵉ) LEÇON

Petit dialogue entre le lecteur et l'auteur

1 Vous avez ce livre entre les mains et vous vous demandez s'il est pour vous ; **(1) (2)**

2 alors, tournez le dos au vendeur un instant et écoutez ce dialogue : **(1)**

3 — Que voulez-vous dire par « la pratique du français » ?

4 — Je vous vois venir, vous ! Dites, parlez-vous français ? **(3)**

5 — Mais oui. Du moins, je me fais comprendre. Je peux dire ce que je veux et les autres... **(4)**

6 — Vous voulez dire que vos interlocuteurs vous comprennent. — Pardon ? **(5)**

7 — Donc, ce livre est en effet pour vous. Vous avez de bonnes bases grammaticales

JE N'AI PAS COMPRIS COMMENT L'UTILISER. IL Y A SÛREMENT UN TRUC...

NOTES

(1) Remember that the words for the parts of the body are not usually personalised in French, i.e. the possessive adjective is not generally used. *Vous avez les yeux rouges:* Your eyes are red. *Il s'est lavé les mains:* He washed his hands.
However, we would use a possessive if the noun is modified by an adjective: *Il s'est lavé ses mains sales:* He washed his dirty hands. A possessive adjective is also used where there may be a confusion as to the 'possessor': *Je connais son visage:* I know his/her face.

1st LESSON

Little dialogue between the reader and the author

1 You have this book between your hands and you are wondering if it is for you;

2 so, turn your back to the salesman for a minute and listen to this dialogue:

3 — What do you mean by 'the practice of French'?

4 — I see what you're going to say. Tell me, do you speak French?

5 — Yes indeed. At least, I make myself understood. I can say what I like and the others...

6 — You mean that the people you are speaking to understand you. — Pardon?

7 — So, this book is indeed for you. You have a good base in grammar

NOTES

(2) *Se demander* (literally, to ask oneself) is best rendered as to wonder. *Parfois, je me demande s'il a raison:* Sometimes, I wonder whether he is right. *Vous vous demandez pourquoi je vous ai téléphoné, n'est-ce pas?:* You are wondering why I 'phoned, aren't you?
To wonder at a person or something that takes your breath away needs the verb *s'émerveiller* from which we get the adjective *merveilleux* (marvellous, wonderful).

(3) An idiom meaning: I know what's coming; I know what you're getting at. Notice the use of the infinitive both in this idiom and the expression in the next line.

(4) *Je me fais comprendre:* I make myself understood. *Il y avait un tel bruit qu'il ne pouvait pas se faire entendre:* There was such a noise that he could not make himself heard.
Where English would use a past participle in such expressions, French uses the infinitive.

(5) One of the characteristics of French is its use of complicated-looking nouns or verbs, usually of classical origin, where English would use a compound noun, a noun-preposition group or a phrasal verb. Using the correct word - *le mot juste* - is very important in speaking or writing good French.
Getting the hang of such words is a question of exposure then trial and error. The noun *un interlocuteur* means simply the person one is talking to or is in contact with; in good French it is this word and not the paraphrase that one should use.
We look at this question in greater detail in Lesson 33.

8 et un vocabulaire assez riche, mais il vous manque le « petit quelque chose ». **(6)**

9 — Le petit quoi ? — Le petit quelque chose qui fait que vous vivez la langue ;

10 vous connaissez ses particularités de style, ses humeurs,

11 ses « trucs » ; vous savez que la langue est le reflet du pays et des gens qui la parlent. **(7)**

12 Bref, vous avez besoin de la pratique.

13 C'est bien plus que les textes ; c'est un voyage à travers la France et le français que nous ferons ensemble. **(8)**

14 — Alors, on y va ? Mais d'abord, voyons ce que l'avenir nous réserve...

EXERCICES

1. J'ai trop fumé ; j'ai mal à la tête. **2.** Elle s'est demandée pourquoi Jean avait téléphoné. **3.** Il n'a pas assez d'argent ; il lui manque dix francs. **4.** Je n'ai pas compris comment l'utiliser. Il y a sûrement un truc. **5.** C'est bien plus qu'un simple livre d'exercices. **6.** Je l'ai vue à travers la fenêtre.

Mettez les mots qui manquent.
Fill in the blanks.   Each dot represents a letter.

1 *Il se . . . . sans problèmes !*

He will make himself heard with no problems!

2 *Il . . . . dix francs pour prendre un taxi,*

He is ten francs short for a taxi

3 *donc il . . . . sûrement son avion.*

so he will miss his plane for sure.

8 and a fairly rich vocabulary but you need the 'little something'.

9 — The little what? — The little something which means that you live the language;

10 You know its peculiarities of style, its moods,

11 its idiosyncracies; you know that the language is the reflection of the country and the people who speak it.

12 In short, you need practice.

13 It's much more than texts; it's a journey across France and French that we will make together.

14 — Well, shall we go? But first, let's see what the future has in store for us...

NOTES

(6) *Manquer* is an awkward verb to use correctly. Its basic meaning is to miss or to lack. Look at these different constructions:

Il est 10 heures; il manquera son train: It is 10 o'clock; he will miss his train.

Il me manque dix francs: I am ten francs short.

Il manque deux boutons à ma chemise: My shirt has two buttons missing.

Do you see how the *il* in the last two examples is impersonal? In English we say: I need... or I miss... whereas French uses the dative: To me is missing... etc.

As we said, this is a rather complex usage. Memorise our examples and we will return to the subject later in the book.

(7) *Un truc* is almost a vocabulary in itself. Used familiarly, it means a thing, a whatname and so on.

You will often hear it (a) when explaining something mysterious; a French person will say *Il y a un truc:* There's something unusual/odd/wrong/I don't understand; (b) when describing how to carry out a manœuvre or series of operations; here the phrase means: There's a knack to it.

In sentence 11 we would have to translate it by 'idiosyncracies' which rather makes *truc* (that indefinable 'something') lose its charm.

Becoming familiar with such words and their uses is what we mean by *la pratique du français.*

(8) Another way of saying *beaucoup plus que.*

EXERCISES: 1. I have smoked too much; I have a headache. **2.** She wondered why John had telephoned. **3.** He doesn't have enough money; he is ten francs short. **4.** I didn't understand how to use it. There must be a knack to it. **5.** It is far more than a simple book of exercises. **6.** I saw her through the window.

4 *Le voilà comme d'habitude,* . . . *mains dans* . . .

poches.

There he is as usual, his hands in his pockets.

5 *Elle* . *'a* . . . . *dos.*

She turned her back on me.

****
DEUXIEME (2ᵉ) LEÇON

L'horoscope (1)

1 Bélier : Vous avez bien travaillé mais vous avez encore des choses à apprendre.
2 Vous ferez de grands progrès en travaillant tous les jours. **(2)**

3 Taureau : Vous êtes en train de vivre une période difficile, mais quand vous finirez ce livre
4 tout ira bien. Le 21 novembre sera un bon jour pour vous.

Les mots qui manquent
The missing words

1. fera entendre 2. lui manque 3. manquera 4. les - les 5. m - tourné le.

The golden rule for using our method is: Don't rush things. Do a lesson every day. Let us worry about the grammar and the vocabulary. Don't look for explanations straight away. Enjoy yourself.

****

2nd LESSON

The horoscope

1   Aries: You have worked well, but you still have some things to learn.

2   You will make great progress by working every day.

3   Taurus: You are living a difficult period, but when you (will) finish this book

4   everything will be (will go) fine. The 21st November will be a good day for you.

NOTES

(1) Remember that the '**h**' is never pronounced. Words beginning with this letter present a pronunciation problem when used with the plural definite article *'les'*: should we make the liaison? Some nouns begin with what the French call *'un h aspiré'* which - just to confuse - is **not** pronounced! We can recognise these words because the singular article *le/la* is not elided. Some examples are: *le haricot* (bean), *le hasard* (luck, chance), *la haie* (hedge) and *le havre* (haven - the name of a famous port) and the number eight: *le huit mai* (May 8th).

In the plural form we must never run on the final **s** of *les; les haricots* is pronounced: lay aricoh; *les harpes:* lay arp (harps). But *l'hôpital ___. les hôpitaux:* layzopitoh.

However, even the French sometimes make mistakes with these words, so don't be put off. A good dictionary will usually indicate by an asterisk those words beginning with a *'h aspiré'*.

(2) Certain nouns which we call 'collective' in English have no plural form, like 'furniture', 'information', 'damage'; in French, the words have both singular and plural forms: *un meuble* (a piece of furniture), *les meubles* (furniture), *une information* (a news item), *les informations* (information, news), *un progrès ___. les progrès*. We will point out others as they come up.

5   Gémeaux : Malgré quelques difficultés au départ, vous pourrez désormais vous débrouiller partout. **(3) (4) (5)**

6   Apprenez vos verbes irréguliers !

7   Cancer : Si vous y passiez un peu plus de temps, vous pourriez apprendre plus vite.

8   Ne vendez pas votre voiture à un homme aux cheveux noirs. **(6)**

9   Lion : Il ne faut pas que vous preniez votre étude trop sérieusement. C'est un plaisir et une distraction. **(7)**

10   — De quel signe du Zodiaque êtes-vous ?
     — Vous plaisantez !

11   Nous, les Scorpions, nous ne croyons pas à ces choses-là ! **(8)**

NOTES

(3) *Malgré:* despite. There is an equivalent expression, whence the English word comes: *en dépit de.* The former is the more usual.

(4) *Désormais:* from now on. *Désormais, vous n'aurez pas le droit d'arriver en retard:* From now on, you will not be allowed to arrive late. An equivalent word is *dorénavant,* which has the same meaning.

*****

EXERCICES

1. Désormais, nous pourrons apprendre le français facilement. **2.** Malgré nos précautions, la tempête a fait beaucoup de dégâts. **3.** Qui est cette femme aux yeux bleus là-bas ? **4.** De quelle nationalité êtes-vous ? — Vous plaisantez ! Je suis Chinois. **5.** Passez-y plus de temps. Vous verrez les résultats. **6.** Les autres signes du Zodiaque sont la Vierge, la Balance, le Scorpion et le Sagittaire. **7.** Le Capricorne, le Verseau et les Poissons.

5   Gemini: Despite some difficulties at the begin-
     ning, you will be able, from now on, to get by
     everywhere.
6   Learn your irregular verbs!
7   Cancer: If you spent a little more time, you would
     be able to learn quicker.
8   Don't sell your car to a man with black hair.
9   Leo: You must not take your study too seriou-
     sly.   It is a pleasure and an entertainment.

10 — What sign of the Zodiac are you?   — You're
     joking!
11   We Scorpios don't believe in those things!

NOTES

(5) A French concept 'par excellence': *se débrouiller:* means to get by,
    to manage, to make out... anything that involves using one's wits.
    To be called *'débrouillard'* is a high compliment. Look at these
    examples:
    Elle se débrouille avec trois mille francs par mois!: She manages on
    3.000 F a month!
    Je ne sais pas comment vous allez le faire; débrouillez-vous!: I don't
    know how you're going to do it; that's your business!
    Tu te débrouilles bien en allemand!: You get by well in German!
(6) *Une femme aux cheveux longs:* a woman with long hair.
    Un homme aux moustaches blanches: a man with a white
    mustache.
    (Notice the plural noun in each case.)
    We use this turn of phrase when we wish to describe the attribute
    (*long* hair; *white* mustache, etc.); otherwise we would say *un
    homme moustachu. L'homme barbu là-bas:* The man over there
    with a beard; *L'homme à la barbe grise:* The man with a grey beard.
(7) We could avoid the subjunctive by using an infinitive: *il ne faut pas
    prendre...,* etc.
(8) In familiar, spoken language, *nous* is very often replaced by *on,* and
    especially in phrases like: *Nous, les...,* where the verb in conjugated
    with this impersonal form. *Nous, les Français, nous aimons le bon
    vin:* We French like good wine. *Nous, les jeunes, on veut du travail:*
    We young people want work.
    In written French we must use *nous* for both pronouns.

EXERCISES: 1. From now on, we'll be able to learn French easily. 2.
Despite our precautions, the storm did a lot of damage. 3. Who is
that woman with the blue eyes over there? 4. What nationality are
you? You're joking! I'm Chinese. 5.   Spend a little more
time.   You'll see the results. 6. The other signs of the Zodiac are:
Virgo (the Virgin), Libra (the scales), Scorpio (the scorpion) and
Sagittarius. 7. Capricorn, Aquarius and Pisces (the fish).

Leçon 2

Mettez les mots qui manquent.
Fill in the blanks.

1 *Ne me dérangez pas. Je* . . . . *de* . . . .

un article passionnant.

Don't disturb me. I'm in the middle of reading a fascinating article.

2 . . . . . . *quelques difficultés, il* . . . . . . *se*

. . . . *tout seul.*

Despite some difficulties, he will be able to get along on this own.

3 *Il* . . . . *ce médicament;*

il est trop fort.

You mustn't take this medicine; it's too strong.

****

TROISIEME (3e) LEÇON

Faisons connaissance

1 Nous allons suivre l'histoire de deux jeunes gens dans leur vie de tous les jours :
2 nous verrons leurs préoccupations et leurs plaisirs **(1)**
3 et de cette façon, nous saurons peut-être mieux comment on vit aujourd'hui en France. **(2) (3)**

*****

4   *Nous avons . . . . . . quelques choses à faire,*

et puis nous . . . . . . prêts.

We still have some things to do and then we'll be ready.

5   *. . . . les Français, ... pas trop*

les règlements.

We French don't like rules too much.

Mots qui manquaient :

1. suis en train - lire **2.** Malgré - pourra - débrouiller **3.** ne faut pas prendre **4.** encore - serons **5.** Nous - nous n'aimons.

****

3rd LESSON

Let's get acquainted

1   We're going to follow the story of 2 young people in their everyday life:
2   we will see their worries and their pleasures
3   and in this way, we will know better perhaps how people live today in France.

NOTES

(1) Remember to check up on irregular verbs from time to time. Our advice: don't try and learn whole lists of verbs. Choose one, memorise it, then do a few transposition exercices (e.g. *je verrai* __ *ils verront; tu verras* __ *vous verrez;* etc.). Only by doing this sort of brief exercise will you move from memorising to assimilating. The verb here is, of course, the future of *voir.*

(2) *Savoir: je saurai, tu sauras, il/elle/on saura, nous saurons, vous saurez, ils sauront.*

(3) Here is the impersonal use of *on* (contrasted with the idiomatic usage in Lesson 2); although often translated as 'one' it is more the equivalent of 'people'. *On dit qu'il est très riche:* People say that he's very rich.

Leçon 3

4 Place aux dames ! Voici Anne-Marie ; elle a vingt-deux ans et elle est agent de voyages. **(4)**

5 Elle travaille à Paris, avenue de l'Opéra et habite la banlieue ouest. **(5)**

6 Elle est passionnée de musique et adore le cinéma.

7 Et voici Laurent ; ce jeune homme de vingt ans est en deuxième année de Lettres à la Sorbonne. **(6) (7) (8)**

8 Ils se connaissent depuis six mois. **(N.1)**

9 Ils se sont rencontrés par hasard, au Quartier Latin,

10 mais leur première rencontre n'a pas été très romantique.

11 Ecoutons plutôt la version d'Anne-Marie.

EXERCICES

1. Je comprends mieux comment on vit en France la vie de tous les jours. **2.** Essayez ceci ; vous verrez, c'est très efficace. **3.** Il est passionné d'art et elle adore la musique. **4.** Elle travaille ici depuis six mois ; elle est ingénieur. **5.** On s'est rencontré en vacances cette année. **6.** Tu veux dire : « Nous nous sommes rencontrés... ». C'est mieux.

4   Ladies first!   Here is Anne-Marie; she is 22 and she is a travel agent.

5   She works in Paris, Avenue de l'Opéra and she lives in the west suburb(s).

6   She's mad about music and she loves the cinema.

7   And here's Laurent; this young, 20-year-old man is in his second year of literature studies at the Sorbonne.

8   They have known each other for 6 months.

9   They met by chance in the Latin Quarter,

10   but their first encounter was not very romantic.

11   Let's listen instead to Anne-Marie's version.

NOTES

(4) In a language where every noun is either masculine or feminine we sometimes find anomalies. For example *une personne* (a person) is feminine regardless of whether the person referred to is a man or a woman. Job-names are mainly masculine and this can give us sentences like *Le Ministre du temps libre, Madame Leblanc.* Although this seems awkward, it is quite accepted.

(5) It is quite common to leave out *à* with verbs like *habiter* and *travailler,* or in turns of phrase like *Je connais un café à Montmartre, rue des Abbesses...* etc. Of course, it is perfectly correct to construct the phrase using the preposition.

(6) Beware of the feminine form *Laurence; Dominique* is both a male and female first name, so is *Claude.*

(7) An unusual use of the noun to refer to literature studies (although we find a parallel usage in English: a man of letters, i.e., a literate man, usually a writer). If he received a doctoral degree Laurent would write *Docteur ès Lettres* after his name. The word *ès,* only found in this context, is an ancient contraction of the words *en* and *les.*

(8) *La Sorbonne:* this famous university - the oldest in Europe - was founded in 1257 by Robert de Sorbon and is today the heart of the Latin Quarter.

EXERCISES: 1. I understand better how people live in France   their everyday life.   **2.** Try this ; you'll see, it's very effective.   **3.** He's mad about art and she loves music.   **4.** She's been working here for 6 months; she's an engineer.   **5.** We met on holiday this year.   **6.** You mean: 'We met, etc. (using *nous* instead of *on*)'. It's better.

Mettez les mots qui manquent.
Fill in the blanks.

1 *Nous* . . . . *des années.*

We've known each other for years.

2 *Vous* . . . . . . *cela la semaine prochaine ; je vous* . . . . . .

à ce moment-là.

You will know that next week; I'll see you then.

3 *Elles* . . . . *dans la même agence* . . . . . .

l'année dernière.

They've been working in the same agency since last year.

****

QUATRIEME (4e) LEÇON

La première fois

1 — Je suis à Paris depuis quatre ans seulement ;
je suis originaire du Havre **(1)**

2   mais je me suis décidée à venir faire carrière
dans la capitale. **(2)**

4 . . . . *vous jouez bien du piano. Est-ce vrai ?*

People tell (me) that you play the piano well. Is that true?

5 . . . . . *Anne-Marie ; elle* . . . . . . — . . . . *ans*

et elle est . . . . . *de* . . . .

Here's Anne-Marie ; she's 22 and she's a travel agent.

Mots qui manquaient :

1. nous connaissons depuis 2. saurez - verrai 3. travaillent - depuis 4.
On dit que 5. Voici - a vingt-deux - agent - voyages.

Remember, don't force yourself to do too much, and don't worry about things that aren't explained immediately. You'll see them again later.

****

4th LESSON

The first time

1 — I have been in Paris for only four years; I come
from Le Havre

2 but I decided to come and make (my) career in the
capital.

NOTES

(1) *Le Havre:* the article behaves in the usual way in compounds. *Il va
au Havre:* He's going to Le Havre. *Elle vient du Mans:* She comes
from Le Mans. This also applies with the plural noun: *Ils ont un
appartement aux Ulis:* They have a flat in Les Ulis.

(2) Many verbs have two forms - transitive and reflexive - where
English only has one: *Il bat son chien:* He beats his dog. *Il se bat avec
son chien:* He fights with his dog. *Ça m'a décidé à partir:* That made
up my mind to leave. *Je me suis décidé à partir:* I decided (i.e. all by
myself) to leave. We will point out other examples as they appear.
Notice the agreement of the past participle: reflexive verbs agree
with the preceding direct object, i.e., the person herself.

Leçon 4

3	J'avais des amis qui y travaillaient ; ils m'ont dit qu'il y avait du travail. **(3)**
4	Je suis venue en janvier et j'ai commencé aussitôt dans l'agence où je suis aujourd'hui.
5	J'avais une mobylette à l'époque et un jour je suis allée faire une course au Quartier Latin. **(4) (5)**
6	En sortant du magasin, j'ai vu un type en train d'enfourcher ma mobylette ! **(6)**
7	J'ai crié tout de suite : « Hé ! Qu'est-ce que vous faites ? »
8	Le type me répond : « Ben, je rentre chez moi. Pourquoi ? » **(7)**
9	Je lui dis : « Alors prenez le métro ou le bus, mais laissez-moi ma mobylette ! »
10	Le pauvre ! Il a rougi jusqu'aux oreilles ; il croyait qu'elle était à lui **(8)**
11	parce que, juste à côté, il y en avait une autre presque pareille !

EXERCICES

1. Nous nous sommes décidés depuis hier. **2.** Nous y allons tous ensemble. **3.** En sortant du magasin elle a vu un type sur une mobylette. **4.** Elle a crié et il a rougi jusqu'aux oreilles. **5.** A cette époque j'habitais au Havre. **6.** Elles sont arrivées au mois de mars et elles ont commencé aussitôt à travailler.

Mettez les mots qui manquent.
Fill in the blanks.

1 *Il . . . . une autre à côté qui . . . .*

There was another one nearby which was his.

2 *J'aime Le Havre ; j' . . . . . des amis qui*

. . . .

I like Le Havre; I had some friends who worked there.

3   I had friends who worked here, they told me there was work.

4   I came in January and I began straight away in the agency where I am today.

5   I had a moped at the time and one day I went to do an errand in the Latin Quarter.

6   Coming out of the shop, I saw a guy straddling my moped!

7   I shouted straight away: 'Hey! What are you doing?'

8   The guy answered: 'Er, I'm going home. Why?'

9   I said to him: 'Well, take the métro or the bus but leave me my moped!'

10   The poor thing! He blushed to the roots (ears); he thought it was his

11   because, just next to it, there was another one almost the same!

NOTES

(3) This little word takes a bit of practice to master. It basically means 'there' or in 'this/that place'. *Vous connaissez Le Havre? J'y suis né:* Do you know Le Havre? I was born there. Or, more idiomatically, *Je n'y connais rien:* I know nothing about it. *Allez-y!:* Go ahead! Look at each use and memorise it; we will give you a rule on.

(4) Lit: at the epoch; a very common expression when speaking about the past: 'at the time'; we sometimes find an equivalent expression in the present: *à notre époque:* nowadays.

(5) *Une course* is a race, but in the expression: *faire des* (or *une*) *course(s)* it means: to run an errand. *Un coursier* is an errand boy. We find more and more the unfortunate expression *faire du shopping,* of which we can only say that it is easy to remember.

(6) One of our aims in this book is to provide you with examples of current idiomatic usage for recognition. We don't suggest that you imitate such speech. *Un type* is the equivalent of a guy in Anglo-American.

(7) See above comments. A very common phenomenon when narrating past events: the speaker switches to the present tense to make the story more vivid. There is, of course, no grammatical rule governing this.

(8) Or ... *qu'elle était la sienne.* Do you remember your pronouns? *C'est le mien* or *c'est à moi.*

EXERCISES: 1. Our minds have been made up since yesterday. **2.** We're going there all together. **3.** Leaving the shop, she saw a guy on a moped. **4.** She shouted, and he blushed to the roots. **5.** At that time I was living in Le Havre. **6.** They arrived in the month of March and they began to work straight away.

Leçon 4

3 *Il . . . . . une voiture et il . . . . faire*

. . . .

He had a car and he went to do an errand.

4 *Nous . . . . aussitôt : « Qu'est- . . . . .*

. . . . . . »

We shouted immediately: 'What are you doing?' (familiar form)

****

CINQUIEME (5e) LEÇON

La suite...

1 Ecoutons Laurent quand il raconte la suite de cette rencontre. **(1)**

2 — Oh là là ! J'étais tellement gêné que je ne savais pas où me mettre. **(2)**

JE L'AI TROUVÉE SYMPATHIQUE ET NOUS NOUS SOMMES MIS A BAVARDER...

3 J'ai invité la jeune fille à boire un verre à côté, pour m'excuser. **(3)**

5   *Vous . . . . à Paris . . . . . . avril, n'est-ce pas ?*

You've been in Paris since april, haven't you?

Mots qui manquaient :

1. y en avait - était à lui **2.** avais - y travaillaient **3**. avait - est allé - une course **4.** avons crié - ce que tu fais ? **5.** êtes - depuis.

****

5th LESSON

The continuation...

1   Let's listen to Laurent while he tells what happened after the encounter.
2 — Oh Heavens! I was so embarrassed I didn't know where to look (to put myself).
3   I invited the young girl for a drink next door, to apologise.

NOTES

(1) *La suite* (from *suivre:* to follow) is a very useful word. It means 'what follows', 'what happens after' or simply 'the continuation'. *Connaissez-vous la suite de l'histoire ?:* Do you know how the story goes on? In a restaurant, the waiter may ask: *Voulez-vous la suite ?:* Do you want the next course? *A suivre* at the end of a chapter etc. means: to be continued.

(2) *Gêner quelqu'un* is to embarrass, to upset or to get in the way of somebody. *Son bras me gênait :* His/her arm was in my way. *J'étais gêné par sa conduite :* I was upset by his/her behaviour. *Stationnement gênant* on a road sign (lit: annoying parking) means that the *contractuelles* (the meter-maids) will be so *gênées* they will give you a *P.V. : procès-verbal* (a parking ticket). *Cela vous gêne si je fume ?:* Does it disturb you if I smoke?

(3) See lesson 4 note 2. *Excuser quelqu'un :* to forgive someone. *Excusez mon retard :* Forgive my being late. *S'excuser :* to apologise. An example of bad usage is when foreigners - and French people - say *Je m'excuse* instead of *Excusez-moi* to apologise for something (we should ask the other person's forgiveness).

Leçon 5

4   Nous avons bu un café et nous nous
       sommes mis à bavarder de tout et de rien.
       (4)

5   Je l'ai trouvée très sympathique ; elle ne
       connaissait pas grand-monde à Paris, **(5) (6)**

6   alors je lui ai proposé d'aller au restaurant le
       lendemain.

7   Elle a hésité un petit peu, puis elle a fini par
       accepter :

8   — Voulez-vous un autre café ? — Si vous
       voulez. — Garçon, deux cafés, s'il vous plaît.
       (7)

9   — Dites, que faites-vous demain soir ? — Rien.
       Pourquoi ?

10   — Je pensais... c'est-à-dire... enfin, si vous
       voulez, nous pourrions aller dîner ensemble.

11   — Je ne sais pas... j'habite en banlieue et puis
       je travaille demain.

12   — Pas de problème. Je vous raccompagnerai
       après.

13   — En mobylette, je suppose...

EXERCICES

1. Il était tellement gêné qu'il ne savait pas où se mettre.
2. Je l'ai trouvée sympathique et nous nous sommes mis
à bavarder. **3.** Ils ont hésité mais ils ont fini par accepter.
4. Si vous êtes libre, venez boire un verre. — Si vous
voulez. **5.** Il ne connaît pas grand-chose en latin, mon
frère. **6.** Vous pouvez me raccompagner après la fête ?

Mettez les mots qui manquent.
Fill in the blanks.

1 *Nous* . . . . *une bière, et nous* . . . .

   . . . *à bavarder.*

   We drank a beer and we began to chat.

4 We drank a coffee and we set to chatting about everything and nothing.

5 I found her very nice; she didn't know many people in Paris

6 so I suggested going to a restaurant the next day.

7 She hesitated a little, then she finally accepted:

8 — Do you want another coffee? — Please. — Waiter, two coffees please.

9 — Tell me, what are you doing tomorrow evening? — Nothing. Why?

10 — I thought... I mean... well, if you like, we could go and have dinner together.

11 — I don't know... I live in the suburbs, and besides I'm working tomorrow.

12 — No problem. I'll take you back afterwards.

13 — By moped, I suppose...

NOTES

(4) An idiomatic usage, equivalent to the English 'we got to...'. *Ils se sont mis à chanter :* They got to singing. *Je me suis mis au tennis :* I have taken up tennis. *Bavarder* means to chat, sometimes excessively. *Il est bavard :* He's a chatterbox.

(5) Agreement of the past participle with the preceding direct object (i.e. *la* = Anne-Marie).

(6) *Grand* is used in two compound expressions, often with a negative verb. *Je ne connais pas grand-monde ici :* I don't know many people here. *Elle ne fait pas grand-chose :* She doesn't do much. Remember that *grand* also means tall and great.

(7) This polite way of acceptance is rather off-putting for the English speaker. It appears as if the person is replying to your offer by: If you insist, only if you want. In fact, it has the same value as *Avec plaisir* or just *S'il vous plaît.*

EXERCISES: **1.** He was so embarrassed he didn't know where to look. **2.** I found her very nice and we got to talking. **3.** They hesitated, but they finally accepted. **4.** If you're free, come and have a drink. — With pleasure. **5.** He doesn't know much about Latin, my brother. **6.** Can you take me home after the party?

2 *Si vous voulez, nous* . . . .

restaurant.

If you want, we can go to a restaurant.

3 *Il . . . . à dîner. Il me*

. . . . après.

He has invited me to dinner. He will bring me home after.

4 *Il . . . . comprendre l'histoire.*

He finally understood the story.

5 *. . . . . , que . . . . . . — . . . ce soir ?*

— Je suis pris.

Tell me, what are you doing this evening? — I'm busy.

****

SIXIEME (6e) LEÇON

Où aller dîner...

1 Il y a un tel choix de restaurants et de cuisines en France

2 que parfois on ne sait pas où donner de la tête.

3 Alors on prend souvent un guide qui commente le choix : **(1)**

4 *Chez Irène :* Ce charmant petit bistro vous offre - et c'est bien le mot - **(2) (3)**

Mots qui manquaient :

1. avons bu - nous sommes mis 2. pouvons aller au 3. m'a invité - raccompagnera 4. a fini par 5. Dites - faites-vous.

Have you noticed that the language is fairly idiomatic? We have deliberately refrained from trying to translate it literally, but instead we give you the nearest equivalent. Don't let this worry you: it's the beginning of full assimilation of another language.

****

6th LESSON

Where to go to have dinner

1 There is such a choice of restaurants and of cuisines in France

2 that often one doesn't know where to turn.

3 So one often takes a guide-book which comments on the choice:

4 *Chez Irène:* This charming little bistro offers you - and it's really the word

NOTES

(1) *Un guide* can be either a person or a guide-book. Two of the most famous restaurant guides are the *Michelin* and the *Gault et Millau.*

(2) *Un bistrot* or *bistro* is a very special French institution; it's a small restaurant, usually serving simple family food. They are unfortunately becoming rarer as the name becomes more widely used. *Un bistro* is also slang for a café. The word comes from the Russian adverb 'Quickly!' (bwistro) which the Russian officers, during the occupation of Paris in 1815, would shout to café-waiters.

(3) The correct word because *offrir* has not only the English sense of to offer or to propose, but also: to give, as a present. *Il m'a offert une jolie bague :* He gave me (as a present) a pretty ring. *Puis-je vous offrir un verre ?:* May I buy you a drink? So, this restaurant is obviously a very good bargain.

5 un remarquable menu à 40 francs S.N.C. Plein comme un œuf. **(4) (5)**

6 *Le Matefaim :* Ce restaurant de quartier affiche complet tous les soirs. N'oubliez pas de retenir. **(6) (7)**

7 *Aux Savoyards :* Dans un cadre pas luxueux pour un sou, **(8)**

8 on sert une cuisine raffinée avec un excellent rapport qualité-prix.

9 *Aux Armes de Bordeaux :* Il manque au cuisinier le petit « rien » qui fait la différence. Décor paysan, prix parisiens. **(N.2) (9)**

10 *A la Bonne Franquette :* Le décor est terne, la cuisine quelconque **(10)**

11 et l'addition ruineuse. A éviter à tout prix.

EXERCICES

1. La maison vous offre l'apéritif, messieurs. **2.** J'ai retenu une table au nom de Perrier. — Pour combien de personnes ? **3.** C'est la fin du mois et je n'ai pas un sou. **4.** Il y avait une telle foule que je suis parti avant la fin. **5.** Ce bistro est plein comme un œuf ; il affiche complet tous les soirs. **6.** Il y avait un tel choix que je ne savais pas où donner de la tête.

Mettez les mots qui manquent.
Fill in the blanks.

1 *Il . . . . . . trois boutons . ma chemise.*

Three buttons are missing from my shirt.

2 *Ce restaurant . . . . à . . . .*

This restaurant is to be avoided at all costs.

3 *Il . . . . cette remarquable lampe en marbre.*

He gave us this remarkable marble lamp.

5   a remarkable menu at 40 francs service not included.   Full up.

6   *Le Matefaim:* This neighbourhood restaurant is full every evening.   Don't forget to reserve.

7   *Aux Savoyards:* In surroundings which are not at all luxurious

8   they serve a refined cuisine with an excellent price-quality ratio.

9   *Aux Armes de Bordeaux:* The cook lacks the little 'something' which makes the difference.   Rustic decor, Parisian prices.

10 *A la Bonne Franquette:* The decor is dull, the cuisine ordinary

11 and the bill ruinous.   To be avoided at all costs.

NOTES

(4) Remember that *un menu* is a fixed price menu. In a restaurant, you would ask to see *la carte* if you wanted the bill of fare.

(5) *S.N.C.* = *service non compris:* service not included.

(6) Or... *est plein tous les soirs.* We use the former expression to speak of restaurants or shows: when they are full and can take no more, they put up a sign *Complet* (full up). To put up a sign is *afficher*, hence our expression (*une affiche :* a poster or bill).

(7) To book a plane-ticket, a train-journey, etc. we say *réserver.* For a restaurant-table, we use *retenir* (lit. to retain); it can also be used for theatre-tickets, etc. *J'ai retenu deux places pour demain :* I've reserved two seats for tomorrow.

(8) *Un sou* is an old unit of money which still survives in idiomatic expressions. For example: *Elle n'a pas un* (or *le*) *sou :* She hasn't got a penny. *Un sou est un sou :* A penny's still a penny. The expression *il/elle n'est pas - pour un sou* means he/she isn't in the least -.

(9) The word literally means peasant. Our English word has feudal (or unsophisticated) connotations. Although it can be used to mean an oaf, etc., the root of the word is visible (*le pays :* the country) and it is used widely to indicate things or people from the country. Here the writer is contrasting the rusticity of the decor and the urbanity of the bill.

(10) A word to be careful with, which we will see later in more detail. It can mean 'whatever', 'any' or, as here, ordinary, uninspired, 'any old cooking'.

EXERCISES: 1. The aperitif is on the house, gentlemen. **2.** I've reserved a table in the name of Perrier. — For how many people? **3.** It's the end of the month and I haven't got a penny. **4.** There was such a crowd that I left before the end. **5.** This bistro is jam-packed; it's full up every evening. **6.** There was such a choice that I didn't know where to turn.

4 *Il n' . . . . . . bête . . . . un . . .*

He's not in the least stupid.

5 *Le décor est . . . . . , la cuisine est . . . .*

et les prix . . . .

The decor is dull, the cuisine is ordinary and the prices are ruinous.

****

SEPTIEME (7e) LEÇON

REVISION ET NOTES

(At the end of every week of six lessons, you will find a revision lesson which will review the main points covered in the preceding week, with more complete explanations of more complex points.)

Verb tenses: This week and next week we will revise the verb tenses we have learned so far. These are:
le présent ; le futur ; le passé composé ; l'imparfait ;
we will also look in more detail at:
le conditionnel; le subjonctif (avec falloir); les verbes pronominaux with both the respective and reciprocal meanings.
If you are not sure of the basic rules, check up in a grammar-book.

Idioms: A good definition of an idiom is that it is an expression where the meaning cannot be gleaned from the different parts. A figurative expression is where the words keep their original meanings but are applied metaphorically. It is important to assimilate such expressions without translating; they are an integral part of the French language, both in everyday speech and in more refined written language. We can often - but not always - find equivalents in English but it is important to relate an expression to a situation and to assimilate its sense

Mots qui manquaient :

1. manque - à 2. est à éviter - tout prix 3. nous a offert 4. est pas - pour - sou 5. terne - quelconque - sont ruineux.

*****

****

7th LESSON

and its usage. Look back again at the following and try to visualise them:
il ne savait pas où donner de la tête ; elle ne connaît pas grand-monde ; c'était plein comme un œuf ; ils affichent complet tous les soirs ; and revise idiomatic turns of phrase like:
on s'est mis à bavarder or *il a fini par accepter.*
Each time you come across an expression, underline it. From time to time, flip back through the book and revise them.

Les verbes pronominaux : French uses the pronominal form *(se)* much more widely than English. In fact, almost every French verb can exist in this form. We say such verbs are either (a) reflexive or (b) reciprocal.
(a) *Il se lave à l'eau froide ; elle s'est regardée dans la glace.* In these examples the action 'reflects' back on the person doing it; we usually express this in English by an active form: he washes in cold water or, to avoid ambiguity, we use a reflexive pronoun: she looked at herself in the mirror.
(b) We say a verb is reciprocal when a same action is shared by one or several partners:
Ils se connaissent bien : They know each other well.
Ils ne se parlent plus : They no longer speak to one another.
On se voit assez souvent : We see each other quite often.
It is hard to give rules without becoming far too involved.

Pay particular attention to verbs that are pronominal in French and which in English are expressed by an active form (e.g. *Elle se sert d'un dictionnaire :* She uses a dictionary) or by a passive *Ça ne se dit pas :* That is not said.

Agreement of past participle in compound tenses.

As usual the past participle agrees with the preceding direct object; this is usually the reflexive pronoun, i.e., doer of the action (*me ; te ; se ; nous ; vous ; se*).

Elle s'est lavée : She washed.

However, if the object comes **after** the verb, there is no agreement.

Elle s'est lavé les mains : She washed her hands.

Sometimes, too, the reflexive pronoun may be an indirect object so, again, no agreement:

Nous nous sommes demandé....: We wondered...

Manquer: Apart from its use in expressions like:
J'ai manqué le train : I missed the train,

****

HUITIEME (8e) LEÇON

La circulation

1   Comme dans toutes les grandes villes un peu partout, Paris connaît des problèmes de circulation,

IL A PRIS SA VOITURE POUR ALLER TRAVAILLER

2   surtout aux heures de pointe. **(2)**

this little verb has several idiomatic uses. Like here, in the impersonal form:

Il manque trois boutons à cette chemise : There are three buttons missing from this shirt.

Il me manque deux francs : I'm 2F short.

Ça manque de sel, ton plat : Your dish needs salt,
or here, for an attribute:

Il manque de politesse : He's lacking in politeness.

Ils ne manquent pas d'imagination: They have no shortage of imagination.

Do you see the idea? Now, try and learn these expressions which are the most difficult:

Il me manque : I miss him.

Je lui manque : He/she misses me.

Tu me manques : I miss you.

Notice that the subject/object order is inverted compared to English.

****

8th LESSON

Traffic

1   As in all large towns almost everywhere, Paris has traffic problems

2   especially at rush-hours.

NOTES

(1) *La circulation* is used to refer to the flow of cars etc. The strict definition of *le trafic* applies to illicit trade like *le trafic des armes ou des stupéfiants* (arms or drug traffic). Due to a common phenomenon of exchange back and forth between French and English, *le trafic* took on the English sense of 'flow of vehicles'; we find it in expressions like *le trafic aérien ou le trafic routier* (air or road traffic). A traffic jam = *un embouteillage ;* a traffic accident = *un accident de la circulation.*

(2) *La pointe d'un couteau :* the point of a knife. *Pointu :* pointed. *La technique de pointe :* high technology. *L'heure de pointe :* rush hour. A related word is *un point* which we see used in line 8 in an idiomatic way; *faire le point sur l'affaire :* to discuss the latest developments of the affair; *le point de l'actualité :* the most up-to-date news. There is a news-magazine called *'Le Point'.*

3 On a beau dire que les Français sont individualistes, **(N.1)**

4 cela n'empêche qu'ils ont tendance à prendre leurs voitures...

5 tous en même temps et souvent pour aller au même endroit !

6 Le résultat s'appelle « embouteillages » ou « bouchons ».

7 Pour rouler à Paris, il faut des nerfs solides, une vieille « bagnole » et beaucoup de patience. **(3) (4)**

8 — F.I.P. Il est quinze heures ; voici le point sur la circulation : **(5)**

9 On roule encore très mal sur les périphériques et tous les grands boulevards sont bloqués ;

10 quant à la rue de Rivoli, on a tendance à y prendre racine. **(6)**

11 Un conseil : si vous devez sortir, prenez le métro ! **(7)**

NOTES

(3) To drive a car: *conduire une voiture. Elle conduit bien :* She drives well. *La conduite en montagne :* mountain driving. The verb gives us the idea of controlling a vehicle; but we use the verb: to drive, in a much broader way, e.g. 'I was driving down to Lyon when...' etc. Here, we are not really concerned with the idea of 'controlling a vehicle'; but the verb 'to drive' gives us an extra piece of information (i.e. travelling by car etc.). French would not use the verb *conduire* but would say *Je descendais à Lyon* adding *en voiture* if it is necessary to say how one was travelling.
In the same way, if we are discussing the movements of cars rather than the control of them, we use the verb *rouler :*
Je roulais à 120 km/h : I was doing 120 kmh.
Ça roule mal le samedi : traffic (i.e. flow) is bad on Saturdays.

EXERCICES

1. N'oublie pas : en France on roule à droite ! **2.** On va faire le point sur vos dépenses. **3.** Quant à lui, je ne suivrai jamais ses conseils. **4.** Il a pris sa voiture pour aller travailler, **5.** mais il y avait de tels embouteillages qu'il a été en retard. **6.** Si tu dois sortir, prends un taxi.

3	Even though the French are said to be individua-lists,
4	this doesn't prevent them from having a tendency to take their cars...
5	all at the same time and often to go to the same place !
6	The result is called 'traffic jams' or 'bottle-necks'.
7	To drive in Paris, you need steady nerves, an old car and a lot of patience.
8	— F.I.P. It's 3.00 p.m.; here is the latest traffic report:
9	Driving is difficult on the circular expressway and all the Major Boulevards are blocked;
10	as for the rue de Rivoli, there is a tendency to take root there.
11	A word of advice: if you must go out, take the métro !

NOTES

(4) Originally a slang word meaning an old wreck of a car, 'a heap' etc. (this is how we have used it here); *une bagnole* is now a familiar word for a car. There is no English equivalent to this usage.

(5) *France Inter Paris (F.I.P.)* is something of an institution; it is a radio station broadcasting to the Paris area and mainly playing music. Its traffic reports are useful and the calm, almost seductive voices of its female announcers - making jokes about the jams while trapped drivers fume - have passed into popular mythology. Notice the 24-hour clock is used in broadcasting, as almost everywhere. There is no equivalent to a.m. or p.m.

(6) An expression meaning: as for... *Quant au problème de la dévaluation...*: As for the problem of devaluation... *Quant à moi, je pense...*: As for me, I think...

(7) See lesson 2 note 2. Another noun which has singular and plural form in French and one collective form in English.
Un conseil : a piece of advice.
Ses conseils sont d'habitude excellents : His/her advice is usually excellent.
Conseiller quelqu'un : to advise someone.
Un conseiller : a councillor or an adviser. *Le Conseil d'Etat :* the State Council.

EXERCISES: 1. Don't forget: in France we drive on the right! 2. Let's check up on your spending to date. 3. As for him, I'll never follow his advice. 4. He took his car to go to work, 5. but there were such traffic jams that he was late. 6. If you must go out, take a taxi.

Mettez les mots qui manquent.
Fill in the blanks.

1 . . . . , *elle* . . . . *ma voiture.*

   As for her, she'll drive my car.

2 *On* . . . . *de prendre le métro ; ce n'est pas*

   toujours facile.

   It's all very well to say 'take the métro'; it's not always easy.

3 *Un* . . . . *ça roule mal ; surtout* . . . *heures*

   . . . .

   Driving's difficult almost everywhere, especially at rush hours.

****

NEUVIEME (9e) LEÇON

Les taxis

1 Si on n'a envie ni de conduire ni de prendre
   le métro, on peut toujours essayer de
   prendre un taxi. **(1)**

2 Il y a des milliers de taxis à Paris, sauf quand
   il pleut, alors on n'en trouve nulle part. **(2)**

3 Si vous en faites la demande, le chauffeur
   doit vous remettre un reçu, appelé « une
   fiche »,

NOTES

(1) *Il n'a ni couteau ni fourchette:* He has neither a knife nor a fork.
Je ne veux ni l'acheter ni l'emprunter: I don't want to buy it or to
borrow it. The construction with *ni... ni* is more commonly used
in French than its counterpart in English. The verb must be in the
negative form (although in popular spoken French, the tendency

4 *Quant à nous, nous* . . . . *laisser*

la voiture . . *garage.*

As for us, we tend to leave the car in the garage.

5 *Le Directeur a* . . . . *de nos ventes pour*

avril.

The Manager brought us up to date on our sales for April.

Mots qui manquaient :

1. Quant à elle, - conduira 2. a beau dire 3. peu partout - aux - de
pointe 4. avons tendance à - au 5. fait le point.

Remember that an idiomatic expression not only has more
than one translation but often, in translation, changes a
whole sentence structure in order to put across the
equivalent meaning.

****

9th LESSON

Taxis

1 If you want neither to drive nor to take the metro
   you can always try and take a taxi.
2 There are thousands of taxis in Paris, except
   when it rains, and then you can't find one
   anywhere.
3 If you ask for it, the driver must give you a receipt
   called *'une fiche'*

NOTES

    is to drop the *ne* before the verb, giving the impression of an
affirmative). If we don't use the *ni... ni* construction but *Je ne*
veux pas l'acheter and we wish to add another object, we must
still use *ni: Je ne veux pas l'acheter... ni l'emprunter.*
(2) Another negative construction: *Je ne l'ai vue nulle part:* I haven't
seen her anywhere. Remember, the verb must be in the negative
form.

4 qui contient des renseignements. En voici un extrait :

5 « Gares SNCF : la prise en charge est majorée de deux francs sur les stations signalées par une pancarte. **(4) (5)**

6 Bagages : bagages à main, première valise ou premier colis GRATUIT.

7 Colis encombrants (skis, vélos, voitures d'enfants) : un franc cinquante chaque, sans franchise.

8 Il est d'usage de donner un pourboire au conducteur, mais celui-ci ne peut l'exiger. » **(6) (7)**

9 — Taxi ! Emmenez-moi à la rue de Sévigné, s'il vous plaît.

10 — Montez. La rue de Sévigné est en sens unique ; je la prendrai par la rue de Rivoli. **(8)**

11 — Cela vous dérange si je fume ? — Pas du tout. Allez-y.

12 Voilà. Nous sommes arrivés. — Combien vous dois-je ? — Cent deux francs. **(N.2)**

13 — En voici cent vingt. Gardez la monnaie. — Merci, monsieur.

NORMALEMENT ON DONNE UN POURBOIRE AU CHAUFFEUR, MAIS IL NE PEUT PAS L'EXIGER

NOTES

(3) *Société Nationale des Chemins de Fer Français :* National Railway Company (*une société* = a company). A nationalised industry since the 1930s. *un cheminot* = a railwayman.

4 which contains information. Here is an extract from it:

5 'SNCF stations; the pick-up charge is increased by two francs at ranks indicated by a placard.

6 Baggage: hand baggage, first suitcase or first parcel FREE.

7 Bulky parcels (skis, bikes, baby carriages): 1F.50 each without exemption.

8 It is customary to give a tip to the driver, but he cannot demand it.'

9 — Taxi! Take me to rue de Sévigné, please.

10 — Get in. The rue de Sévigné is one-way; I'll take it from the rue de Rivoli.

11 — Do you mind if I smoke? — Not at all. Go ahead.

12 Here you are. We've arrived. — How much do I owe you? — 102F.

13 — Here's 120. Keep the change. — Thank you, sir.

NOTES

(4) An expression either nominal or verbal with many meanings, *prendre en charge* needs a different translation for each situation. Its basic meaning is to take charge of, or to take responsibility for. In this case, *la prise en charge* is the sum of money first indicated on the meter when the taxi driver 'takes you in charge'.

(5) Remember *une gare* is a railway station; *une station de taxis, de bus*: a bus station or stop, a taxi rank (remember also that the verb *stationner* means to park).

(6) *Celui-ci, celle-ci*, we know, means: this one here. *Je veux un chou rouge ; donnez-moi celui-ci :* I want a red cabbabe; give me this one. But in formal written French we use *celui-ci* to help avoid any confusion which could come about in a sentence where two or more nouns have the same gender. For example, in sentence 8, both *conducteur* and *pourboire* are masculine so, in theory, if we had continued the sentence '... mais il ne peut l'exiger' *il* could refer to either the driver or the tip. We thus replace *il* by *celui-ci*. The noun thus referred to is the latter of the two (or the last of a longer list). Since the confusion is really only theoretical (a tip could hardly demand a driver!), we would use the *il* construction in spoken language. We will see later how English, having no genders, is often obliged to repeat a noun to avoid confusion.

(7) The verb *pouvoir* and *oser* - to dare - can, in formal language, be negated by using only the *ne* particle. *Je n'ose le dire:* I daren't say it. In spoken French this tends to sound stilted.

(8) *Monter dans une voiture:* to get into a car.
Descendre de la voiture: to get out of the car.
Also true for *un bus, un avion* (a plane) etc.

EXERCICES

1. Je veux une autorisation ; j'en ai fait la demande. **2.** On n'en trouve nulle part depuis des mois. **3.** « Normalement on donne un pourboire au chauffeur de taxi, **4.** mais il ne peut pas l'exiger ». **5.** Cela vous dérange si j'ouvre la fenêtre ? — Pas du tout. **6.** Combien vous dois-je ? Vingt-deux francs ? En voici vingt-cinq.

Mettez les mots qui manquent.
Fill in the blanks.

1   *Je n'en . . . . le temps . . l'envie, mais allez-y.*

    `I have neither the time nor the desire, but you go ahead.

2   *Il . . . . un bruit et il . . . .*

    de la voiture.

    He heard a noise and he got out of the car.

3   *J'aimais beaucoup Londres . . . . quand . . . .*

    I liked London a lot, except when it was raining.

****

DIXIEME (10ᵉ) LEÇON

Un taxi futé (1)

1   Conduire un taxi est un métier difficile et il faut avoir le sens de l'humour.
2   Un jour, un Américain un peu chauvin saute dans un taxi à Paris. (2)

NOTES

(1) We can say *un chauffeur de taxi:* a taxi driver; if we just speak of the driver, we say *le conducteur*. In familiar French *un taxi* can also be the driver as well as the vehicle!
Futé means smart or clever. Most adjectives formed from verbs are formed from the past participle.

EXERCISES: 1. I want an authorisation; I've asked for/applied for one. **2.** We haven't been able to find any for months. **3.** Normally you give a tip to the taxi driver, **4.** but he can't demand it. **5.** Do you mind if I open the window? — Not at all. **6.** How much do I owe you? 22F? Here's 25.

4   *Elle . . a cherché partout ; on . . . trouve . . . . .*

    . . . .

She looked for it/some everywhere, you can't find it/them

anywhere.

5   *La . . . . de . . . . . est juste devant . .*

    . . . .

The taxi-rank is just in front of the station.

Mots qui manquaient :

1. ai ni - ni **2.** a entendu - est descendu **3.** sauf - il pleuvait **4.** en - n'en - nulle part **5.** station - taxis - la gare.

****

10th LESSON

A smart taxi-driver

1   Driving a taxi is a difficult trade and a sense of humour is needed.

2   One day, a rather chauvinistic American jumps into a taxi in Paris.

NOTES

(2) Here is a classic example of an eponym. Nicholas Chauvin was a marshal in Napoleon's army and, despite defeats and downfalls, remained unswervingly, blindly faithful to the Little Corporal. His name became synonymous with, and later used to describe blind, narrow-minded nationalism.

3 — Gare Saint-Lazare s'il vous plaît. Le taxi longe les quais de la Seine devant la Tour Eiffel. **(3)**

4 — C'est ça votre Tour ? Il a fallu combien de temps pour la construire ? **(4)**

5 — Environ cinq ans, je crois. — Chez nous, il faudrait cinq mois ! .

6 — Ils continuent et passent devant les Invalides. **(5)**

7 — Et ça ? Ils ont mis combien de temps pour le faire ? **(6)**

8 — Ah, ça, monsieur, environ dix ans. — Autant ? Chez nous il ne faudrait que dix semaines. **(7)**

9 — Le client continue ses propos pendant une demi-heure et le chauffeur s'énerve.

10 — Tout à coup, le taxi prend la rue Royale et VLAN ! Il rentre dans l'église de la Madeleine ! **(N.3)**

11 — Alors il se retourne vers son client ahuri et lui dit :

12 — Excusez-moi, monsieur. Je ne comprends pas. Ce n'était pas là hier !

EXERCICES

1. Le navire longeait la côte très lentement. **2.** Il lui a fallu six heures pour entrer dans le port. **3.** — Je passe devant cette église tous les jours. **4.** — Combien de temps a-t-il fallu pour la construire ? **5.** Il m'a dit : « Prends ton temps » et j'ai mis trois heures ! **6.** Elles se sont énervées et elles ont eu un accident.

Mettez les mots qui manquent.
Fill in the blanks.

1 *Actuellement* . . . . *le mur de la prison.*

At the moment we are walking the length of the prison wall.

3 — Gare Saint-Lazare please. The taxi goes along the banks of the Seine in front of the Eiffel Tower.

4 — That's your Tower? How much time was needed to build it?

5 — About 5 years I think. — Back home, it would take 5 months!

6 They continue and drive past the Invalides.

7 — And that? How long did it take them to do that?

8 — Ah, that, sir, about 10 years. — As much as that? Back home, it would only take 10 weeks.

9 The customer continues his statements for half an hour and the driver gets angry.

10 Suddenly, the taxi takes the rue Royale and BAM! He smashes into the Madeleine church!

11 Then he turns back to his dumbfounded customer and says to him:

12 — Excuse me, sir. I don't understand. It wasn't there yesterday!

NOTES

(3) A useful word when giving directions or physical descriptions. *Longez la voie ferrée pendant 1 kilomètre:* Walk along the railway track for 1 kilometer. *La route longe un bois:* The road runs along the edge of a wood. (The imperfect is *je longeais* with an *e* to keep the 'g' sound soft.)

(4) Here is the impersonal use of *falloir ;* when speaking of time, the nearest English equivalent is: to take. *Il me faut dix minutes:* it takes me ten minutes. *Combien de temps vous faut-il ?:* How much time do you need? (A rather more elegant question-form than in sentence 4.) Notice all the different tenses and moods.

(5) *Les Invalides,* constructed in 1670, was initially a military hospital. The remains of Napoleon Bonaparte are inhumed in a chapel just behind.

(6) Another way of saying: to take time, but in a personalized way. *J'ai mis deux heures:* It took me two hours. *Prenez votre temps:* Take your time.

(7) (See also lesson 9 notes 1 and 2.) *Elle n'a que dix minutes :* She only has 10 minutes. *Je n'ai que ceci à vous donner :* I have only this to give you. We will see *ne... que* used with verbs later on.

EXERCISES: 1. The ship moved slowly along the coast. **2.** It took six hours to get into the port. **3.** I go past this church every day. **4.** How long did it take to build? **5.** He said: 'Take your time' and I took three hours! **6.** They got angry and they had an accident.

2 *Il . . . . dix ans pour le finir.*

It would only take 10 years to finish it.

3 *. . . . ., il s' . . . .*

Suddenly, he got angry.

4 *. . . . . avez-vous . . . pour*

arriver ?

How long did it take you to arrive ?

5 *J' . . été . . . . . par ce qu'il a dit.*

I was flabbergasted by what he said.

****

ONZIEME (11e) LEÇON

Il faut sortir de temps en temps (1)

1 Que fait-on quand on a envie de sortir le soir
et qu'on ne sait pas où aller ?

2 Eh bien, on regarde dans le journal ou encore
dans une revue spécialisée, comme « Paris-
rama ».

3 « En exclusivité cette semaine : Jean Aumont dans « L'épouvantail ». **(2)**

4 Pour cinéphiles, reprise de : « Der Blaue
Engel » avec Marlène Dietrich. En V.O. **(3) (4)**

NOTES

(1) This is an expression often used derisively to tease someone for a
lack of knowledge of current events, etc., like 'Have you been living
up a tree?'

(2) *Epouvanter:* to scare someone. *Une pièce épouvantable:* a terrible
play. *Un film d'épouvante:* a horror film.

(3) French uses many more 'intellectual words' than English (see lesson
33) thanks to its classical origins. The two suffixes *-phile* and *-
phobe* are an example: *un bibliophile, un anglophobe.* Now, the

Mots qui manquaient :

1. nous longeons **2.** ne faudrait que **3.** Tout à coup - 'est énervé **4.**
Combien de temps - mis **5.** ai - ahuri.

ELLES SE SONT ÉNERVÉES ET ELLES ONT EU
UN ACCIDENT

****

11th LESSON

You have to go out from time to time

1 What do you do when you want to go out in the
   evening and you don't know where to go?
2 Well, you look in the paper or, again, in a
   specialised revue like 'Paris-rama'.
3 'Exclusive distribution this week: Jean Aumont in
   'The Scarecrow'.
4 For cinema-lovers, re-run of 'The Blue Angel' with
   Marlene Dietrich.   In German.

NOTES

   same words exist in English but they sound pompous or learned
   (depending on one's point of view); we would use a Germanic
   structure for the first - a book-lover - and a paraphrase for the
   second: anti-English. In French, these words are quite natural.
(4) Foreign films in France are either dubbed *(doublés)* in which case
   'V.F.' is written after the title *(version française),* or they are sub-
   titled *(sous-titrés),* and we find 'V.O.' after the title *(version
   originale).* So, in this sentence the *version originale* is German.

5 Nouveauté : un film écrit et réalisé par Michel Vion : « Vive le Roi ».

6 Ce film, drôle et tendre, a déjà battu tous les records d'entrées dans les salles parisiennes. »

7 Si l'on n'a pas envie d'aller au cinéma, on peut choisir dans la rubrique « Autres spectacles et manifestations ». **(6)**

8 Il y a de très bonnes pièces de théâtre, ou encore le café-théâtre ou bien les chansonniers ; **(7)**

9 mais si l'on trouve qu'il y a trop de choix, on peut simplement

10 flâner sur les Champs-Elysées et regarder les queues devant les cinémas !

11 — Tu as vu le dernier Duffaut ? — Non, pas encore. **(8) (9)**

12 — On y va ? — Quoi, maintenant ? C'est trop tard !

13 — Il est huit heures moins dix. On a encore dix minutes avant la séance.

QU'EST-CE-QU'ON FAIT CE SOIR ?

EH BIEN ALLONS AU THÉÂTRE

EXERCICES

1. Qu'est-ce qu'on fait ce soir ? — Eh bien, allons au théâtre. **2.** Elle n'a pas encore vu ce beau film de Jean Aumont. **3.** Il bat tous les records en ce moment. **4.** Je n'avais pas envie de voir cette pièce, mais c'était très bien en fait. **5.** Qu'est-ce que tu as envie de faire ? **6.** Je n'ai pas encore décidé.

5 New: a film written and directed by Michel Vion: 'Long Live the King'.

6 This tender and funny film has already broken all box-office records in Parisian cinemas.'

7 If we don't want to go to the cinema, we can choose from the heading, 'Other shows and happenings'.

8 There are some very good plays or, again, the 'café-théâtre' or the 'chansonniers';

9 but if you find that there is too much choice, you can simply

10 stroll on the Champs-Elysees and look at the queues in front of the cinemas!

11 — Have you seen the latest Duffaut? — No, not yet.

12 — Shall we go? — What, now? It's too late!

13 — It's ten to eight. We still have ten minutes before the programme.

NOTES

(5) *Réaliser* is another verb with many uses. In the cinema it means to direct a film. *Le réalisateur:* the director.

(6) *Une manifestation* generally means a (political) demonstration but, since it comes from the verb *manifester:* to reveal, to show (often for feelings), the noun is found in expressions like *une manifestation sportive:* a sporting event. To understand it correctly, one must know the context.

(7) *Les chansonniers* have no real equivalent. They are balladeers who write songs about current events, especially politics; the songs are often humourous but sometimes critical, ironic or just rude.

(8) *As-tu vu...?* or, in common parlance *tu as vu...?* Spoken at speed, there is often an elision of the first of the two vowels: *T'as vu...?* We **don't encourage** such habits but we intend to point them out to you where they exist.

(9) French makes no difference between the last (i.e. final) and the latest, most recent.
Le dernier roman de Victor Hugo: Victor Hugo's last novel.
Le dernier film de Godard: Godard's latest film.

EXERCISES: **1.** What shall we do/what are we doing this evening? — Well, let's go to the theatre. **2.** She hasn't yet seen that beautiful film by Jean Aumont. **3.** It's breaking all the records at the moment. **4.** I didn't want to see that play but in fact it was very good. **5.** What do you want to do? **6.** I haven't yet decided.

Leçon 11

Mettez les mots qui manquent.
Fill in the blanks.

1 *Il y a le* . . . . *Godard, ou* . . . . . . *la pièce*

de Feydeau.

There's the latest Godard, or otherwise the Feydeau play.

2 *Notre équipe* . . . . . . *l'Allemagne la semaine prochaine.*

Our team will beat Germany next week.

3 *Les* . . . . *n'ont pas* . . . .

cette saison.

The Germans haven't yet won this season.

****

DOUZIEME (12ᵉ) LEÇON

Le cinéma

1 La France a une grande tradition en matière de
cinéma. **(1)**
2 Depuis les grands « maîtres » comme Abel
Gance, Jean Renoir ou Marcel Carné,
3 jusqu'aux cinéastes de la « Nouvelle vague »
tels Truffaut et Lelouch. **(2) (3)**
4 Le « septième art » doit beaucoup au talent
des réalisateurs et des acteurs français.
5 Mais aujourd'hui le cinéma est en crise : les
gens vont de moins en moins au cinéma.

NOTES

(1) *La matière:* the substance, the matter. *En quelle matière est-il
construit?* What substance is it built of?
On yoghourt and curd cheese containers in France, you will find the
percentage of *matière grasse* (fat content).
Il est expert en la matière: He's an expert in the subject. (What's the
matter?: *Qu'est-ce qu'il y a?*)

4 *On* . . . . . . *une* . . . . — . . . . . *avant*

le début du match.

We've still got half an hour before the beginning of the match.

5 *Vous n'* . . . . *pas* . . . . . *de sortir ? Eh bien, restons*

à la maison.

You don't want to go out?   Well, let's stay at home.

Mots qui manquaient :

1. dernier - encore 2. battra 3. Allemands - encore gagné 4. a encore - demi-heure 5. avez - envie.

****

12th LESSON

The cinema

1 France has a great tradition in cinema.
2 From the great 'masters' like Abel Gance, Jean Renoir or Marcel Carné
3 to the film-makers of the 'New Wave' like Truffaut or Lelouch.
4 The 'Seventh Art' owes a lot to the talents of French directors and actors.
5 But today the cinema is in crisis: people are going less and less to the cinema.

NOTES

(2) Notice the construction with *depuis... jusqu'à:* it can be used for time: *Depuis le début jusqu'à la fin:* From the beginning to the end; or for distance: *Depuis la gare jusqu'au bureau:* From the station to the office. It is used here in a temporal sense.

(3) *'La Nouvelle vague'* was the name given to a movement started by young French film-makers in the late 1950s which tried to break away from the traditional story-telling approach which had been prevalent for many years. Its leading proponents were François Truffaut and Jean-Luc Godard.

6   En mil neuf cent soixante (1960), trois cent cinquante-quatre millions de spectateurs sont passés aux guichets **(N.4)**

7   mais en mil neuf cent soixante-dix, ce chiffre n'était que de cent soixante-dix millions,

8   soit la moitié. **(4)**

9   En moyenne, le Français va trois fois par an voir un film.

10 Une autre statistique : un Français sur cinq cents mesure plus d'un mètre quatre-vingts

11 mais c'est toujours celui-là qui sera devant vous au cinéma !

12 *Le Réalisateur :* — Votre scénario est excellent, mais il n'est pas du tout original ;

13 c'est la copie exacte des « Enfants du Paradis » de Carné. **(5)**

14 *Le jeune auteur :* — Et alors ? Ce n'était pas un merveilleux film, « Les Enfants du Paradis » ?

ILS ÉTAIENT DEUX MILLE À LA MANIFESTATION

EXERCICES

1. Je te dois vingt francs. — Non, pas à moi, à lui. **2.** Si vous ne trouvez pas le titre, cherchez dans la table des matières. **3.** Un Français sur trois va au cinéma toutes les semaines. **4.** Ils étaient deux mille à la manifestation, soit dix pour cent des habitants. **5.** Depuis le début du siècle jusqu'à aujourd'hui, nous avons eu deux guerres mondiales.

6   In 1960, 354 million spectators went through the turnstiles

7   but in 1970, this figure was only 170 million

8   in other words, half.

9   On average the French go three times a year to see a film.

10 Another statistic: one Frenchman in 500 measures more than 1 m 80

11 but it's always he who will be in front of you at the cinema!

12 *Director:* — Your screenplay is excellent, but it isn't at all original;

13 It's copied directly from the 'Enfants du Paradis' by Carné.

14 *Young author:* — So what?   Wasn't 'Enfants du Paradis' a marvellous film?

NOTES

(4) *Soit* is the 3rd person singular present subjunctive of the verb *être* but it is sometimes used when giving figures or statistics in two different forms. *Deux cents personnes, soit dix pour cent:* 200 people, or in other words, 10%. *Cinq mille francs, soit la moitié de son salaire:* 5 000 F, or half his salary. The word means 'in other words' and is invariable.

(5) Notice what happens to titles, place names, etc., which begin with the definite article. We have seen *Elle est du Havre:* She's from Le Havre. Here, the title of the film (a master-piece, by the way) is *Les Enfants du Paradis*. If we have a partitive article before *(de)* we must make the two agree.
... *copie des « Enfants du Paradis ». Il est l'auteur du « Voyou ».* He's the author of 'Le Voyou'.
Paradis in the film title refers to the upper circle of a theatre which, in English theatre jargon, is called 'The Gods'.

EXERCISES: 1. I owe you 20 F.   — Not to me, to him.   **2.** If you can't find the title, look in the list of contents.   **3.** One Frenchman in three goes to the cinema every week.   **4.** There were 2000 people at the demonstration, in other words 10% of the inhabitants.   **5.** From the beginning of the century up to today, we have had two world wars.

Mettez les mots qui manquent.
Fill in the blanks.

1 *Bertrand Blier est le scénariste* . . . «. . . . .».

Bertrand Blier is the scriptwriter of 'Les Valseuses'.

2 *Je* . . . . *deux* . . . . . *francs.*

I owe him 200 F.

3 *Ce* . ´ . . . . *un film merveilleux.*

It wasn't a marvellous film.

4 *Il a pris un taxi* . . . . . . *l'aéroport* . . . . . ´ .

la maison.

He took a taxi from the airport to his home.

****

TREIZIEME (13ᵉ) LEÇON

Quelques expressions (1)

1 — Ne tournez pas autour du pot. Expliquez-
vous tout de suite.
2 — Inutile de continuer ; c'est chercher une
aiguille dans une botte de foin. (2)
3 — Je n'ai pas pu savoir ce qu'il voulait dire ; il
coupe toujours les cheveux en quatre ; (3)

NOTES

(1) Although we have said that the meaning of an idiom cannot
usually be guessed from its constituent parts, English and
French have a common heritage which even extends to some
idiomatic expressions which are the same, or very similar, in
both languages. Here is a selection of some of those. In the
translation, we have put the nearest English equivalent.

(2) *Une botte* in this expression is equivalent to the old English
expression 'a bottle of hay' (a bunch - the word comes from old
French). We use *une botte* nowadays for a bunch or a bundle - *une
botte de carottes*. (*Des bottes* can also mean: boots).

Ecrivez ces dates :

1984 ....

1726 ....

1066 ....

1800 .... '

1409 ....

Mots qui manquaient :

1. des « Valseuses » **2.** lui dois - cents **3.** n'était pas **4.** depuis - jusqu'à.

Corrigé

1984: mil (or dix) neuf cent quatre-vingt-quatre.
1726: mil (or dix) sept cent vingt-six.
1066: mil soixante-six.
1800: mil (or dix) huit cents.
1409: mil quatre cent neuf or quatorze cent neuf.

****

13th LESSON

Some expressions

1 — Don't beat about the bush. Explain yourself immediately.

2 — It's useless continuing; it's like looking for a needle in a haystack.

3 — I couldn't find out what he meant; he's always splitting hairs,

NOTES

(3) *Vouloir dire:* the expression for 'to mean', when one is explaining one's words, intentions, etc. *Ce n'est pas ce que je voulais dire:* That's not what I meant. *Qu'est-ce que vous voulez dire?:* What do you mean?

The use of 'to mean' for 'to intend' (I meant to do it but I forgot) is translated by *avoir l'intention de: j'avais l'intention de le faire, mais j'ai oublié.*

The verb *signifier* also has the sense of 'to mean' when we are speaking of representation. *Que signifie ce mot?:* What does this word mean?

4 et qui plus est, il ment comme un arracheur de dents. **(4) (5)**

5 — Il va sûrement sortir en ville ce soir ; il est sur son trente et un. **(6)**

6 — Elle se sent bien ici ; elle est comme un poisson dans l'eau ;

7 et qu'est-ce qu'elle travaille bien ! — Elle vaut son pesant d'or.

8 — On ne sait pas ce qu'il devient ; on n'a pas de nouvelles. — Pas de nouvelles, bonnes nouvelles.

9 — Qu'est-ce qu'il m'énerve celui-là. Il fourre son nez partout.

10 — Tiens ! Voilà Henri ! Quand on parle du loup, on en voit la queue !

11 — Il m'a traité de lâche ; j'étais hors de moi ! **(7)**

12 — Ne vous en faites pas pour lui ; il a plusieurs cordes à son arc. **(8)**

13 — Qu'est-ce que j'avais peur ! J'avais la chair de poule !

EXERCICES

1. Que voulez-vous dire par cela ? **2.** Excuse-moi ! J'avais l'intention de t'écrire, je te l'assure. **3.** Ne vous en faites pas comme ça ; **4.** il va simplement vous arracher une dent ! **5.** Les deux conducteurs se sont traités de tous les noms. **6.** Qu'est-ce qu'elle travaille bien !

4 and what's more, he lies in his teeth.

5 — He's certainly going out on the town tonight; he's dressed up to the nines.

6 — She feels good here; she's like a fish in water;

7 and doesn't she work well! — She's worth her weight in gold.

8 — We don't know what's become of him; we haven't got any news. — No news is good news.

9 — How he gets on my nerves, that one! He sticks his nose into everything.

10 — Hey! Here's Henry! Speak of the devil (and you tread on his tail!).

11 — He called me a coward; I was beside myself with anger!

12 — Don't worry about him; he's got several strings to his bow.

13 — How scared I was! I had goose-flesh!

NOTES

(4) *Mentir* = to lie (prevaricate).

(5) A wonderful expression for which there is no real equivalent. The scene is a mediaeval market-place; the tooth-puller (*arracher:* to pull out, off) is standing with his pliers in his blood-stained hands, shouting 'Come on, I won't hurt you'. Well, would **you** believe him? The expression refers to a habitual liar.

(6) *En ville* is not quite 'on the town'; it is a slightly snobbish expression, the town referred to is that composed of the members of its high(ish) society.
Un dîner en ville: a social engagement-style dinner.

(7) *Traiter* literally means to treat, but in this context, or with an epithet after the verb, it means: to call someone a name. *Traiter quelqu'un de tous les noms:* To call someone all the names under the sun.

(8) Another idiomatic use of *faire*, always in this expression, with *en*. It means: to worry (infinitive *s'en faire*). It is most often found in the negative, in the expression *ne vous en faites pas (pour quelqu'un ou quelque chose)*.

EXERCISES: **1.** What do you mean by that? **2.** Excuse me, I meant to write to you, I assure you. **3.** Don't worry like that; **4.** he's only going to pull a tooth out! **5.** The two drivers called one another all the names under the sun. **6.** How well she works!

Mettez les mots qui manquent.
Fill in the blanks.

1 *Il* . . . . *autour* . . . . . .

He beat about the bush.

2 *Elle* . . . . . *toujours les* . . . . *en* . . . . . .

She always splits hairs.

3 *Il* . . . . . *sur son* . . . . . . *et* . . *hier soir.*

He was dressed up to the nines yesterday evening.

****

QUATORZIEME (14e) LEÇON

REVISION ET NOTES

1 The word *beau* has many idiomatic uses, but this is one of the most idiosyncratic. With the infinitive following, it gives the idea of an action which brought no results. Look at the following examples:
J'avais beau chercher, je ne trouvais pas.
Il avait beau crier, elle n'entendait pas.
The first sentence could be rendered as: Look as I may, I found nothing; the second as: He shouted in vain (because) she didn't hear. Do you see the idea of trying but not succeeding? The construction, thus: *Vous avez beau courir, vous ne la rattraperez pas:* It doesn't matter how fast you run, you won't catch her up.
Obviously, each of these sentences can be expressed differently. Don't worry about trying to construct sentences with this, or other idiomatic constructions: just build up a repertoire of phrases and use them when appropriate, learning others by example.

2 Since our aim in this book is to present as many different examples of current French as is useful, we will

4 *C'est chercher* . . . . *dans une*

. . . .

It's like looking for a needle in a haystack.

5 *Ils* . . . . . . *leur* . . . . . . *d'* . .

They're worth their weight in gold.

Mots qui manquaient :

1. a tourné - du pot **2.** coupe - cheveux - quatre **3.** était - trente - un **4.** une aiguille - botte de foin **5.** valent - pesant - or.

****

14th LESSON

show you both the 'bad' (i.e. careless) and the 'elegant' (i.e. language which is normally only found nowadays in written form).

So, we know that there are basically three ways of asking a question:

a) With the raised intonation: *Vous fumez?*

b) With an auxiliary phrase: *Est-ce que vous fumez?*

c) By inversion: *Fumez-vous?*

This would also be considered the ascending order of 'correctness'. The second form is probably the most common, the third form is found with the *vous* form but rarely with the other pronouns, especially *je,* mainly because of the sound. So it would be possible to say: *Fumé-je?:* Do I smoke? (The acute accent is necessary to prevent a sound like: fyoomzh) but it is hardly ever found, except used in a self-mocking way.

However, there are certain accepted expressions and it is quite usual to hear: *Combien vous dois-je?*

3 The more we speak and read French, the more we become aware of the differences between the two languages and how translation is often impossible because of the genius of each language. English, for

Leçon 14

example, has many more words to describe visual and aural perception. A good example is the translation of the verb *luire* which can be rendered as to glimmer, to gleam, to glow, to glint or to glisten. In the sentence in question the taxi driver crashes into a building. In English, we can say: to ram into; to crash into; to slam into; whereas French is restricted to describing the movment - *rentrer dans* or *s'écraser sur*. The more we become aware of such differences (which do not necessarily make one language richer than the other) the more we can assimilate French as a living language rather than a set of translations.

4   Here are some notes about numbers.

(I) When do we put an *s* on *vingt* and *cent?* If there is no other figure after them; e.g. 80 = *quatre-vingts* but 83 *quatre-vingt-trois;* 200 = *deux cents* but *deux cent cinquante.*

****

QUINZIEME (15ᵉ) LEÇON

Au café, Anne-Marie raconte son passé

1   J'avais dix-huit ans et je venais de finir l'école ; je n'avais pas envie d'aller à l'Université. **(1)**

2   Je connaissais des gens que j'avais rencontrés en vacances à La Baule, **(N.1) (2)**

3   et qui travaillaient dans une agence de voyages à Paris.

4   Ils venaient de mon pays, mais ils étaient partis pour Paris deux ans auparavant. **(1) (3) (4)**

NOTES

(1) *Je viens de...:* an idiomatic expression meaning I have just... *Nous venons d'arriver:* We have just arrived. This is the past-perfect tense. (Contrast the idiomatic usage - *venir de* + infinitive with the literal use in line 4.) This whole text is based on past-tense revision: pay special attention to each verb when re-reading.

(2) Agreement of past participle with preceding direct object: *J'ai rencontré les gens* but *Les gens que j'ai rencontrés.*

Of course, these details do not change the pronunciation.

(II) With *un million* and upward we must use *de* if we specify the content. *Trois millions de Français:* 3.000.000 Frenchmen.

(III) *Un milliard* poses a problem between English and American; it means one thousand million, which the Americans call a billion. A billion in English is one million million. There is a French word *un billion* (just as there is an English word milliard) but neither is used. For an English billion, the French would say *mille milliards.*

(IV) The year. First, the word *mil* is a contraction of *mille;* both are used (but mil **only** when writing the date).

Next, there are two ways of expressing the year. 1984 is either *mille (or mil) neuf cent quatre-vingt-quatre* (i. e. a figure) or *dix-neuf cent quatre-vingt-quatre* (i.e. the number of hundreds). We have chosen the former way, thinking it to be the more common, but there is no rule governing this. For dates only *mille* can be written as *mil.*

****

15th LESSON

In the café, Anne-Marie relates her past

1 I was eighteen and I had just finished school; I didn't want to go to University.
2 I knew some people whom I had met on holiday at La Baule,
3 and who were working in a travel agency in Paris.
4 They came from around my home, but they had left for Paris two years previously.

NOTES
(3) *Le pays* is the geographical country (*la campagne* is the country as opposed to the town) but, because of the history of the development of France and the great centralisation around the capital, each region has kept an individual identity akin to that of a country apart. This theme will be developed in the book (see lesson 31 et al.). It also explains why un *paysan* is not quite the 'peasant' that dictionaries give as a translation but more of a 'country-dweller'. In dialect un *pays* can mean a person from your 'country' or region.
(4) *Auparavant* is an adverb meaning: before(hand). Unlike *avant* it does not take a complement. *Avant de sortir* but *Il me l'a dit auparavant.* (He told me beforehand.) It is especially found in either indirect speech or sentences set in the pluperfect tense.

5 Je ne trouvais pas d'emploi au Havre et je ne voulais pas y rester.

6 Mes amis m'avaient dit que je pouvais trouver du travail avec eux.

7 J'avais économisé de l'argent en travaillant le week-end comme caissière dans un supermarché **(5)**

8 donc j'ai décidé de tenter ma chance.

9 J'ai demandé à mes parents la permission de partir ;

10 ils avaient compris depuis longtemps que je voulais m'en aller **(6)**

11 donc, malgré leur inquiétude, ils ont accepté.

12 Alors, j'ai fait mes valises et... me voilà ; je suis ici depuis quatre ans **(7)**

13 et je m'y plais beaucoup. Et vous ?

EXERCICES

1. Elle s'en est allée trois semaines en vacances. **2.** Il m'en avait parlé auparavant. **3.** Il a trouvé un nouvel emploi et il gagne beaucoup d'argent. **4.** Elle vient de terminer son nouveau roman. **5.** Vas-y ! Tente ta chance ! Tu pourrais gagner ! **6.** Il était là depuis deux mois mais il ne trouvait pas de travail.

Mettez les mots qui manquent.
Fill in the blanks.

1 *Ce sont les gens* . . . *j'* . . . . *là-bas.*

These are the people whom I met over there.

2 *Ils* . . . . *de* . . . . *pays un an*

. . . .

They had left their region a year previously.

5 I couldn't find a job in Le Havre and I didn't want to stay there.

6 My friends had told me that I could find work with them.

7 I had saved some money by working at the week-ends as a check-out clerk in a supermarket

8 so I decided to try my luck.

9 I asked my parents for permission to leave;

10 they had long since understood that I wanted to go

11 so, despite their misgivings, they accepted.

12 So, I packed my bags and... here I am; I have been here for four years

13 and I like it a lot.   And you?

(Notice that our translation is from one idiom into another - we don't want you to translate word for word.)

NOTES

(5) *La caisse:* the cash desk in a store or check-out in a supermarket; *une caissière:* the cashier or clerk. *La caisse enregistreuse:* the cash register. (*Une caisse* can also mean a case as used for packing goods.)

(6) *S'en aller* is a synonym for *partir:* to leave. *Va-t-en!* Go away!, Get lost!

(7) Although *voici* means: here is/are and *voilà,* there is/are, the latter is more commonly used for both cases, usually accompanied by a gesture.

EXERCISES: 1. She left for three weeks on holiday.   **2.** He had spoken to me about it before.   **3.** He found a new job and he's earning a lot of money.   **4.** She's just finished her new novel.   **5.** Go on!   Try your luck!   You may win!   **6.** He had been there for two months but he couldn't find a job.

Leçon 15

3 *Je* . . . . *la permission avant.*

I had asked for their permission before.

4 *Nous* . . . . *finir nos études.*

We had just finished our studies.

****

SEIZIEME (16ᵉ) LEÇON

Quelques questions

1 — Quel âge avait Anne-Marie quand elle a décidé de quitter Le Havre ?

2 — Où avait-elle rencontré ses amis ? Que faisaient-ils ?

3 — Quand étaient-ils partis du Havre ? Pour quoi faire ? **(1)**

4 — Où Anne-Marie avait-elle travaillé pour gagner de l'argent ?

5 — Quel était l'avis de ses parents sur ses projets ? **(2)**

6 — Depuis combien de temps était-elle à Paris avant qu'elle ne rencontre Laurent ? **(3)**

SES PARENTS N'ÉTAIENT PAS D'ACCORD AVEC SES PROJETS

NOTES

(1) Notice the difference between *Pourquoi?* Why?, and *Pour quoi* usually followed in the interrogative by *faire*: what for? (Which, in old English, was: what for to do?) Quite often, of course, the distinction is minimal. Notice, however, the difference in writing (in

5 *Vous* . . . . *ici ?*

Do you like it here?

Mots qui manquaient :

1. que - ai rencontrés 2. étaient partis - leur - auparavant 3. leur avais demandé 4. venions de 5. vous plaisez.

****

16th LESSON

A few questions

1 — How old was Anne-Marie when she decided to leave Le Havre?
2 — Where had she met her friends? What were they doing?
3 — When had they left Le Havre? What for?
4 — Where had Anne-Marie worked to earn money?
5 — What was her parents' opinion of her plans?
6 — How long had she been in Paris before she met Laurent?

NOTES

the affirmative) between *Je ne sais pas pourquoi elle est venue:* I don't know why she came and *Je ne sais pas pour quoi elle est venue:* I don't know what she came for.

(2) *L'avis:* the critical opinion of a person: *Quel est votre avis?:* What's your opinion? *Je ne suis pas de son avis:* I'm not of his/her opinion. *A votre avis, ça peut coûter combien?:* In your opinion, how much would that cost? The word *l'opinion* is also used, but tends to be more linked with the **way** one thinks.
Un avis is also a notification, or a notice. On municipal bulletin-boards, public notices are headed: *AVIS.* If a registered letter, or the like, is waiting for you at the post-office you receive *un avis de passage* notifying you of the fact. (The English work *advice* is translated by *le conseil.*)

(3) *Avant qu'il ne vienne;* this conjunctional phrase (along with several others we shall see later) is followed by a subjunctive at all times. The presence of what is called the *ne explétif* is the subject of debate among French grammarians. The argument centres around this point: since the action *avant que* relates to has not yet occurred we need some way of bringing out the distinction. Let's add *ne* say some; the subjunctive alone is sufficient insist others. Suffice it to say that *avant que* with *ne* is the more common of the two forms. We recommend you to use it. The sentence could also side-step the problem by saying ... *avant de rencontrer;* (this only works, of course, if the subject of both 'joined' verbs is the same).

Leçon 16

7 — Voici une belle, vieille chanson française ;
écoutez bien :

A la claire fontaine

8   A la claire fontaine, m'en allant promener,
9   J'ai trouvé l'eau si belle que je m'y suis
baigné.
10   Il y a longtemps que je t'aime ; jamais je ne
t'oublierai.
11   Sur la plus haute branche un rossignol
chantait,
12   Chante, rossignol, chante, toi qui as le cœur
gai.
13   Il y a longtemps que je t'aime, jamais je ne
t'oublierai.
14 — Chantez-la avec nous...

EXERCICES

*Nous vous donnons ici les réponses aux questions. Nous
voulons que vous reconstituiez les questions sans vous
référer au texte de la leçon.*

1. Elle avait 18 ans quand elle a décidé de quitter Le
Havre. **2.** Elle avait rencontré ses amis à La Baule. Ils
étaient en vacances. **3.** Ils étaient partis du Havre deux
ans auparavant pour travailler dans une agence de
voyages. **4.** Ses parents n'étaient pas d'accord avec ses
projets. **5.** Elle était à Paris depuis quatre ans avant de
rencontrer Laurent.

Mettez les mots qui manquent.
Fill in the blanks.

1 *Nous* . . . . *il y a deux ans.*

We left Le Havre two years ago.

7 — Here is a beautiful old French song; listen carefully:

At the clear fountain

8 At the clear fountain, as I went a-walking
9 The water was so sweet that I went a-swimming.
10 Long have I loved you; never will I forget you.
11 Upon the highest branch a nightingale was singing.
12 Sing, nightingale, sing you whose heart is gay.
13 Long have I loved you, never will I forget you.
14 — Sing it with us...

2 *Quand je vous* . . . . , *vous*

. . . . *dans une banque ;*

When I met you, you were working in a bank;

3 *Je* . ´ . . . . *jamais ce que vous* . ´ . . . .

. . .

I'll never forget what you said to me.

4 *Elle* . ´ . . . . *baignée.*

She swam there.

5 *Finissez la bouteille* . . . . ´ . . . ´*arrive.*

Finish the bottle before he comes.

6 *Je veux vous voir avant qu'ils* . . . .

I want to see you before they come.

Mots qui manquaient :

1. sommes partis du Havre 2. ai rencontré - travailliez 3. n'oublierai - m'avez dit 4. s'y est 5. avant qu'il n' 6. ne viennent.

DIX-SEPTIEME (17e) LEÇON

S'il vous plaît...

1 — Excusez-moi, monsieur, mais est-ce que cela vous dérange **(2)**

2   si j'ouvre la fenêtre ? Il fait horriblement chaud ici.

3 — Mais pas du tout, madame. Ne bougez pas. Je vais le faire. **(3)**

4   (Au magasin) — Qu'y a-t-il pour votre service, mademoiselle ? **(4)**

5 — Vous permettez que je regarde ? Je cherche un cadeau.

6 — Mais, je vous en prie.

IL FAIT HORRIBLEMENT CHAUD ICI !

7 — Dites donc ! Voulez-vous baisser un peu votre chaîne ? **(5)**

8 — Excusez-moi, monsieur. Je vais le faire tout de suite.

9   (Au téléphone) — Allô ? Bonjour, madame, je vous demande pardon, mais suis-je bien chez M. Prévôt ? — Non, vous faites erreur. **(6)**

10 — Excusez-moi de vous avoir dérangée. — Il n'y a pas de quoi.

17th LESSON

Please...

1 — Excuse me, sir, but will it disturb you
2   if I open the window?   It's terribly hot here.
3 — Not at all, madam.   Don't move.   I'll do it.
4   (In a shop) — May I be of service, miss?
5 — May I look?   I'm looking for a present.
6 — But of course.
7 — Hey!   Will you turn down your stereo a little!
8 — Excuse me, sir.   I'll do it straight away.
9   (On the phone) — Hello?   Good morning, madam, I beg your pardon.   Is that M. Prevot's house?   — No, you've made a mistake.
10 — Excuse me for having disturbed you.   — Don't mention it.

NOTES

(1) French tends to begin a request with *s'il vous plaît* whereas English usually puts **please** at the end of a phrase unless expressing emphasis.
In the type of situation illustrated by the dialogues, we have reproduced the English equivalents, not the translation. 'Polite' French seems much more formal, or even pompous, than English, yet it is not at all so to a French ear.
S'il vous plaît, when written, is often abbreviated to *S.V.P.*
T.S.V.P. = Tourner s'il vous plaît = PTO.
The infinitive of to please is *plaire*.

(2) *Déranger* means to disturb or to put out. In hotels you hang a sign on your door so as not to be disturbed - *ne pas déranger*. *En dérangement,* however, means: out of order.

(3) Using the *aller + infinitive* form brings the action much closer to the present (see also line 8) where the speaker further emphasises by adding *tout de suite* (immediately).

(4) (See comments in note 1.) This very formal phrase (along with another: *Que puis-je pour vous?*) tends to disappear, to be replaced with *Vous désirez?:* What do you want? or *On vous sert?:* Are you being served? or *A qui le tour?:* Whose turn? or - most unfortunately - *A qui?!*

(5) *Une chaîne* is a chain but it is commonly used to mean a stereo unit, because the different parts are linked together. A lot of vocabulary concerning *la hi-fi* is English (*le 'tuner', le 'woofer', le 'boomer', le 'tweeter'*, etc.).

(6) *Allô* is **only** used on the telephone and is really a means of discovering if one has been heard (the French never give their name or number when answering the phone); it should be followed by a polite word like *Bonjour* ou *Bonsoir*.

63

11 — (Dans un bus) — Pardon, monsieur, mais permettez-vous que je m'assoie à votre place ?

12 Je suis désolée, mais je suis enceinte. — Mais bien sûr !

13 — Je sais que ça ne se voit pas ; ce n'est que depuis hier, **(N.2)**

14 mais que c'est fatigant !

EXERCICES

1. Ne bougez pas ! Je vais l'ouvrir. **2.** Je vous demande pardon, mais suis-je bien chez M. Lemarc ? **3.** Vous permettez que je regarde? — Je vous en prie. **4.** Oh, excusez-moi de vous avoir dérangé. — Il n'y a pas de quoi. **5.** Vous êtes malade ? Ça ne se voit pas.

Mettez les mots qui manquent.
Fill in the blanks.

1 *Cela vous . . . . si j' . . . . . la porte ?*

Will it disturb you if I open the door?

2 *Il . . . . sa . . . . tout de suite.*

He'll turn down his stereo straight away.

3 *. . . . . - . . . . que je . . . . . . votre place ?*

May I take your place?

****

*****

11 (In a bus) — Excuse me, sir, but may I take your seat?

12 I'm very sorry, but I'm pregnant. — But of course!

13 — I know it doesn't show; it's only since yesterday

14 but how tiring it is!

EXERCISES: 1. Don't move! I'll open it. **2.** I beg your pardon, but is this M. Lemarc's house? **3.** May I look? — Please do. **4.** Oh, excuse me for having disturbed you. — Don't mention it. **5.** You're sick? It doesn't show.

4 *La cabine est* . . . . , *je suis*

. . . . . .

The phone-box is out of order. I'm very sorry.

5 *Est-ce que la nouvelle voiture* . . . . . . *votre femme ?*

Does the new car please your wife?

Mots qui manquaient :

1. dérange - ouvre **2.** va baisser - chaîne **3.** Permettez-vous - prenne **4.** en dérangement - désolé* **5.** plaît à.

* In line 12, *désolé* takes an extra 'e' since it is a woman speaking.

****

*****

DIX-HUITIEME (18ᵉ) LEÇON

Incidents

1 — Où vas-tu ? — A la poste. Je dois envoyer cette lettre recommandée. **(1)**

2 — Tu pourrais me prendre des timbres ? Je n'en ai plus.

3 — D'accord. Tu en veux combien ? — Oh, prends m'en dix.

4 Je te rembourserai tout à l'heure, O. K. ? — O. K. Salut. **(3) (4)**

5 — Pardon, madame ; je voudrais un renseignement s'il vous plaît. — Guichet vingt-deux.

6 — Ah voilà. Excusez-moi, monsieur, pourriez-vous me dire... — C'est fermé.

7 — Mais enfin ! Ne pourriez-vous pas me donner un renseignement ? **(5)**

8 — Je vous en ai donné un. On est fermé. — Ça alors ! **(5)**

Incidents

1 — Where are you going? — To the post office. I have to send this registered letter.

2 — Could you get me some stamps? I've none left.

3 — O. K. how many do you want? — Oh, get me ten.

4 — I'll pay you back later, O. K.? — O. K. 'Bye.

5 — Excuse me, madam, I would like some information, please. — Counter 22.

6 — Ah, here we are. Excuse me, sir, could you tell me... — It's closed.

7 — Oh come on! Couldn't you give me some information?

8 — I gave you some. We're closed. — Well I never!

NOTES

(1) *Une lettre recommandée* is a registered letter. If you want proof that the addressee has received it, you ask for *une lettre recommandée avec accusé de réception,* meaning you will receive a slip signed by the addressee upon receipt. *Accuser réception* means to acknowledge receipt.

(2) (see lesson 15, note 5) Another common phenomenon of popular spoken French, is to drop the *u* of the *tu* form before another vowel. This would give us a sound like *T'en veux combien ?* Although it avoids a hiatus, it is considered incorrect and is never written.

(3) Another example of vocabulary difference: English has 'to pay back' and 'to reimburse' (which is more technical), one from its Germanic origins and the other from Latin. French has only the latter (see also lesson 33).

(4) *Salut!* is a familiar greeting among friends, meaning 'Hi' or 'Bye!' It should not be used with strangers. Incidentally, there is a theory that the ubiquitous O. K. derived from a trysting arrangement between French sailors and American maidens during the American Revolution, when they agreed to meet *aux quais* (on the docks)!

(5) Two expletives, the first expressing impatience, the second incredulity *Comment? Vous n'en avez plus? Mais enfin?* What? You don't have any left? Oh, come on!
Elle lui a volé sa bague! — *Ça alors!:* She stole the ring from him! — Well, I never.

9   Dans un compartiment de wagon-lit, deux hommes essaient de s'endormir.

10   Ou plutôt l'un deux - et il n'y arrive pas car l'autre ne cesse de gémir : **(7)**

11   — Oh que j'ai soif ! C'est horrible, j'ai si soif !

12   L'autre ne tient plus ; il se lève et va au wagon-bar.

13   Il achète une bouteille d'eau minérale, revient et la donne à l'assoiffé. **(N.3)**

14   — Maintenant qu'il a bu, je vais dormir, dit-il, en fermant les yeux.

15   mais il n'y arrive toujours pas car l'autre commence à gémir : — Que j'avais soif ! Mon Dieu que j'avais soif !

EXERCICES

1. Combien voulez-vous de bouteilles ? — Prenez m'en trois. **2.** Ne pourrais-tu pas me rembourser tout de suite ? **3.** Je ne cesse de te répéter que je n'ai plus d'argent. **4.** Je ne tiendrai plus s'ils continuent de chanter. **5.** Comment ? Vous ne venez pas ? Mais enfin ! **6.** J'ai essayé mais je n'y arrive pas. — Ça alors !

Mettez les mots qui manquent.
Fill in the blanks.

1   *Maintenant* . . . *vous* . . . . . *je* . . . . *m'* . . . .

Now you have drunk, I'll fall asleep.

2   *Je veux des timbres. — Combien* . . . . - . ?

I want some stamps. — How many do you want?

3   *Prends* . . . *une vingtaine ; je te* . . . .

Get me about 20; I'll pay you back.

68

9 In a sleeping-car compartment, two men are trying to get to sleep.

10 Or rather one of them - and he isn't succeeding since the other doesn't stop groaning:

11 — Oh I'm thirsty! It's horrible, I'm so thirsty!

12 The other can't bear it; he gets up and goes to the bar-car.

13 He buys a bottle of mineral water, comes back and gives it to the thirsty one.

14 — Now that he has drunk, I will sleep, he says, closing his eyes.

15 But he still doesn't succeed because the other begins to moan: — How thirsty I was! My God, how thirsty I was!

NOTES

(6) One of the few words in French to begin with a 'w'; like this one, all the others are foreign, usually English (e.g. *un watt, un week-end, un western*). Such *mots d'emprunt* (loan words) use (something like!) the English pronunciation [oueekend; ouestern] etc. *Un wagon(-lit)* is pronounced with a 'v'. Another English expression to pass into French was *water-closet* or *W.C.* (pronounced vaysay)!

(7) *Car* is a conjunction and it is used when explaining a situation or a judgement, like 'since' in English. *Vous ne le trouverez pas chez lui car il est sorti il y a dix minutes:* You won't find him at home since he went out ten minutes ago.
Parce que (because) explains the motive or the reason for an action. *Elle est tombée parce qu'il y avait du verglas:* She fell because there was ice.
The two are often interchangeable, but *car* (like all conjunctions) never begins a sentence.

EXERCISES: 1. How many bottles do you want? — Get me three. **2.** Couldn't you pay me back immediately? **3.** I keep telling you that I've no more money. **4.** I won't hold out any longer if they keep singing.**5.** What? You're not coming? Oh, come on! **6.** I tried but I can't manage. — Well I never!

4 *Il n'y . . . . . . pas . . . l'autre ne . . . . . de*

ronfler.

He doesn't manage since the other keeps snoring.

5 . . . . — . . . . m'aider ?

Couldn't you help me?

****

DIX-NEUVIEME (19e) LEÇON

Le pessimiste et l'optimiste

1 — L'argent rentre par petites gouttes et s'en va
au galop, dit-on souvent.

2 Que l'on touche un bon salaire, des honoraires ou des appointements, **(1) (2)**

3 que l'on reçoive les allocations de chômage
ou que l'on joue dans le métro pour gagner
son pain, **(3) (4)**

MAIS TU ES FAUCHÉ !

4 il y aura toujours des factures à régler, des
relevés à payer et des dépenses à faire. **(5)**

5 Gagner de l'argent devient de plus en plus
dur, d'autant plus que le pouvoir d'achat

6 est rongé par l'inflation, même si on ne jette
pas l'argent par la fenêtre.

Mots qui manquaient :

1. que - avez bu - vais - endormir 2. en veux-tu 3. m'en - rembourserai
4. arrive pas - car - cesse 5. Ne pourriez-vous pas.

****

19th LESSON

The pessimist and the optimist

1 — Money comes in in drops and goes galloping out,
they often say.

2 Whether one earns a good salary, fees or income,
3 whether one receives unemployment benefit, or
plays in the metro to earn one's bread,

4 there will always be bills to settle, bills to pay and
expenditure to make.

5 Making money is becoming harder and harder, all
the more so since one's purchasing power

6 is eaten away by inflation, even if one doesn't
throw money out of the window.

NOTES

(1) We are going to look at the subjunctive in greater detail next week but here is an example of its use when in English, we say: whether..., where two actions depend on the same verb or vice versa. Whether you go or not, you will have to pay: *Que vous y alliez ou non, vous devrez payer.* Whether you walk or run, you'll never catch him: *Que vous marchiez ou que vous couriez, vous ne le rattraperez jamais.* Remember *Que* + subjunctive.

(2) A worker earns *un salaire,* a doctor or a lawyer *des honoraires (masc.), une femme de ménage* (a cleaning lady) earns *des appointements.* Most workers in France are either *des salariés* or *des artisans* (craftsmen). Few people are paid weekly wages, and most salaries are paid directly into a bank account.

(3) Again, we see the impersonal use of *on;* the possessive form (i.e. one's in English) is the same as for his and her, i.e., *son* or *sa* depending on the gender of the noun, not the sex of the speaker.

(4) Notice the similarity of the expression *gagner son pain* with the English one. *Un gagne-pain* is an occupation that brings in the money; there is no real expression for a bread-winner (plural *des gagne-pain,* invariable).

(5) *Un relevé* is literally something that has been taken up from, a reading; it is used, for example, in *un relevé de compte (bancaire):* a bank statement. The expressions *un relevé d'électricité* or *de téléphone* therefore, literally refer only to the figures noted down but, by transference, they have come to mean the electricity and 'phone bills'.

7   Certes, il y a toujours des banques ou des Caisses d'épargne pour vous conseiller, **(6)**

8   ou bien vous pouvez acheter des actions à la Bourse

9   mais, à la fin, on tire toujours le diable par la queue. **(7)**

10 — Tant pis ! Moi, je suis optimiste. Tiens, je vais manger un plateau d'huîtres.

11 — Mais tu es fauché ! Avec quoi veux-tu les payer, tes huîtres ? **(8)**

12 — Eh bien, avec la perle que je trouverai dedans ! Salut !

EXERCICES

1. Il est au chômage; il ne touche pas de salaire depuis six mois. **2.** Il doit tirer le diable par la queue ! **3.** Non, il a d'autres gagne-pain, **4.** mais, quand même, il ne jette pas l'argent par la fenêtre. **5.** Des huîtres ? Mais tu es fauché ! — Tant pis ! **6.** Ce mois va être dur ; il faut régler ces factures et payer le relevé de téléphone.

Mettez les mots qui manquent.
Fill in the blanks.

1 *Il* . . . . . . *toujours des* . . . . *à faire.*

   There will always be expenditure.

2 *Que tu y* . . . . . . *ou non, moi, j'* . . . .

   Whether you go or not, I'll go!

3 *C'est dur,* . ´ . . . . *je viens de*

   payer la facture.

   It's hard, all the more so since I've just paid the bill.

7 Of course, there are always banks and savings banks to advise you

8 or you can buy shares on the Stock Exchange

9 but, in the end, you always burn the candle at both ends.

10 — Hard luck! Me, I'm an optimist. I'll go and eat a tray of oysters.

11 — But you're broke! What do you think you are going to pay for the oysters with?

12 — Well, with the pearl that I'll find inside! So long!

NOTES

(6) *Certes* is a literary form of *Bien sûr* (of course).

(7) This picturesque idiom means simply 'to have a hard time financially, to be hard up'.

(8) *Etre fauché* is a familiar expression for *ne pas avoir d'argent*. It means 'to be broke'.

EXERCISES: 1. He is unemployed; he hasn't earned a salary for six months. **2.** He must be really hard up! **3.** No, he has other money-earning activities, **4.** but all the same, he doesn't throw money out of the window. **5.** — Oysters? But you're broke! — Hard luck! **6.** This month is going to be hard; I have to settle these bills and pay the 'phone bill.

4 . . . *vous* . . . . *des honoraires ou que vous*

. . . . *un salaire*

Whether you receive fees or you earn a salary

5 *vous* . . . . . *des impôts à payer.*

you will have taxes to pay.

6 . . . . *devient de plus en plus dur.*

Earning one's bread is becoming harder and harder.

Mots qui manquaient :

1. y aura - dépenses **2.** ailles - irai **3.** d'autant plus que **4.** Que - receviez - touchiez **5.** aurez **6.** Gagner son pain.

Leçon 19

VINGTIEME (20ᵉ) LEÇON

L'argent (1)

1 — Voilà ; cela vous fait deux cent cinquante francs. Comment voulez-vous régler ? En espèces ? **(2)**

2 — Non, par chèque s'il vous plaît. — Bien. Avez-vous une pièce d'identité ?

3 — Voici mon permis de conduire. A l'ordre de qui dois-je mettre le chèque ?

4 — Oh, laissez-le en blanc ; nous avons un tampon. **(3)**

5 (Vu dans un café) Nous avons un accord avec la banque.

6 Ils ne servent pas de vin, et nous n'acceptons pas les chèques.

7 — Je croyais qu'il avait du mal à boucler ses fins de mois **(4)**

8 mais voilà qu'il m'achète pour quatre cents francs de marchandises et il me règle en espèces ! **(5)**

9 Il n'y a pas eu un hold-up ces jours-ci ? **(6)**

NOTES

(1) *L'argent* is money, yes, but it also means silver. *Un plateau en argent:* a silver tray. The adjective *argenté* can thus mean either silvery (*gris argenté:* silvery-grey) or 'moneyed': *des touristes argentés:* well-heeled tourists.

(2) There are several expressions for 'to pay cash': *payer en espèces* (current); *payer en liquide* (popular but current) or... yes, *payer cash!* Please avoid the last one.

(3) Since all salaried workers must have a bank account, payment by cheque in France is fairly simple. You usually only need *une pièce d'identité* (identity card, driver's licence, passport, etc.) as guarantee. On the cheque are the words *Payer à l'ordre de:* Payable to... One usually asks for the name of the payee and, quite often, is told to leave it blank since the establishment has a rubber stamp *(un tampon)* with its name. The verb is *tamponner.* (Remember that a postage stamp is *un timbre* and the verb *affranchir.*)

20th LESSON

Money

1 — There we are, that makes 250F. How do you want to pay? Cash?

2 — No, by cheque, please. — Fine. Do you have some form of identification?

3 — Here is my driving licence. To whom must I make the cheque payable?

4 — Oh leave it blank; we have a stamp.

5 (Seen in a café) We have an agreement with the bank.

6 They don't serve wine, and we don't accept cheques.

7 — I thought he had a hard time making ends meet

8 but he goes and buys 400F-worth of goods from me and he pays cash!

9 There hasn't been a hold-up recently, has there?

NOTES

(4) An idiomatic expression. *Boucler* is to buckle (*une boucle:* a buckle or a curl). Since most workers are paid at the end of the month, it is sometimes difficult to join the (relatively prosperous) beginning to the (meagre) end. Similar to, but less literary than *tirer le diable par la queue.*

(5) Be careful of the construction of sentences with the verb *acheter. Acheter quelque chose à quelqu'un* usually means: to buy from someone. *Il a acheté des roses à la fleuriste:* He bought roses from the florist. With the pronoun: *Il lui a acheté des roses:* He bought roses from him/her. But there is an ambiguity possible: since *à* indicates movement **towards** something or someone. *Elle a acheté un cadeau à son mari* would mean: She bought a present for her husband. (He would be a niggard if he were to **sell** her one!) And even more confusing are the prepositions. *Il nous a acheté du chocolat* could mean that he bought chocolate **from** us or **for** us. Usually, as with the example of the present, the context makes things clear. Should ambiguity persist, we would form the sentence differently. *Il a acheté un cadeau pour sa femme,* or *pour elle.* (Note the 's' after *cent,* since there is no other figure following.)

(6) *Ces jours-ci* or *ces mois-ci* means recently.
Un hold-up (like all foreign loan-words, it is invariable) is the accepted expression for, well, a hold-up. The verb would be *attaquer une banque* or *dévaliser* (rob) *une banque.*

10 — Les traites arrivent à échéance à la fin de la
     semaine ; **(7)**

11   peut-on faire un virement sur notre compte
     courant ?

12 — Il vaut mieux, sinon nous allons signer des
     chèques en bois ! **(8)**

13 — Je ne veux pas de vos cartes de crédit ici.

14   Je veux être payé rubis sur l'ongle. **(9)**

15 — L'argent, c'est comme les femmes ; il faut
     s'en occuper un peu,

16   sinon, il va faire le bonheur de quelqu'un
     d'autre !

EXERCICES

1. Vous pouvez régler en espèces, par chèque ou avec
une carte de crédit. **2.** Devrais-je faire un virement
bancaire ? — Il vaudrait mieux. **3.** Voilà qu'il m'achète un
bracelet pour sa femme. **4.** Y a-t-il eu un accident de la
circulation récemment ? **5.** Elle a du mal à boucler ses fins
de mois, n'est-ce pas ? **6.** Ils ont tamponné mon
passeport à la douane.

Mettez les mots qui manquent.
Fill in the blanks.

1 . . . . *a-t-* . . . . *quelque chose ces jours-ci ?*

   Has he bought anything from you recently?

10 — The drafts fall due at the end of the week;
11 can we make a transfer to our current account?
12 — We better had, if not we'll be signing rubber cheques!
13 — I don't want any of your credit cards here.
14 I want to be paid cash on the nail.
15 — Money is like women; you must look after it a little
16 otherwise it goes to make the happiness of someone else!

NOTES

(7) As in English, a draft comes from the verb 'to draw' so *une traite* comes from the old verb *traire* meaning 'to pull'. We still find it in the expression *traire une vache:* to milk a cow (by pulling, of course). The modern verb is, of course, *tirer.*

(8) In English we have rubber cheques because they 'bounce'; in French, they are made of wood because they make a hollow noise when they fall! The official expression is *un chèque sans provision* (not to be confused with *un chèque en blanc:* a blank cheque).

(9) An interesting expression, meaning to pay all one owes at once and in full. It is akin to 'cash on the nail' in English, but the two nails are totally different. The English **'nail'** was a dock-side mooring post where quayside transactions were carried out in cash. The French expression means 'to do something to the full - to drain one's glass so that only one drop of red wine (ruby-coloured) remains to cover a fingernail'! Hence, to pay in full.

EXERCISES: 1. You may pay in cash, by cheque or with a credit card. **2.** Should I make a bank transfer? — You better had. **3.** He goes and buys a bracelet from me for his wife. **4.** Has there been a traffic accident recently? **5.** She has trouble making ends meet, doesn't she? **6.** They stamped my passport at the Customs.

2 *Les* . . . . *à échéance.*

The drafts have fallen due.

3 . . . - . . *payer en* . . . . *(. . . . . . .) ?*

Can one pay cash? (Insert one or two words.)

4 *A l'* . . . . . *de qui* . . . . - . . *mettre* . . . *chèque ?*

To whom must I make my cheque payable?

5 *Nous ne* . . . . *pas* . . *vin et ils*

n' . . . . *pas* . . . *chèques.*

We won't serve wine and they won't accept cheques.

****

VINGT-ET-UNIEME (21e) LEÇON

REVISION ET NOTES

1 *... que j'avais rencontrés:* This is what we call the *plus-que-parfait* or the 'past perfect' tense and usually corresponds to the English 'had' + past participle.
A vingt ans, j'avais fini mes études: By the time I was 20, I had finished my studies.
Elle m'en avait déjà parlé: She had already told me about it.
Those verbs which conjugate with *être* follow the same pattern.
J'étais venu vous voir: I had come to see you.
Je m'étais réveillé très tôt ce jour-là: I had woken up very early on that day.
However, when the English sentence uses a past perfect with 'for' or 'since' *(depuis)* French uses the imperfect.
Elle était à Lyon depuis trois mois: She had been in Lyon for three months. Used in construction with the imperfect it expresses an idea of habit in the past; *Quand il avait déjeuné, il faisait la sieste:* When he had eaten, he used to take a siesta. As in English, the *plus-que-parfait* should never be used without another determining phrase, but often French seems to confuse the issue by making a statement in the *plus-que-parfait* and leaving the second part of the sentence unspoken. A very common example is the expression: *Je vous l'avais dit:* Usually uttered when the speaker sees that the other person has ignored advice or warning, we might put it like this in English: 'I told you so' and, understood, 'but you wouldn't listen to me' (i.e. I told you before you carried out the action).

Mots qui manquaient :

1. Vous - il acheté 2. traites sont arrivées 3. Peut-on - espèces (liquide)
4. ordre - dois-je - mon 5. servirons - de - accepteront - les.

****

21st LESSON

Such a usage is difficult to make rules for because, for one, the language obeys the situation rather than the grammatical precept. However, be on the look-out for the cases where it occurs.

The use of the *plus-que-parfait* differs when a conjunction of time is added to the sentence (e.g. *Aussitôt que... Dès que... etc.).* We will see this in more detail when we look at the 'past historic' tense.

2 *Ça ne se voit pas.* This impersonal use of the reflexive mood is very common and helps avoid a passive construction (we have already noted the extensive use of *on* in this context). Look at these examples:

Il est malade: He's sick.
Ça ne se voit pas: It doesn't show (i.e. it can't be seen).
Il est Allemand: He's German.
Cela ne s'entend pas: You can't hear it (i.e. it isn't heard).
Elle était en colère: She was angry.
Ça se comprend!: That's understandable!
Dire « non » à son directeur, ça ne se fait pas: Saying 'no' to one's director is just not done.

Notice how regular French usage is (*Cela* or *ça* + reflexive *se* + 3rd person singular) as compared to English.

A very common expression is *Ça ne se dit pas en français* (That isn't good French); it is often used to correct foreigners who use a spoken (i.e. 'incorrect') form when written French would demand something else. The irony is that, most often, *ça se dit!*

3 Look at the following adjectival forms:

soif (thirst) *assoiffé; un assoiffé:* a thirsty person
triste (sad) *attristé:* saddened
faim (hungry) *affamé; un affamé:* a hungry person
or with some verbs:
doux - douce (soft, sweet); *adoucir:* to soften

****

VINGT-DEUXIEME (22ᵉ) LEÇON

Soyez le bienvenu (1)

1 — Bonjour, monsieur Perrier ; bienvenue à Lyon. Avez-vous fait bon voyage ?

2 — Ça a été, je vous remercie. Ce train est en effet remarquable. **(2) (3)**

3 — Le T.G.V. ? N'est-ce pas ? Maintenant, on peut faire le trajet en deux fois moins de temps. **(4) (5)**

4 N'avez-vous pas d'autres bagages ? Non ? Alors, allons chercher un taxi. **(6)**

5 — Excusez-moi du retard ! J'aurais été deux fois plus vite si j'avais pris un taxi ; **(N.1)**

NOTES

(1) *Soyez* (fam. *sois*) is, as we know, the subjunctive of *être*. It is used also for the imperative. *Soyez tranquille:* Don't be worried. *Sois sage!:* Be good!
Le bienvenu is literally 'the welcome person' so the expression means: Be the welcome person. The word agrees in gender. *Soyez la bienvenue, chère Madame.* But be careful: we say *souhaiter la bienvenue à quelqu'un* (to a man or a woman).
Bienvenue à Marseille: Welcome to Marseille.
'A welcome' in the abstract sense is *un accueil* [akeuy]. *Il m'a fait un bon accueil:* He gave me a good welcome. *Un comité d'accueil:* a welcoming committee. In a public building or an office, *l'accueil* is the reception desk.
Incidentally, *Fulgence Bienvenüe* was the Belgian engineer who designed the Parisian Metro in 1897. Montparnasse metro station bears his name: *Montparnasse-Bienvenüe*.

futé - (sharp) of a person; *affûter:* to sharpen (a knife etc.)
Always look for the root word to help you understand:
Il était adossé contre un mur. Root word is *le dos:* the
back. He was leaning back against the wall.
Elle est alitée depuis deux semaines. Root word is *le lit:*
the bed. She has been bedridden for two weeks.

****

22nd LESSON

Welcome

1 — Good morning Mr Perrier; welcome to Lyon. Did
you have a good trip?

2 — It was fine, thank you. That train is really
remarkable.

3 — The T.G.V.? Isn't it? Now you can do the
journey in half the time.

4 — Don't you have any other baggage? No? Well,
let's go and look for a taxi.

5 — Excuse me for being late! I would have been
twice as fast if I had taken a taxi;

NOTES

(2) A more elegant way of saying *merci*. The verb *remercier* means
'to thank'.

(3) *En effet* (in fact) used after the verb reinforces the sense of the
verb, like the adverb 'really'.
Elle a en effet de bonnes idées: She really does have good ideas.

(4) *T.G.V. Train à Grande Vitesse:* The High Speed Train.
N'est-ce pas? This simple interjection replaces all the English tag
questions like '— isn't it?' '— haven't you?' '— do you?' etc.
However, whereas such 'tags' are extremely frequent in English,
n'est-ce pas? a rather elegant term, is less used.

(5) *Un trajet:* is a journey (another word is *un parcours*); *un voyage* is a
trip - *un voyage d'affaires:* a business trip. Travel, in the abstract, is
les voyages. A famous expression is *Les voyages forment la
jeunesse:* Travel shapes youth. *Un agent de voyages:* a travel
agent. *Voyager:* to travel.
In business contexts we hear the word *un déplacement* (lit: a
displacement) for 'a business trip'. *Il est en déplacement:* He's
travelling for his job. *Frais de déplacement:* travelling expenses.

(6) *Chercher:* to find; used with *aller* as in line 14, it means to fetch.
Veux-tu aller me chercher mes pantoufles?: Will you go and fetch
my slippers?

6   je connais mal les rues de Paris et je me suis perdu. Et quelle circulation affreuse !

7 — Je vous en prie, ne vous excusez pas. L'essentiel est que vous soyez arrivé.

8 — Vous êtes bien aimable. Votre bureau est-il encore loin ?

9 — A une vingtaine de kilomètres. — Cela vous gênerait-il de conduire ? **(7)**

10 — Du tout ! Passez-moi les clés. Hop ! Allons-y. **(8) (9)**

11 — Salut, Jean. Enfin te voilà. J'espère que tu n'es pas trop fatigué ? **(10)**

12 — Non, ça va merci. Où allons-nous maintenant ?

13 — Nous allons prendre le bus pour aller jusqu'à la maison. C'est tout ce que tu as comme bagages ? **(11)**

14 — Non, les autres sont à la consigne. — Bon, allons les chercher. **(12) (6)**

EXERCICES

1. Ne t'excuse pas ! L'essentiel est que tu sois heureuse. **2.** La circulation est en effet affreuse ! — Mais prenez un taxi. **3.** Elle s'est perdue une bonne vingtaine de fois. **4.** Avez-vous aimé votre repas, madame ? — Ça a été, merci. **5.** J'espère que tu n'es pas trop fatigué pour marcher jusqu'à la maison. **6.** Michelle ! Allez me chercher le dossier Rimbaud, s'il vous plaît. **7.** Excusez-moi du retard. — Je vous en prie.

Mettez les mots qui manquent.
Fill in the blanks.

1 *Si j' . . . ., j' . . . . un taxi.*

If I had known, I would have taken a taxi.

6 I know the streets of Paris badly and I got lost. And what atrocious traffic!

7 — Please, don't apologise. The most important thing is that you have arrived.

8 — You are very kind. Is your office far still?

9 — About 20 kilometres. — Would you mind driving?

10 — Not at all! Pass me the keys. Hup! Let's go.

11 — Hi, John. Here you are at last. I hope you're not too tired?

12 — No, I'm O. K. thanks. Where are we going now?

13 — We'll take a bus to go home. Is that all the luggage you have?

14 — No, the rest is in the left-luggage. Er, let's go and fetch it.

NOTES

(7) Adding the suffix *-aine* to multiples of ten gives the idea of 'about that number'. *Il a une trentaine de chemises:* He has about thirty shirts. Applied to a person, *Elle a la soixantaine,* means: She's in her sixties (if we add *bien sonnée* it means well into her sixties, etc.).
Although we say 'multiples of ten' we usually only find the compound up as far as sixty, then one hundred. (N.B. *une douzaine:* a dozen, i.e., exactly 12, and *une quinzaine:* a fortnight).

(8) A shorter version of *Pas du tout!:* Not at all.

(9) *Une clé* can also be written *une clef*. Note these expressions: *fermer à clé(f):* to lock; *ouvrir:* to open **or** to unlock. *Une clé(f) anglaise:* a spanner. And the beautiful expression: *prendre la clé(f) des champs:* to run off, to head for freedom.

(10) Notice the change in register between this dialogue and the two others.

(11) *Jusqu'à* (until, to) can be used for physical distances whereas 'until' in English can only be used with expressions of time. In sentences like *Je t'accompagnerai jusqu'au bout de la rue* it has the same sense as 'I'll go with you as far as the end of the road'.

(12) *Une consigne* means a (military or official) order but we most commonly find it in airports and stations where *la consigne automatique* means 'left-luggage' lockers. If you see *bouteille consignée* on your bottle of soft drink, it means that a deposit has been paid on the bottle.

EXERCISES: 1. Don't apologise! The most important thing is that you be happy. **2.** The traffic really is atrocious! — But take a taxi. **3.** She got lost a good 20 times or so. **4.** Did you like your meal, madam? — It was fine. **5.** I hope you're not too tired to walk as far as the house. **6.** Michelle! Go and fetch me the Rimbaud file please. **7.** Excuse me for being late. — Don't mention it.

Leçon 22

2 *Vous faites* . . . . *la distance en* . . . .

. . . . *temps.*

You do twice the distance in half the time.

3 *Elle se* . . . . *si elle* . . . . .

. . . .

She would have got lost if she had driven.

4 *Le magasin* . . . - . . . . *ouvert ?*

Is the shop still open?

5 *Tes valises sont* . . . . , *n'* . . . - . . *pas ?*

Your suitcases are in the left-luggage locker, aren't they?

```
*************************************
```

VINGT-TROISIEME (23e) LEÇON

Un voyage en avion

A l'aéroport
1 — Air France annonce le départ de son vol AF
    809 à destination de Copenhague.
2 — Embarquement immédiat à la porte numéro
    quatre.
A la porte
3 — Mesdames, messieurs, nous allons procéder
    à l'embarquement.
4   Veuillez ne plus fumer et présenter vos
    cartes d'accès à bord à l'hôtesse. (1)

```
*****
```

Mots qui manquaient :

1. avais su - aurais pris 2. deux fois - deux fois moins de 3. serait perdue - avait conduit 4. est-il encore 5. à la consigne - est-ce.

If you can't remember a turn of phrase, look back to the text. Some people feel they are 'cheating' when they do this. A ridiculous idea!

****

23rd LESSON

A plane trip

At the airport
1 — Air France announces the departure of its flight AF 809 for Copenhagen.
2 — Immediate boarding at gate No. 4.
At the gate
3 — Ladies and gentlemen we are going to proceed with boarding.
4 — Please stop smoking and present your boarding cards to the hostess.

NOTES

(1) (See also lesson 22 note 1) *Veuillez* is the subjunctive (2nd person plural of *vouloir*) and is very commonly used in giving polite orders. *Veuillez me suivre, s'il vous plaît:* Follow me, please. It is more forceful than *Voulez-vous me suivre.* Being so formal, it is not used with the *tu* form. On public notices, requesting people to obey a certain order, we often find *Prière* (lit: a prayer). *Prière de tenir la main courante:* Please hold the moving hand-grip (sign on an escalator in the metro).

Dans l'avion

5 — Bienvenue à bord de cet Airbus d'Air France. Nous allons décoller dans quelques instants. **(N.2) (2)**

6 Veuillez vérifier que la tablette et le dossier de votre siège sont relevés

7 et éteindre votre cigarette jusqu'à l'extinction du signal lumineux. **(3) (4)**

En vol

8 — Voici votre plateau-repas, monsieur. Désirez-vous boire quelque chose ? **(5)**

9 — Je prendrais bien un jus de fruit. Un jus de pamplemousse.

10 Combien vous dois-je ? — C'est offert, monsieur. — Merci bien ! **(6)**

11 — Nous allons procéder à la distribution des cartes de débarquement

12 pour tous les passagers qui ne sont pas ressortissants de la C.E.E. **(7)**

13 Mesdames, messieurs, nous allons bientôt atterrir. Veuillez éteindre vos cigarettes

14 et ne plus fumer jusqu'à ce que vous soyez à l'intérieur de l'aérogare. **(8)**

15 Nous venons d'atterrir à Copenhague où l'heure locale est seize heures vingt.

16 Nous espérons que vous avez passé un agréable moment en notre compagnie **(9)**

17 et nous souhaitons vous revoir bientôt sur nos lignes. Au revoir.

NOTES

(2) *Coller* means to stick (*la colle* = glue); so *décoller* means to unstick, which is pretty much what a plane does when it takes off! *Le décollage:* take-off, *atterrir:* to land, *l'atterrissage (masc.):* landing.

(3) Another habit in formal announcements is to 'singularise' them by addressing *Madame, Mademoiselle, Monsieur* (the opening line of the evening news) then, instead of talking about *vos,* the singular *votre* is used.

(4) We have already seen that we can avoid using the subjunctive by following a clause that normally demands it by a noun or an infinitive. Here, and in line 14, we see a time clause *jusqu'à* with, and without, the subjunctive;

In the plane

5 — Welcome on board this Air France Airbus. We are going to take off in a few moments.

6 Please check that your tray and seat-back are upright

7 and extinguish your cigarette until the illuminated sign goes out.

In flight

8 — Here's your meal-tray, sir. Would you care for something to drink?

9 — I'd love a fruit juice. A grapefruit juice.

10 How much do I owe you? — It's free sir. — Thanks a lot!

11 — We're going to proceed with the distribution of landing cards

12 for all passengers not members of the E.E.C.

13 Ladies and gentlemen, we will soon be landing. Please extinguish your cigarettes

14 and don't smoke again until you are in the terminal.

15 We have just landed at Copenhagen where local time is 4.20 p.m.

16 We hope you spent an enjoyable time in our company

17 and we wish to see you again soon on our lines. Goodbye.

NOTES

jusqu'à son arrivée: until his/her arrival;
jusqu'à ce qu'il arrive: until he arrives;
jusqu'à ce que le signal lumineux soit éteint (line 14 without subjunctive) *jusqu'à l'arrivée dans l'aérogare.*

(5) An elegant - and formal - way of saying *Voulez-vous...?*

(6) *Offrir* means more that just to offer. It also means to give. The sense here is that the drink is free.

(7) 'Formalese' and jargon are the same everywhere. Instead of saying *qui ne sont pas de la C.E.E.* or something simple, an official will use this horrible word. The root is, of course, *sortir* so *un ressortissant* is 'someone who comes out of', i.e., 'a native or citizen of'. French seems to like formal usage. The Anglo-Saxon is used to a more pragmatic form of expression.
C.E.E. = *la Communauté Economique Européenne.*

(8) See note 4.

(9) *La compagnie* has, like in English, the meaning both of companionship and a commercial venture. A more common word for a commercial company is *une société.*

EXERCICES

1. Veuillez ne pas déranger le pilote. **2.** Désirez-vous manger quelque chose ? — Ça coûte combien ? — C'est offert. **3.** Prière de ne rien jeter à terre. **4.** Je la garderai jusqu'à ton retour. **5.** Nous allons atterrir dans quelques instants. Veuillez éteindre vos cigarettes. **6.** J'espère te revoir bientôt.

Mettez les mots qui manquent.
Fill in the blanks.

1 *Je le* . . . . *jusqu'à* . . . .

I will keep it until you come back (with the verb).

2 . . . . *vérifier que* . . . . . . *les fenêtres*

. . . . *à clé.*

Please check that all the windows are locked.

3 *Je* . . . . *un jus de* . . . .

I'd love a glass of grapefruit juice.

4 *Prière de* . . . .

Please stop smoking from now.

****

VINGT-QUATRIEME (24e) LEÇON

Qui s'excuse s'accuse...

1 — Michelle et Claude devaient déjeuner ensemble mais Claude fait envoyer ce mot : **(1)**

*****

EXERCISES: **1.** Please do not disturb the pilot. **2.** Do you care for something to eat? — How much does it cost? — It's free. **3.** Please throw nothing on the ground. **4.** I will keep it until your return. **5.** We're going to land in a few moments. Please put out your cigarettes. **6.** I hope to see you again soon.

5   *J'attendrai . . . .'il me . . . . . une*

proposition.

I'll wait until he makes me an offer.

Mots qui manquaient :

1. garderai - ce que tu reviennes **2.** Veuillez - toutes - sont fermées **3.** prendrais bien - pamplemousse (masc.) **4.** ne plus fumer **5.** jusqu'à ce qu - fasse.

****
24th LESSON

Who apologises accuses himself

1   Michelle and Claude were supposed to have lunch together but Claude has this note sent:

NOTES

(1) We already know the past tense of *devoir* (must). *Je devais payer une amende:* I had to pay a fine; but often, we find *être obligé de* in the past tense and *devais - devait - devaient,* etc. takes on the meaning 'was/were supposed to'. *Il devait me téléphoner à cinq heures:* He was supposed to call me at five o'clock. *Elle était obligée de partir tôt:* She had to leave early.

Leçon 24

2 — Chère Michelle, j'ai enfin trouvé du travail : je commence aujourd'hui même,

3 alors je doute que je puisse me libérer pour déjeuner avec toi et j'en suis désolé,

4 mais ce n'est que partie remise. Je t'embrasse. Claude. **(2)**

5 Michelle lui envoie la réponse suivante :

6 — Mon cher Claude, que je suis contente pour toi !

7 Bien sûr, je suis désolée que tu ne puisses pas venir,

8 j'avais plein de choses à te raconter mais, comme tu dis,

9 ça sera pour un autre jour. C'est dommage que nous ne nous voyions pas

10 mais je te félicite et je te dis à bientôt. Michelle.

11 Un journaliste de la télévision s'entretient avec un député. **(3) (4)**

12 — Je regrette, Monsieur le Député, mais je comprends mal votre comportement et votre logique :

2 — Dear Michelle, at last I have found some work: I
    begin this very day,

3   so I doubt that I'll be able to free myself to have
    lunch with you and I'm very sorry

4   but it's just postponed, not cancell-
    ed. Kisses. Claude.

5   Michelle sends him the following reply:

6 — My dear Claude, how happy I am for you!

7   Of course, I'm sorry that you cannot come,

8   I had a load of things to tell you but, as you say,

9   it will be for another day. It's a pity that we
    can't see one another

10   but I congratulate you and say: see you
    soon. Michelle.

11   A T/V journalist is interviewing a Member of
    Parliament.

12 — I regret, sir, but I find it hard to understand your
    behaviour and your logic:

NOTES

(2) *Remettre* (past participle *remis*). The English verb is more flexible
than the French, thanks especially to the use of post-prepositions.
Hence *remettre* can mean: to put back on (*Il a remis son chapeau:*
he put his hat back on); to put back (*Remettez ce vase à sa place:*
Put this vase back in its place); to deliver by hand (*On m'a remis
cette lettre*) and many more, the prefix *re* not necessarily meaning
'again'. The sense we see in this sentence is the one of 'to
postpone, to put off'. *Ne remettez jamais à demain ce que vous
pouvez faire aujourd'hui:* Never put off until tomorrow what you
can do today. *Une partie remise* is literally a drawn game (it will be
played again later) but in the expression *c'est* (or *ce n'est que*) *partie
remise* it means: we're just postponing it for another time.
(If you see signs in stores with *Remise* (*de 5%* for example) it
means a reduction.)

(3) *S'entretenir:* to discuss with, to negotiate.
Les entretiens: discussions, talks. This verb is found in formal
contexts (politics, commerce, television interviews). In the latter
context it is being replaced more and more by the barbaric verb
interviewer (noun: *une interview*). Try to avoid it.
The reflexive *s'* is vital because, without it, *entretenir* means to keep
something up, to maintain. *Des produits d'entretien:* household
cleaning products.

(4) The French parliament is divided into an upper house: *le Sénat* (*un
sénateur:* a senator) and a lower house: *l'Assemblée Nationale.*
Un député is a member of the lower house, like a Member of
Parliament in England or a Congressman in the U.S.A.

13   je suis étonné que vous ayez voté contre un
     projet de loi **(5) (6)**
14   visant à la modernisation des écoles mater-
     nelles et primaires
15   et voilà que, deux mois plus tard, vous votez
     des crédits importants **(7)**
16   pour l'amélioration de la vie à l'intérieur des
     prisons. Etonnant, n'est-ce pas ?
17 — Mais pas le moins du monde, répond
     l'homme politique,
18   je suis même surpris que vous n'y ayez pas
     songé : **(8)**
19   c'est simplement qu'il n'y a aucune chance
     que je retourne à l'école...

EXERCICES

1. Ce n'est que partie remise. Nous nous verrons la semaine prochaine. **2.** J'ai déjà songé à cette solution, mais c'est trop dangereux. **3.** Voilà qu'il m'écrit deux ans plus tard ! **4.** Il n'y a aucune chance pour que tu gagnes au Loto. **5.** Elle est ~~ssée~~, elle a plein de choses à faire. **6.** Le Président s'est entretenu avec les députés.

Mettez les mots qui manquent.
Fill in the blanks.

1 *Je suis désolé que vous* . . . . *venir.*

   I'm very sorry you are unable to come.

2 *Elle était* . . . . *que tu n'* . . . . *pas téléphoné.*

   She was astonished that you didn't 'phone.

3 *Ils regrettent qu'ils ne* . . . . . . *pas* . . . . . .

   They regret that they are not rich.

13 I'm surprised that you voted against a bill

14 aiming at the modernisation of nursery and primary schools

15 and here you are, two months later, voting for large credits

16 for the improvement of life inside prisons. Surprising, isn't it?

17 — But not in the least, replies the politician,

18 I'm even surprised that you haven't thought of it:

19 it's simply that there is no chance that I will go back to school...

NOTES

(5) *Voter:* to vote *une voix:* an individual vote; the word is used when giving the number of votes *(trois mille voix contre deux mille);* but when vote is used in the theoretical sense (the right to vote, to take part in a vote, etc.) we use *un vote, le droit de vote, participer au vote. On vote pour quelqu'un mais on vote quelque chose.* You vote for someone but you vote something (i.e., bring it into acceptance).

(6) *Une loi:* a law or, in parliamentary terms, an Act. Before it is voted the proposition, or Bill, is *un projet de loi (un projet:* a project, a plan).

(7) *Important.* The word has two senses. *Un homme important:* an important man (of consequence); *une augmentation importante:* large increases. *Important* has thus a sense of physical size missing from the English adjective. A good indicator to the quality of a French/English dictionary is to look at this word (in the French part) and see if the extra sense is mentioned. Most don't...

(8) *Songer* means to dream, especially in old French. *Le Songe d'une Nuit d'Eté* is the French translation of 'A Midsummer Night's Dream'. In more modern French, the physical act (?) of dreaming is expressed by *rêver* and the idea of imagining an event is now expressed by *songer. Je n'aurais jamais songé à lui demander:* I would never have dreamed of asking him. *Il ne faut pas y songer!:* You mustn't dream of it! Briefly put - *rêver* is asleep, *songer* is awake!

EXERCISES: 1. It's just postponed. We'll see one another next week. **2.** I have already thought of that solution but it's too dangerous. **3.** Here he is writing to me two years later! **4.** There is no chance that you will win the Loto. **5.** She's in a hurry; she has a load of things to do. **6.** The President had discussions with the Members of Parliament.

4 *Quel dommage . .'elle . . . . occupée ce soir.*

What a shame she's busy this evening.

5 *Je suis surpris . . . vous m' . . . . posé cette question.*

I'm surprised that you asked me that question.

****

VINGT-CINQUIEME (25e) LEÇON

Réclamations (1)

1 — Allô, le Garage Lamotte ? Passez-moi l'atelier, je vous prie.

2 L'atelier ? J'ai déposé ma voiture ce matin pour une révision ; **(2)**

3 non seulement vous avez oublié de vérifier les freins mais vous ne l'avez pas vidangée. **(3)**

4 Il faut que j'aie cette voiture demain matin au plus tard ! **(4)**

5 Je veux que vous m'envoyiez quelqu'un la chercher tout de suite, **(N.3)**

6 et j'exige qu'elle soit réparée au plus vite, sinon vous aurez de mes nouvelles ! **(5)**

7 Voulez-vous que je vous dise ce que je pense de votre entreprise... ?

8 — Merci, non, monsieur, mais par contre, j'aimerais que vous me donniez vos nom et adresse. — Oh...

Mots qui manquaient :

1. ne puissiez pas **2** . étonnée - aies **3**. soient - riches **4**. qu' - soit **5**. que - 'ayez.

****

25th LESSON

Complaints

1 — Hello, the Lamotte Garage? Put me through to the workshop, please.

2 Workshop? I left my car this morning for a service;

3 not only have you forgotten to check the brakes but you haven't done the oil change.

4 I must have that car tomorrow morning at the latest!

5 I want you to send me someone to fetch it immediately

6 and I demand that it be repaired at the double, if not you'll be hearing from me!

7 Do you want me to tell you what I think of your business?

8 — No thank you, sir, but on the other hand, I'd like you to give me your name and address. — Oh...

NOTES

(1) *Réclamer* is to complain, but in an official sense. If you complain about the weather or the food, you would use the verb *se plaindre*. *Le service des réclamations* is the complaints department.

(2) *Une révision* (for a car) a service; *un service* (in an office) a department (see line 9).

(3) The object is *la voiture*, so that the past participle must agree. *Vidanger*: literally means to empty, to drain, but for a car we use it to mean 'change the oil' as well as just draining the sump. *Une vidange:* an oil change.

(4) *Au plus tard:* at the latest; *au plus tôt:* at the earliest; *au plus vite:* at the double!

(5) *On n'a pas eu de ses nouvelles:* We haven't heard from him. *Donnez-moi de vos nouvelles:* Let me know what's happening to you. *Pas de nouvelles, bonnes nouvelles:* No news is good news. But, when spoken in a menacing tone, the expression *Vous aurez de mes nouvelles!* is not a promise but a threat.

9 — Les Galeries Farfouillette ? Passez-moi le service après-vente s'il vous plaît. Le poste vingt. **(6)**

10 Allô, monsieur Leblanc est-il là ? C'est de la part d'une cliente.

11 — Je regrette, madame, mais monsieur Leblanc s'est absenté quelques instants.

12 Voulez-vous patienter, ou préférez-vous que je vous passe une autre personne ? **(7)**

13 — Dans ce cas, je préfère laisser un message. Qu'il rappelle madame Béraut. Merci. **(8)**

EXERCICES

1. Passez-moi l'atelier. C'est de la part d'un client. 2. Je veux que ce soit fait au plus vite. — Ça sera mardi au plus tôt. 3. Déposez votre voiture à neuf heures au plus tard pour une vidange. 4. Non seulement il a fait une réclamation, mais il a écrit à son député. 5. Elle s'est absentée quelques instants. Voulez-vous patienter ? 6. J'ai eu de ses nouvelles pas plus tard qu'hier.

Mettez les mots qui manquent.
Fill in the blanks.

1 *Je veux que vous* . . . . *combien vous* . . . . .

I want you to tell me how many you will be.

2 *Il* . . . . *nous* . . . . . *une réponse demain* . .

. . . .

We must have an answer by tomorrow at the latest.

3 *Non seulement* . . . .′ . . . . *mais il a exigé*

Not only did he complain but he demanded

4 *que sa femme* . . . . . . *une lettre au directeur.*

that his wife write a letter to the director.

9 — Galeries Farfouillette? Put me through to the after-sales department, please. Extension 20.

10 Hello, is Mr Leblanc there? It's a customer speaking.

11 — I'm sorry, madam, but Mr Leblanc has slipped out for a few minutes.

12 Will you hold on or would you prefer me to put you through to someone else?

13 — In that case, I prefer to leave a message. Have him call back Mrs Béraut. Thanks.

NOTES

(6) As we will see in later lessons, some words change their meaning depending on whether they are masculine or feminine. There are about 30 of these but we will only learn the most important ones. Here we see *un poste:* a telephone extension, or a post (job); *une poste:* a post office.

(7) Subjunctive.

(8) We have already seen *Soyez* and *Veuillez* used as imperatives. Here is how we use other verbs in that way. The exclamatory construction *Que* + subjunctive is often equivalent to the English: Let + subjunctive. *Que justice soit faite!:* Let justice be done! But it is used more commonly - and less declamatorily - in everyday French. We use it when we wish to impose our will on a third person or an event. *Qu'il me dise s'il veut le billet:* Have him tell me if he wants the ticket. *Qu'elle m'écrive pour le confirmer:* Have her write to confirm. As you can see, these sentences are spoken to one person and relate to a third person.

Appeler, rappeler, jeter and other verbs that end in *-eler* or *-eter* double the final consonant before a mute *e.* For example, I write *vous jetez* because you hear the second *e* but I write *je jette,* the final *e* being mute. *Il m'appelle* but *Appelez-moi* (*rappelle* in line 13 is, of course, subjunctive).

EXERCISES: 1. Put me through to the workshop. It's a customer speaking. **2.** I want it done at the double. — It will be Tuesday at the earliest. **3.** Drop off your car at 9.00 at the latest for an oil change. **4.** Not only did he lodge a complaint, but he wrote to his M.P. **5.** She's slipped out for a few minutes. Will you hold on? **6.** I had news from him/her no later than yesterday.

5 . . 'il . . . . . un effort ! Ce n'est pas trop difficile.

Let him make an effort. It's not too difficult.

****

VINGT-SIXIEME (26e) LEÇON

Un cadeau d'anniversaire (1)

1   Un homme vieux et tout rabougri se présente au bureau du directeur d'un grand magasin parisien. (2)

2 — Que puis-je pour vous ? dit la secrétaire. — Je veux acheter le magasin.

3 — Pardon ? Je ne suis pas sûre que je vous aie bien compris. (N.3)

4   Je doute fort que vous puissiez acheter un pareil magasin comme ça.

5   Je ne pense pas qu'il soit à vendre. Mais l'homme s'obstine : — Présentez-moi au directeur.

6   Le directeur est tout aussi étonné et il croit à une mauvaise plaisanterie. (3)

7 — Admettons que vous possédiez les moyens, qu'en feriez-vous ? (4)

NOTES

(1) *Un anniversaire:* a birthday. But the French word has a wider meaning: it also means an anniversary. *L'anniversaire de mariage:* the wedding anniversary. For larger numbers, we find *le centenaire:* the centenary, *le bicentenaire:* the bicentenary.
One also finds expressions like *Les vingt-cinq ans de Maryse:* Maryse's 25th birthday.

Mots qui manquaient :

1. me disiez - serez 2. faut que - ayons - au plus tard 3. il s'est plaint 4. écrive 5. Qu' - fasse.

****

26th LESSON

A birthday present

1   An old and wizened man presents himself in the office of the manager of a Parisian department store.

2   — What can I do for you? says the secretary.   — I want to buy the shop.

3   — Pardon? I'm not sure I understand you.

4   I strongly doubt that you can buy such a store just like that.

5   I don't think it's for sale.   But the man insists:
      — Introduce me to the manager.

6   The manager is just as surprised and he thinks it is a bad joke.

7   — Let's say that you have the means, what would you do with it?

NOTES

(2) *Un grand magasin.* Apart from the literal description, this expression also means a department store. Each department is called *un rayon.*

(3) In this story we see two verbs (also line 9) for which the English use 'to think'. *Je crois qu'elle va venir:* I think she will come. The verb here means 'I think, but I'm not sure'. *Est-il député? — Je crois.* Is he a member of Parliament? — I think so. In this case, *croire* is less strong than *penser.* When we wish to follow the verb by an indirect object, we use the preposition *à.*
Elle croyait à une plaisanterie: She thought it was a joke. Followed by a direct object, we use *en. Ils croient en Dieu:* They believe in God (*une croyance:* a belief).
Réfléchir means literally 'to reflect'. *Les miroirs réfléchissent les images:* Mirrors reflect images. But, for a person: *Voici ma proposition; réfléchissez-y:* Here's my proposition; think it over. *Après mûre réflexion, j'ai décidé:* After thinking it over for a long time...

(4) From the verb *admettre:* to admit. *Les chiens ne sont pas admis dans les magasins d'alimentation:* Dogs are not admitted into food stores.
In a discussion, the imperative has the sense of: Let's assume that... *Admettons que vous ayez raison:* Let's assume that you are right. The subjunctive follows the imperative because the position is hypothetical.

8 — Cela me concerne, mais disons que c'est un cadeau pour ma femme.

9 Le directeur réfléchit et se dit : —- Il vaut mieux que je me débarrasse de cet individu. **(3) (5)**

10 — Bien, dit-il à haute voix. J'accepte de vendre... pour quarante milliards de francs ! **(6)**

11 — Puis-je téléphoner ? répond l'homme. — Faites donc. **(7)**

12 Le vieil homme décroche le combiné et fait un numéro au cadran. **(8)**

13 — Allo, Sandra ? Oui, c'est moi. Ça marche pour les Galeries Tartempion. **(9)**

14 Pour le règlement, tu cherches sous le lit. Là, tu trouveras deux valises. C'est entendu ? **(10)**

15 Bien. Alors, apporte-moi la petite ! **(11)**

NOTES

(5) *Se débarrasser de quelque chose (quelqu'un):* to get rid of something (somebody). The verb *embarrasser* means to hamper, to get in the way: *Est-ce que ma valise vous embarrasse?:* Is my suitcase in your way? By extension it can mean to embarrass. *Je serais embarrassé de vous expliquer:* I would find it difficult (i.e. embarrassing) to explain to you.
The opposite - to remove a hindrance - is obtained by the prefix *dé-*. To remove an obstacle. *Débarrasser la table:* to clear the table. The reflexive removes the encumberment from oneself. — *Le vieux canapé? Je m'en suis débarrassé:* The old sofa? I got rid of it. In an appartment *le débarras* is a storage cupboard. (Out of sight, out of mind. *Loin des yeux, loin du cœur.)*

(6) *A haute voix:* aloud. *Une voix forte:* a loud voice.

(7) A rather elegant reply, using the auxiliary, to a request. *Puis-je vous poser une question? — Faites donc:* May I ask you a question? — Go ahead.

EXERCICES

1. Décrochez le combiné et faites votre numéro. **2.** Je ne l'ai jamais vue dans un pareil état. **3.** Il a réfléchi au problème, mais il n'est pas sûr d'avoir raison. **4.** Débarrassez-vous de vos manteaux et puis je vous présenterai au directeur. **5.** Je ne crois pas à tout cela. — Bien, c'est votre affaire. **6.** Il vaut mieux ne rien dire pour l'instant. — C'est entendu.

8 — That's my business, but let's say that it's a present for my wife.

9 — The manager thinks it over and says to himself — I'd better get rid of this character.

10 — Well, he says aloud. I accept to sell for forty thousand million francs!

11 — May I telephone? replies the man. — Go ahead.

12 — The old man lifts the receiver and dials a number.

13 — Hello Sandra! Yes it's me. It's O. K. for the Galeries Tartempion.

14 For the payment, you look under the bed. There you will find two suitcases. Understood?

15 Good. Then bring me the small one!

NOTES

A more mundane - and common - reply would be *Je vous en prie* or *Allez-y*.

(8) Again we see an example of the plasticity of English (a dial - to dial) which French cannot follow. *Un cadran:* a dial; *faire* (or, in official language on post-office signs, *composer*) *un numéro au cadran:* to dial a number. Everyday language would allow just *faire un numéro.*

(9) A very common idiom *Ça marche,* means: it works. *La radio ne marche plus:* The radio no longer works. But applied more generally it means: things are going well; its O. K. *Ça marche pour votre projet:* Your plan has the go-ahead. *Sa théorie ne marche plus:* His/her theory no longer applies.
Mettre en marche (un appareil): to turn on (an appliance). Again, (see note 8), to translate the 'on' button French is obliged to say *le bouton de mise en marche.*

(10) *C'est entendu:* it's understood. *Qu'entendez-vous par cela?:* What do you understand by that? *Ces prix s'entendent toutes taxes comprises:* These prices are inclusive of tax (i.e. we understand and accept that taxes are included).

(11) There are two ways of expressing the verb to bring, depending on whether what is brought is a person or an object.
Garçon, apportez-moi deux cafés!: Waiter, bring me two coffees! *Chacun a apporté sa contribution:* Everyone brought his contribution. *Apporter* is thus used for objects. *Amenez votre amie dîner à la maison:* Bring your (girl)friend home to dinner. *Le Président amènera quatre ministres en visite officielle:* The President will bring four ministers on an official visit. *Amener* is used for people.

EXERCISES: 1. Lift the receiver and dial your number. 2. I have never seen her in such a state. 3. He has thought the problem over but he's not sure he's right. 4. Take off your coats and then I'll introduce you to the manager. 5. I don't believe in all that. — Well, that's your business. 6. You'd (we'd) better say nothing for the time being. — Understood.

Leçon 26

Mettez les mots qui manquent.
Fill in the blanks.

1 *Je ne crois pas qu'il . . . les . . . . . .*

I don't think he has the means.

2 *. . . . . que vous . . . . raison, qu' . .*

. . . . . . -vous ?

Let's assume you are right, what would you do with it?

3 *Je . . . . . fort qu'ils . . . . l'acheter comme ça.*

I strongly doubt they can buy it just like that.

****

VINGT-SEPTIEME (27e) LEÇON

Révisons « avoir » (1)

1 — Votre mari n'a pas bonne mine. Quel âge a-
t-il ? **(2)**

2 — J'ai bien peur que vous ne me croyiez pas. Il
a quinze ans.
3 — Comment, quinze ans ? Mais il a l'air
beaucoup plus âgé. **(3)**

4 *Je ne suis pas* . . . *qu'il* . . . . *l'homme que vous*

recherchez.

I'm not sure he's the man you're looking for.

5 *Il* . . . . *vous* . . . .

tout de suite.

You had better get rid of it straight away.

Mots qui manquaient :

1. ait - moyens 2. admettons - ayez - en feriez 3. doute - puissent 4. sûr - soit 5. vaut mieux - en débarrasser.

****

27th LESSON

Let's revise 'to have'

1 — Your husband doesn't look well. How old is he?
2 — I'm really afraid you won't believe me. He's fifteen.
3 — What fifteen? But he looks much older.

NOTES

(1) In this lesson we will see numerous examples of where French uses the verb *avoir* for idioms in which English uses *être*. Pay close attention.

(2) *Avoir bonne/mauvaise mine:* to look well/ill. Although *une mine* means a mine, when applied to a person or object, it refers to its appearance. *Il a une mine de bandit* [bondi]: He looks like a bandit. *Faire mine de...* means: to put on the appearance of. *Elle a fait mine de me croire:* She pretended to believe me. *Le restaurant ne paie pas de mine:* The restaurant isn't much to look at.

(3) *Comment?!* as an interjection at the beginning of a phrase has the sense of: What do you mean? *Comment, vous fermez à cinq heures?:* What do you mean, you close at five o'clock? It is more an expression of incredulity than a question.

Leçon 27

4   Comment se fait-il que vous ayez la quarantaine et que votre époux ne soit qu'un... gamin ? **(4) (5)**

5 — J'ai honte de vous l'avouer : il est né dans une année bissextile

6   et il n'a un anniversaire que tous les quatre ans !

7 — Qu'y a-t-il ? Vous avez l'air souffrant. Ça ne va pas ?

8 — Mais si ! Seulement, j'ai froid, j'ai sommeil, j'ai mal à la tête.

9   et mal au dos... et, en plus, c'est mon anniversaire.

10 — Heureusement qu'il n'a lieu qu'une fois par an ! **(6)**

11 — J'en ai assez de son soi-disant sens de l'humour ! Il ne dit que des bêtises. **(7)**

12 — Mais non, tu te trompes. En réalité, il a beaucoup d'esprit. **(8) (9)**

13   Il a dit une très belle phrase l'autre jour

14   « On a toujours tort d'avoir raison. » Amusant, n'est-ce pas ?

NOTES

(4) *Comment se fait-il...?* An invariable question meaning: How is it that... *Comment se fait-il qu'il n'ait jamais d'argent?:* How is it that he never has any money? It is usually followed by the subjunctive.

(5) An example of how our two languages readily borrow words. Although *un gamin* was originally a dialectical word from the East of France, it came to signify the typical street-smart Parisian urchin (immortalized by the character of Gavroche in Hugo's *'Les Misérables'* - see lesson 52). In modern usage, it is a familiar word for a child (the feminine is *une gamine*). The word passed into

EXERCICES

1. Je me suis trompé de porte et j'ai réveillé les voisins. **2.** Je trouve cet homme fort spirituel. — Moi, je le trouve bête. **3.** Comment, vous ne pouvez pas venir ? Nous ne faisons cette réunion qu'une fois tous les quatre mois ! **4.** Vous avez l'air souffrante, ma chère amie. Ça ne va pas ? **5.** J'en ai assez de ce soi-disant intellectuel. **6.** Sais-tu ce qu'il m'a dit l'autre jour ? Quelle mauvaise plaisanterie !

4   How is it that you are in your forties and your husband is just... a kid?

5 — I'm ashamed to admit it to you: he was born in a leap-year

6   and he only has a birthday every four years!

7 — What's the matter? You seem to be in pain. Are you unwell?

8 — Of course I'm not! Only I'm cold, I'm tired, I have a headache

9   and my back hurts... and, what's more, it's my birthday.

10 — Fortunately, it only takes place once a year!

11 — I'm fed up with his so-called sense of humour. He only says stupid things.

12 — No, you're mistaken. In reality he's very witty.

13   He said a very pretty sentence the other day

14   'One is always wrong to be right.' Amusing, isn't it?

NOTES

English with the sense of the street-urchin and its feminine form is used to describe a girl of impish or pert appearance. The word *un/une gosse* is more a slang term.

(6) *Un lieu:* a place. *C'est un lieu où on peut se détendre:* It's a place where one can relax. *Avoir lieu:* to take place. *La réunion annuelle a lieu en juin:* The annual meeting takes place in June.
Un lieu-dit is the smallest demographic appellation for a group of houses or just a place.

(7) *Une bête:* an animal. *Une bêtise:* a stupid thing (to do or say). *Il est bête!:* He's stupid!

(8) *Avoir tort:* to be wrong - *se tromper:* to make a mistake, to be mistaken. Followed by a direct object: *Elle s'est trompée d'autobus,* we translate by: She took the wrong bus. *Ils se sont trompés d'heure:* They mistook the time. *Il n'y a pas à s'y tromper:* There is no mistake about it. As an active verb *tromper* means to deceive or to be unfaithful to someone. *Il trompe sa femme:* He is unfaithful to his wife.
(In art and architecture English uses the expression 'a trompe l'œil' for a dummy window, or a painted facade [i.e. it deceives the eye]).

(9) *Un esprit* is literally a spirit. *Le Saint-Esprit:* the Holy Ghost, but *avoir de l'esprit* means to be witty. The adjective is *spirituel*.

EXERCISES: 1. I took the wrong door and woke up the neighbours. **2.** I find that man very witty. — I find him stupid. **3.** What do you mean, you can't come? We only have this meeting once every four months! **4.** You seem to be in pain, my dear friend. Are you unwell? **5.** I've had enough of that so-called intellectual. **6.** Do you know what he said to me the other day? What a bad joke!

Leçon 27

Mettez les mots qui manquent.
Fill in the blanks.

1 *Elle n' . . . . . pas . . . . la dernière fois*

que je l'ai . . .

She didn't look well the last time I saw her.

2 *Je . . . . toujours . . nom quand je . . . . parle.*

I always get their names wrong when I talk to them.

3 *Vous devriez . . . . ! Ce n'est . . ' . . . . !*

You should be ashamed! He's only a kid!

****

VINGT-HUITIEME (28e) LEÇON

REVISION ET NOTES

1 **J'aurais été** *deux fois plus vite si* **j'avais pris** *un taxi.*
This is the third form of the conditional - the past
conditional. The auxiliary in the conditional form is
followed by the past participle.
Let's remind ourselves briefly of the other two forms.
(a) *Si vous* **prenez** *un taxi, vous* **aurez** *votre train.* If you
take a taxi, you will get your train. PRESENT + FUTURE.
(b) *Si vous* **preniez** *un taxi, vous* **auriez** *votre train.* If you
took a taxi, you would get your train. IMPERFECT +
CONDITIONAL.
(a) *Si vous* **aviez pris** *un taxi, vous* **auriez eu** *votre train.*
If you had taken a taxi you would have got your train.
PAST PERFECT + PAST CONDITIONAL.
The form - which is very similar to English - presents no
particular difficulties but you must enunciate clearly.
Practise reading these sentences aloud.
*Si vous aviez fait comme je vous l'ai dit, vous n'auriez pas
eu ces ennuis:* If you had done as I told you, you would
not have had these problems.

4 *Elles* . . . . . . *de rentrer toutes seules.*

 — *Comment,* . . . . ?

They are afraid to go back home alone. — What do you mean, afraid?

5 *Il* . *l'* . . . *beaucoup* . . . . *mais* . . . .

He looks much older but, in reality,

6 *il* . *'* . . . . *vingt-cinq ans.*

he's only 25 years old.

Mots qui manquaient :

1. avait - bonne mine - vue 2. me trompe - de - leur 3. avoir honte - qu'un gamin 4. ont peur - peur 5. a 'air - plus âgé - en réalité 6. n'a que.

****

28th LESSON

Elle n'aurait pas pu réussir son examen si vous ne l'aviez pas aidée: She wouldn't have passed her exam, if you had not helped her.
Si j'y avais pensé avant, j'aurais apporté les photos: If I had thought of it earlier, I would have brought the photos.

Be careful:
(I) for verbs which conjugate with *être*
Si j'avais su, je serais venu hier: If I had known, I would have come yesterday.
(II) for an idiomatic form which drops the *si* and uses a present conditional in the first clause
Elle serait venue plus tôt, elle aurait vu mon frère. This is similar to the inverted form in English: Had she come earlier, she would have seen my brother.
This **is** an inelegant form and we only include it so that you will not be surprised should you come across it.

2 Being (for the most part!) a logical language, French treats proper names in a regular fashion. If we are talking about makes of car, we would speak of *une Renault* because Renault - being a car - is **une** *voiture. Une côte:* a hillside, a coast. But in wine names we would speak of *un Côtes du Rhône* because *le vin* is masculine.

So, when using a brand-name, the article (and any adjectives) depend on whether the object referred to is masculine or feminine. *Un Airbus* because this plane is *un avion* but *une Honda 125* because a motor-bike is *une moto.*

Remember also that proper names are invariable. We write *des Citroën* but any adjective would be in the plural - *des Citroën neuves.*

3 The subjunctive. This mood tends to worry English speakers but it does exist in our language (e.g. Long live the King); the reason we don't notice it is that the English verb usually has only four or five forms (smoke - smokes - smoked - smoking) whereas French verbs have an average of fifteen forms (check through them yourself). Apart from 'obligatory' uses we know - after conjunctions of time and impersonal expressions like *Il faut que...* the subjunctive is used in French where

(1) there is a feeling or an emotion
(2) one expresses one's wishes or desires or
(3) if there is a doubt, a suggestion or a possibility.

In all these cases there are **two** verbs in the sentence. Re-read this paragraph then look at the following examples:

(1) *Je veux que vous* **veniez** *à dix heures:* I want you to come at ten o'clock. *Voulez-vous que je vous* **dise** *ce que j'en pense?:* Do you want me to tell you what I think of it? *J'aimerais que vous me* **fassiez** *ce travail:* I want you to do this job for me. (Notice the two verbs.)

(2) *Je suis désolé que tu ne* **puisses** *pas venir:* I'm so sorry you can't come. *Nous sommes surpris que nous*

****

*****

*n'*ayons *pas de ses nouvelles:* We are surprised we don't have news of him/her. *C'est dommage qu'ils* **soient** *obligés de partir:* It's a pity they have to leave.

(3) *Je ne suis pas sûr qu'il* **soit** *à vendre:* I am not sure that it's for sale. *Je doute que vous* **puissiez** *acheter cet appartement:* I doubt that you can buy that flat. *Il vaut mieux que vous* **arriviez** *de bonne heure:* You had better arrive early.
These are good examples to memorise. Try transforming them using other pronouns (e.g. *Elle doute que je* **puisse** *acheter...*). Re-read the examples one more time.
(1) feeling or emotion
(2) wishes or desires
(3) doubt, suggestion, probability

Do you see how the verb in the subjunctive conveys an idea of uncertainty or dependence? This is what 'subjunctive' means - the second verb is 'sub-joined' to the first. The use of the subjunctive mood is governed by situation. Don't make a mountain of it: remember our examples and look out for others in the lessons.

N.B.
(1) Remember the form *Qu'il me téléphone:* an order, or *Qu'elle ne dise rien:* an interdiction.
(2) When we use a verb like *Je crains que...* (I'm afraid that) in the affirmative form we put an 'expletive **ne**' before the verb in the subjunctive. *Je crains qu'il ne soit trop cher:* I'm afraid it's too expensive. The **ne** has no negative sense (and is often dropped in colloquial speech).

****

*****

VINGT-NEUVIEME (29ᵉ) LEÇON

Un petit peu d'histoire (1)

1 Lisons les notes que Laurent a prises pendant un cours d'histoire sur la Révolution française : (2)

2 « Hiver 1789 : mauvaises récoltes, chômage, froid exceptionnel - et le trésor royal vide. (3)

3 Le roi Louis XVI va réunir les Etats Généraux (il y a trois « états », avec 300 députés chacun

4 pour la noblesse et le clergé, et 600 pour les paysans et les bourgeois : (5)

5 on appelle ce dernier état « Le Tiers état »). (6)

NOTES

(1) Since these are notes, the writer uses the present tense both for facility and because, in spoken narrative and modern fiction, French uses this 'historic present' to involve the listener or reader in the events. If, however, we were to read the same narrative in a history book, we would discover a new tense, which is the subject of Lesson 30.

(2) Be careful: *un cours* is a lesson, *un cycle de cours* is a course of lessons. However, the two words are often confused and in a university setting *un cours* may also be a course of lectures.
We also have the word *une leçon* which is more often used in secondary education (*lycées* etc.) and in figurative expressions. *Ça lui servira de leçon!*: Let that be a lesson for him!

29th LESSON

A little bit of history

1 Let's read the notes that Laurent took during a history lesson on the French Revolution:

2 Winter 1789: bad crops, unemployment, exceptional cold - and the royal treasury empty.

3 The king Louis XVI is to assemble the General Estates (there are 3 'estates' with 300 'députés' each

4 for the nobility and the clergy, and 600 for the peasants and the bourgeois:

5 the latter estate is called 'the 3rd estate'.)

NOTES

(3) *Un trésor:* Treasury or a treasure. The French Treasury is called *Le Trésor Public; les bons du Trésor* are Treasury bonds. If the word treasury is used in other ways than in a title, we find the word *la trésorerie.*

(4) Notice how the French number their kings: *Louis seize, Charles premier,* never the ordinal. *Charles Quint = Charles V.* The definite article is always used before the word *roi.*

(5) This word has strayed from its original meaning of *un citoyen d'un bourg,* i.e., a citizen of a town (we find the latter word in *un faubourg:* a suburb); in the Middle Ages, that citizen had certain privileges and we called him a burgher (one of the bones of contention between France and England was the latter's humiliation of the burghers of Calais, and les *Six bourgeois de Calais* - one of Rodin's finest sculptures is in the gardens of the Houses of Parliament in Westminster).

By extension, the word has strayed came to mean 'middle-class' and often 'narrow-minded, conservative, etc.'; this pejorative meaning persists, but we also find the adjective used quite commonly in *la cuisine bourgeoise:* simple family cooking or *un agent de police en bourgeois:* a plain-clothes policeman (we also find ... *en civil:* in civilian clothes).

(6) *Un tiers* means a third: *les deux tiers* = two thirds, but we find it as an adjective in some titles both historical and ecclesiastical.
Le tiers monde: the third world. (In a sequential order, of course, we would say *la troisième fois,* etc.)
Un tiers also means a third person in contract or legal language, *une assurance au tiers:* third party insurance. You need to recognise rather than use the word.

6 Les Etats discutent sans résultat, les députés du Tiers état se séparent des autres en juin 1789. **(7)**

7 Ils se proclament « Assemblée Nationale » ; le roi s'y oppose d'abord mais finit par accepter.

8 Avec l'accord de Louis, ils forment l'Assemblée Constituante. Le 9 juillet, la monarchie absolue n'existe plus.

9 Mais Louis veut se venger. Le 11 juillet, il rappelle ses troupes à Paris **(8)**

10 et il renvoie le ministre Necker. **(9)**

11 Les Parisiens sont furieux ; ils se rassemblent pour donner l'assaut à la Bastille. **(10)**

12 Ils l'attaquent, libèrent les prisonniers et le gouverneur est décapité.

13 Le roi reprend Necker, accepte la cocarde bleu, blanc, rouge. **(11)**

14 En octobre, la foule va à pied jusqu'à Versailles et force Louis à venir résider à Paris.

15 L'Ancien Régime est terminé. »

NOTES

(7) You will notice that often, a verb is in the reflexive form in French whereas English uses the active (or even the passive) form. It is much better to notice and remember examples than learn sets of rules, but the logic of using the reflexive is simple to understand:
Elle a séparé la classe en trois: She separated the class into three (i.e. the action of separating takes a direct object).
Elle s'est séparée de son mari: She separated from her husband (i.e. the direct object of the separation is herself).

(8) *Il voulait venger son frère:* He wanted to avenge his brother. *Il voulait se venger de son frère:* He wanted to get revenge on his brother. Notice again the use of the reflexive. We find a similar phenomenon in English, where 'get' is often put before a verb to give it a reflexive sense: *je me suis perdu:* I got lost; *ils se sont saoulés:* they got drunk.

*****

6 The Estates discuss without result, the 'députés' of the 3rd estate separate from the others in June 1789.

7 They proclaim themselves the National Assembly; the king opposes it first of all, but finishes by accepting.

8 With the agreement of Louis, they form the Constituant Assembly. On the 9th July, absolute monarchy no longer exists.

9 But Louis wants to get his revenge. On the 11th July, he calls his troops back to Paris

10 and he dismisses the minister Necker.

11 The Parisians are furious; they assemble to assault the Bastille.

12 They attack it, free the prisoners, and the governor is decapitated.

13 The king takes back Necker, accepts the red, white and blue cockade.

14 In October, the crowd marches to Versailles and forces Louis to come and reside in Paris.

15 The Ancien Régime is finished.

NOTES

(9) *Renvoyer* literally means: to send back. *Il a renvoyé le plat à la cuisine:* He sent the dish back to the kitchen. An extended meaning is: to dismiss someone from a job, although we would usually find the word *licencier* in modern usage.
A very picturesque expression is *renvoyer l'ascenseur* (lit. to send back the lift) meaning: to return a favour.

(10) *La Bastille:* the famous prison which was the symbol of the 'despotism' of the *Ancien Régime* (the old order); its storming - on 14th July 1789 - was the opening act of the French Revolution. Incidentally, we tend to get the impression that hundreds of poor souls were set free by a vengeful crowd. In fact, only seven prisoners - two madmen, a lecher and four forgers - were in the prison at the time. The *Fête Nationale* (f) is held every year on the 14th July. (The French do not call it Bastille Day, though, just *le quatorze juillet* or *la Fête Nationale.*) There is even a rather picturesque verb: *embastiller:* to throw into jail.

(11) *Une cocarde* is a rosette or a cockade. The colour of the king's cockade was white, the coulour of the House of Bourbon. Red and blue were the colours of Paris, and the king allowed his colour - white - to be bordered by those of the capital. *Le tricolore:* the Tricolour, or the French flag.

EXERCICES

1. Voici les notes que j'ai prises et voilà les livres que j'ai lus. **2.** Je m'y suis opposé d'abord mais j'ai fini par accepter. **3.** Ils se vengeront de l'insulte, vous verrez. **4.** Elle veut venir habiter Paris. **5.** Ils se sont séparés l'année dernière. **6.** Je me suis servi d'un dictionnaire pour faire le test.

Mettez les mots qui manquent.
Fill in the blanks.

1 *As-tu . . . . beaucoup de notes ? — J'en . . . . pas*

mal.

Did you take many notes? — I took quite a few.

2 *Elle . ' . . . . dans la forêt et . ' . . .*

. . . . .

She went for a walk in the forest and got lost.

****

TRENTIEME (30ᵉ) LEÇON

Les débuts de la Révolution

1 Laurent veut vérifier ses notes, aussi il prend un livre d'histoire et l'ouvre au chapitre correspondant :

2 — La situation en cet hiver de 1789 était catastrophique ;

3 le chômage et les mauvaises récoltes, aggravés par un froid exceptionnel, sapaient le moral du peuple. **(1) (2)**

NOTES

(1) A word that has passed directly into English, 'a sapper', is an army engineer who 'undermines' buildings, etc. *Saper* can be used figuratively or literally. *Les sapeurs-pompiers* is the administrative name for firemen (in everyday language, we refer simply to *les pompiers*).

EXERCISES: 1. Here are the notes I took and there are the books I read. **2.** I opposed it at first but I finished by accepting. **3.** They will get revenge for the insult, you'll see. **4.** She wants to come and live in Paris. **5.** They separated last year. **6.** I used a dictionary to do the test.

3 *Il n'a pas* . . . . *son* . . . . . .

He still hasn't given his agreement.

4 *Où sont les fleurs* . . . . *?*

Where are the flowers that you bought?

5 *Ils l'* . . . . *à* . . . . *à Paris.*

They forced him to come and reside in Paris.

Mots qui manquaient :

1. pris - ai pris 2. s'est promenée - s'est perdue 3. encore donné - accord 4. que tu as achetées 5. ont forcé - venir résider.

****

30th LESSON

The beginnings of the revolution

1 Laurent wants to check his notes, so he takes a history book and opens it at the corresponding chapter:

2 — The situation in that winter of 1789 was catastrophic;

3 unemployment and bad crops, aggravated by exceptional cold, were undermining the morale of the people.

NOTES

(2) Do not confuse *le moral* (the morale, the spirits - *Elle m'a beaucoup remonté le moral:* She really raised my spirits) with *la morale* (morals). *C'est contraire à la morale:* It's immoral. *Faire de la morale:* To moralize. *Moral - e - aux* is also an adjective.

(3) *Compter:* to count up. *Comptez la monnaie!* Count the change, but used figuratively it is equivalent to the English use of 'to number'. *La rue comptait quelque trente maisons:* The street numbered some 30 houses. *Un comptable:* an accountant, *la comptabilité* (in familiar language *la compta*): accountancy. The 'p' is silent: [kontabilitay, konta].

4 Le roi Louis XVI réunit alors les Etats Généraux ; ces trois assemblées **(N.1)**

5 comptaient 300 députés chacune pour le
clergé et la noblesse, **(3)**

6 et 600 pour la bourgeoisie et les paysans : le
Tiers état.

7 Les Etats discutèrent des réformes mais sans
résultat et, en juin 1789,

8 les députés du Tiers état se séparèrent des
autres.

9 Ils se proclamèrent « Assemblée Nationale ».
Le roi s'y opposa mais dut finir par accepter.
(4)

10 Avec l'accord de Louis, les députés formèrent
l'Assemblée Constituante et, le 9 juillet,

11 la monarchie absolue cessa d'exister.

12 Mais Louis voulait se venger de son humiliation : le 11 juillet, il rappela ses troupes à Paris

13 et il renvoya Necker, le ministre qui lui avait
conseillé la modération. **(5)**

14 Les Parisiens furent excédés ; la foule se
rassembla place Royale et se dirigea vers la
forteresse de la Bastille, **(6) (7)**

15 où elle donna l'assaut ; les prisonniers furent
libérés et le gouverneur, de Launay, fut
décapité.

4   The king Louis XVI therefore called together the General Estates; those three assemblies

5   numbered 300 'députés' each for the clergy and the nobility,

6   and 600 for the bourgeoisie and the peasants: the Third estate.

7   The Estates discussed reforms but without result and, in June 1789,

8   the 'députés' of the Third estate separated from the others.

9   They proclaimed themselves the National Assembly. The king was opposed to it but had to finish by accepting.

10   With the agreement of Louis the 'députés' formed the Constituent Assembly and, on 9th July,

11   absolute monarchy ceased to exist.

12   But Louis wished to avenge his humiliation; on July 11th, he called his troops back to Paris

13   and he dismissed Necker, the minister who had advised him to be moderate.

14   The Parisians lost all patience; the crowd gathered in the Place Royale and went towards the fortress of the Bastille,

15   where they attacked; the prisoners were freed and the governor, de Launay, was decapitated.

NOTES

(4) The past historic of *devoir: je dus; tu dus; il dut; nous dûmes; vous dûtes; ils durent*. Notice the circumflex (^) on the 1st and 2nd person plural. We also find a circumflex on the **masculine** singular past participle. *L'argent dû:* owed money, but *en bonne et due forme:* in due form.

(5) Notice the construction: *Je lui ai conseillé la prudence:* I advised him/her to be cautious.

(6) The past historic of *être: je fus; tu fus; il fut; nous fûmes; vous fûtes; ils furent*. Notice again the two circumflexes.

(7) This place - one of the most beautiful in Paris - is now called *la place des Vosges*.

*****

16 Louis, ému par la violence, reprit Necker et accepta la cocarde tricolore. **(8)**

17 En octobre, la foule se rendit à pied au palais de Versailles « chercher le boulanger, la boulangère et le petit mitron ». **(9)**

18 Louis dut venir habiter la capitale ; l'Ancien Régime n'existait plus. — **(10)**

EXERCICES

1. Le peuple n'a pas de pain. — *Qu'ils mangent de la brioche ! **2.** On lui a conseillé la modération. J'espère qu'il a écouté. **3.** Penses-tu qu'on peut lui remonter le moral ? **4.** Ne comptez pas sur lui si vous avez un problème. **5.** Il était excédé par son patron ; il n'en pouvait plus. **6.** Vous avez l'air tout ému. Que s'est-il passé ?

* Marie-Antoinette's reply referred to all the people - thus she uses the plural.

Mettez les verbes au passé simple.
Put the verbs into the past historic.

1 *Il . . . . ses troupes à Paris et . . . .*

le ministre.

He called his troops back to Paris and dismissed the minister.

2 *Ils . . . . . . licenciés et . . . . . . quitter la région.*

They were fired and had to leave the region.

3 *Le directeur . . . . . . le Conseil d'Administration.*

The manager called together the board of directors.

4 *Ils . . . . du projet et s'y*

. . . . favorables.

They discussed the plan and declared themselves in favour.

16 Louis, moved by the violence, took Necker back and accepted the tricoloured cockade.

17 In October, the crowd marched to the palace of Versailles 'to look for bread'.

18 Louis had to come and live in the capital; the Ancien Régime no longer existed. —

NOTES

(8) This is the past participle of the verb *émouvoir* (to move with emotion) which is little used in the active form, but very common in the passive. *Nous étions très émus par sa mort:* We were deeply affected by his/her death. (Notice the agreement of the past participle in the passive - it is an adjective.) *Il parla d'une voix émue:* He spoke in a voice full of emotion.

(9) This was a reference to Queen Marie-Antoinette's famous - or infamous - retort when told that the people had no bread to eat; she is reputed to have said *'Qu'ils mangent de la brioche'*. English has no equivalent for *la brioche* (a sweet, spongy bread) so history has left us with the translation 'Let them eat cake!' (Notice the subjunctive after *Que...*!) *Un mitron* was a baker's apprentice and referred to Louis XVII, the Dauphin. The baker and baker's wife were Louis XVI and Marie-Antoinette.

(10) We use the imperfect and not the past historic, because the 'non-existence' was a continuous action, unlike in line 11 where the verb is 'to cease' (to exist); this cessation took place at a definite fixed point in past time.

EXERCISES: 1. The people has no bread. — Let them eat cake! **2.** He was advised to be moderate. I hope he listened. **3.** Do you think we can cheer him/her up? **4.** Don't count on him if you have a problem. **5.** He lost patience with his boss; he couldn't stand it any more. **6.** You look all upset. What's happened?

5 *La* . . . . . *se* . . . . *et se* . . . .

. . . . *à Versailles.*

The crowd gathered and marched to Versailles.

Mots qui manquaient :

1. rappela - renvoya **2.** furent - durent **3.** réunit **4.** discutèrent - déclarèrent **5.** foule - rassembla - rendit à pied.

TRENTE ET UNIEME (31e) LEÇON

« Hors de Paris, il n'y a point de salut... » (1)

1   — Ah, vous êtes Français ? Vous êtes donc de Paris !
2   Combien de fois ai-je entendu cette réflexion ? Pour bon nombre d'étrangers, la France, c'est Paris.
3   Remarquez, les Français eux-mêmes n'aident en rien : ils divisent leur pays en « Paris » et « la province ».
4   On entend à la radio : « L'autoroute A 6 est bouchée dans le sens Paris-province » ;
5   ou encore : « Jean-Pierre ? Oh, il habite la province ».
6   Il peut vivre à Marseille dans le Midi, à Strasbourg en Alsace, (N.2)
7   au Havre dans le Nord ou encore au diable vauvert (2)
8   mais c'est encore et toujours la province !
9   Cependant, les régions de France sont riches en histoire, en traditions, en couleur locale ; (3)
10   un Bourguignon ou un Breton, un Basque ou un Provençal
11   vous parleront de leur « pays » et en effet, ils sont bien plus que de simples « régions » ; (4)

NOTES

(1) Le salut is salvation. L'Armée du Salut: The Salvation Army. A much more common usage is the familiar greeting Salut!, equivalent to our 'Hi there'!
ne... point is an emphatic ne... pas. The quotation is from 'Les Précieuses Ridicules' by Molière and is itself satirical: Hors de Paris, il n'y a point de salut pour les honnêtes gens.
(2) An expression whose form is as much disputed as its origin. We find au diable vert, le diable auvert and several others. It had its origins perhaps in an allusion to the castle of Vauvert which was miles from anywhere, or from over in the green valleys (old French)

31st LESSON

'Out of Paris there is no salvation...'

1 Ah, you're French? So you're from Paris!
2 How many times have I heard this remark? For a good number of foreigners, France is Paris.
3 Mind you, the French themselves don't help at all: they divide their country into 'Paris' and 'the provinces'.
4 You hear on the radio: 'The A6 motorway is blocked by traffic in the Paris-province direction';
5 or again: 'Jean-Pierre? Oh, he lives in the provinces'.
6 He may live in Marseille in the South, in Strasbourg in Alsace,
7 in Le Havre in the North or again, in the back of beyond
8 but it's still and always *'la province'!*
9 And yet, the regions of France are rich in history, in traditions and in local coulour;
10 a Burgundian or a Breton, a Basque or a Provençal
11 will talk to you of their 'countries' and, in fact, they are really more than simple 'regions';

NOTES

un val - plural *vaux* - now *une vallée;* whatever its origin, the most usual form is the one in line 7, and the meaning of all of them is 'in a lost place', 'in the back of beyond'.

(3) Notice that English would have to put 'and' before the last word in a list. In written French this is unnecessary.

(4) *Ils ont ôté leur chapeau:* They took off their hats.
Ils éteignirent leur cigarette. If the noun and the possessive adjective were in the plural, it would mean that each man was wearing several hats or smoking several cigarettes at the same time. So, when the possessor has only one of the item referred to, we leave the adjective and noun in the singular. However, if we want to insist on variety we would use the plural. For example: *Les commerçants ouvrirent leurs boutiques à quatre heures:* tells me that there were several kinds of shop-keeper and several kinds of shop.
We also use the plural to avoid a ridiculous situation: *Les femmes peuvent amener leurs maris.* If this were to follow the singular rule, the reader may be led to believe that bigamy were the order of the day!

12 ils font de la France l'un des pays les plus
diversifiés d'Europe. **(5)**

13 Si vous le permettez, nous allons partir de Paris
ensemble pour découvrir cette « province »

14 dont on parle tant et que l'on connaît si mal. **(6)**

15 Vous verrez que, comme a dit un auteur
français,

16 La France est le seul pays du monde où, si
vous ajoutez dix citoyens à dix autres, **(7)**

17 vous ne faites pas une addition mais vingt
divisions.

EXERCICES

1. Combien de fois ai-je entendu cette réflexion ! **2.** Bon
nombre d'étrangers pensent que la France, c'est Paris. **3.**
L'année dernière, il est allé en Allemagne, en Angleterre,
au Danemark et au Portugal. **4.** Si vous le permettez, nous
allons changer de sujet. **5.** Nous sommes partis au diable
vauvert chercher sa maison. **6.** C'est un pays dont on
parle beaucoup mais qu'on connaît mal.

Mettez les mots qui manquent.
Fill in the blanks.

1 *Ces régions* . . . . . . *la France un pays très diversifié.*

These regions make France a very diversified country.

12 they make France one of the most diversified countries in Europe.

13 If you will, we shall go out of Paris together to discover this *'province'*

14 of which so much is said and so little is known.

15 You will see that, as a French author said,

16 France is the only country in the world where, if you add ten citizens to ten others,

17 you don't make an addition but twenty divisions.

NOTES

(5) Note the construction *Qu'est-ce que tu vas faire de cette vieille boîte?:* What are you going to do with that old box? Also, *Il a fait de la société l'une des entreprises les plus grandes du pays:* He made the company one of the largest businesses in the country.
Ils ont fait de ce restaurant une merveille de la nouvelle cuisine: They made that restaurant a marvel of the 'nouvelle cuisine'. Look carefully at the word order.

(6) See how we use the passive to translate this sentence. Where *on* cannot be attributed to a fictitious 'you' or 'we', as in line 4, we use the passive voice in English.

(7) Or *le seul pays au monde.*

EXERCISES: 1. How many times have I heard that remark! **2.** A good number of foreigners think that France is Paris. **3.** Last year he went to Germany, to England, to Denmark and to Portugal. **4.** If you will, we'll change the subject. **5.** We went to the back of beyond to find his/her house. **6.** It's a country/region about which a lot is said but little is known.

2 *Ils ont enlevé . . . .*

They took off their coats.

3 *Il est . . . . 'un . . . . . . musicien.*

He is much more than a simple musician.

4 *C'est un film . . . . on . beaucoup . . . . .*

It's a film which has been much talked of.

Leçon 31

5 . . . . , *nous allons sortir de Paris.*

If you will, we'll leave Paris.

****

TRENTE-DEUXIEME (32ᵉ) LEÇON

La Bretagne

1 Nous vous avions promis de visiter quelques régions de France. Eh bien, pour notre premier voyage, allons en Bretagne. **(1)**

2 Cette péninsule, située au Nord-Ouest de la France, lui fut rattachée en 1491.

3 Cette année-là, la duchesse Anne de Bretagne épousa le roi de France, Charles VIII, puis, plus tard, Louis XII. **(2) (3)**

4 Elle apporta la Bretagne en dot ; ce fut un cadeau magnifique. **(4)**

5 Terre relativement pauvre, mais splendide, de landes et de granit, peuplée de Celtes ombrageux et romantiques, **(5) (6)**

6 la Bretagne est surtout un pays de marins. Ils furent corsaires, pirates, découvreurs, **(7)**

NOTES

(1) We sometimes find a pluperfect where we would expect a *passé composé*. Although we are not supposed to use the tense alone there is sometimes an 'understood' qualification - here, *nous vous avions promis... et voilà.*
Notice the alternative construction with the verb *promettre. Je vous ai promis de le faire:* I promised you I would do it. We also find *Je vous ai promis que je le ferais.*

(2) *Cette année-ci:* This year. *Cette année-là:* In that year.
Ce jour-là nous fîmes connaissance avec sa sœur: On that day, we made the acquaintance of his/her sister.

(3) *Marier* is a transitive verb. *Le curé maria le couple:* The priest married the couple. We have a reflexive use: *Ils se sont mariés à l'église:* They got married in church. We can use this form to speak about the two people. *Jean s'est marié avec la fille du banquier:* Jean married the banker's daughter. But it is simpler to use the verb *épouser: Elle épousa le roi de France:* She married the king of France. We can talk of *un époux* and *une épouse* (recognise the English word spouse?) although these words are more used in an administrative context.

Mots qui manquaient :

1. font de 2. leur manteau 3. bien plus qu' - simple 4. dont - a - parlé 5. Si vous le permettez.

****

32nd LESSON

Brittany

1 We promised you that we would visit several regions of France. Well, for our first trip, let's go to Brittany.

2 This peninsula, situated in the North-West of France, was joined to it in 1491.

3 In that year Anne, Duchess of Brittany, married the king of France, Charles VIII then, later, Louis XII.

4 She brought Brittany as a dowry; it was a magnificent present.

5 A relatively poor, but splendid, land of moors and granite, peopled with touchy and romantic Celts,

6 Brittany is above all a region of sailors. They were privateers, pirates and discoverers,

NOTES

(4) Notice the pronunciation [dot] *une dot* = a dowry. Although the verb *doter* literally means to dower, we find it frequently (especially in the past participle) when describing the equipment of something: *Cette école est dotée d'un laboratoire de langues:* This school is equipped with a language laboratory.

(5) We know that the indefinite article is omitted before a profession. *Il a été nommé directeur:* He was appointed manager (but we would say *C'est un directeur très efficace*) and before a nationality. *Sa femme est Argentine:* His wife is Argentinian. Notice the two possibilities *Il est Anglais* or *C'est un Anglais.*
Omission before a concrete noun is a literary effect. *Femme de Louis XVI, Marie-Antoinette naquit en...:* Wife of Louis XVI, Marie-Antoinette was born in...

(6) *Une ombre:* a shadow. *Sans l'ombre d'un doute:* Without the shadow of a doubt. The noun also means: shade. *Il fait quarante degrés à l'ombre:* It is 40° in the shade. The adjective, however, describes people who are quick to take offence.

(7) *Un corsaire* has nothing to do with *la Corse* (Corsica) as some pretend. It is the ancient equivalent of *un coursier:* an errand boy. *Le corsaire* was a ship equiped by private individuals, with government authorisation, to capture or destroy enemy ships. The 'price' was shared among the king, the captain and the crew. Later, the word *corsaire* became applied to the crew. A pirate is a brigand.

7 ils restent parmi les meilleurs pêcheurs du monde.

8 Qu'ils soient des champs - artichauts, oignons, choux-fleurs -, ou de bord de mer - pêche et tourisme -,

9 les Bretons sont fiers et secrets, se réfugiant volontiers dans le particularisme de leur langue et de leur culture.

10 Assez réservés, si vous savez les comprendre et les apprivoiser, vous vous en ferez des amis fidèles, joyeux, mais... susceptibles ! **(8)**

11 Tous les Bretons emploient le français dans la vie quotidienne.

12 Voici, cependant, deux mots bretons utiles qui vous procureront un petit succès à coup sûr : Démad déoc'h (Bonjour à vous) et Kénavo (au revoir). **(9)**

EXERCICES

1. C'est un Français et sa femme est Espagnole. **2.** La voiture est dotée d'un équipement très sophistiqué. **3.** Elle reste parmi les régions les plus pauvres. **4.** Prenez le cheval et faites-en ce que vous pouvez : essayez de l'apprivoiser. **5.** Il serait volontiers parti avec nous s'il avait pu. **6.** Ils arriveront après le match à coup sûr !

Mettez les mots qui manquent.
Fill in the blanks.

1 *Anne . . . . . . le roi et . . . . la Bretagne en dot ;*

Anne married the king and brought Brittany as her dowry;

2 *. . . . . un cadeau splendide.*

it was a splendid present.

7   they remain among the best fishermen in the world.
8   Whether it is of the fields - artichokes, onions, cauliflowers -, or of the seaside - fishing, tourism -,
9   the Bretons are proud and secretive, willingly hiding behind the particularism of their language and of their culture.
10   Fairly reserved, if you know how to understand and to win them over, you will make faithful, joyous... but sensitive friends!
11   All Bretons use French in their everyday life.
12   However, here are two useful Breton words which will obtain you a certain success: *Démad éoc'h* (Good morning to you) and *Kénavo* (Good-bye).

NOTES

(8) When applied to an animal, *apprivoiser* means to tame. (The French title of the Taming of the Shrew is *La Mégère Apprivoisée*) but when applied to a person it means to win someone over, or to 'domesticate' them.

(9) Another use of *coup*. *Il gagnera à coup sûr:* He's bound to win. We usually find the expression in a construction with a future tense.

EXERCISES: **1.** He's a Frenchman and his wife is Spanish.   **2.** The car is fitted with very sophisticated equipment.   **3.** It remains among one of the poorest regions.   **4.** Take the horse and do what you can with it: try and tame it.   **5.** He would willingly have gone with us if he had been able.   **6.** They are bound to arrive after the match.

3 *Il* . . . . *de l'usine et* . . . . . .

. . . . *très efficace.*

He is manager of the factory and he's a very efficient manager.

4 *Ils* . . . . *qu'ils*

. . . .

They promised us that they would come.

****

TRENTE-TROISIEME (33ᵉ) LEÇON

Une question de mots

1 J'ai des problèmes, vous savez. Je suis non seulement myope mais daltonien ; **(1)**
2 en plus j'ai une calvitie avancée (c'est pourquoi je porte une perruque). **(2)**
3 Malgré des consultations hebdomadaires chez un spécialiste, ça ne s'améliore pas. **(5)**
4 La dernière fois, il m'a défendu de boire du café lyophilisé ! **(6)**

NOTES

(1) We have already mentioned that French is a language of almost entirely classical origins - most of its words come from Latin, but it also draws on Greek for word-formation (prefixes, suffixes, etc.) English - which is roughly divided between Latin (via Old French) and Germanic languages - has a dual etymology which often allows two words where French has only one. French nouns and verbs often appear 'intellectual' when compared to their common English counterparts but they are simply the only way of expressing an object or an idea. This lesson will show you some very common ones, with appropriate notes. More important than learning the words is recognising the mechanisms which allow us to translate them by an explanatory noun-group. So the adjectives *myope* and *daltonien* are respectively 'short-sighted' and 'colour-blind' (cf. the German equivalents: kurzsichtig, farbenblind). The

5 *Il . . . . . . 40° à . ' . . . . . dans le Midi.*

It was 40° in the shade in the south of France.

Mots qui manquaient :

1. épousa - apporta **2.** ce fut **3.** est directeur - c'est un directeur **4.** nous ont promis - viendraient **5.** faisait - l'ombre.

****

33rd LESSON

A question of words

1 I have problems, you know. I'm not only short-sighted but colour-blind;

2 what's more, I'm going bald (which is why I wear a wig).

3 Despite weekly visits to a specialist, it's not getting better.

4 The last time, he forbade me to drink freeze-dried coffee!

NOTES

English adjectives 'myopic' and 'daltonian' (from the English chemist John Dalton, who described his own case) are usually only found in scientific contexts. The opposite of *myope* is *presbyte* (long-sighted).

(2) *Etre chauve:* to be bald. The Latin root is 'calvus' so *la calvitie* is baldness. In a similar way *aveugle* means 'blind' (from Greek) but the Latin word is 'coecus' so blindness is *la cécité.*

(3) *Consulter un médecin:* to consult a doctor - but, more commonly, to see a doctor.

(4) *Hebdomadaire* (from Greek 'hebdomas', meaning a week): weekly; *un hebdomadaire:* a weekly (paper, magazine, etc.); *quotidien:* daily; *mensuel:* monthly; *annuel:* yearly.

(5) *S'améliorer:* to ameliorate (from Latin 'melior' meaning: better - cf. *meilleur* in French) but, in everyday English: to get better. *Une amélioration:* an improvement.

(6) *Lyophilisé:* from two Greek words, this adjective describes the process by which instant coffee is made. First it is *frozen* then *dried,* hence - freeze-dried. It is commonly found on jars of instant coffee.

5 En conduisant par temps neigeux, n'oubliez pas de regarder souvent dans le rétroviseur **(7)**

6 et de rétrograder avant de freiner ; cela vous évitera des accrochages. **(8) (9)**

7 Tu parles d'une distraction ! Nous devons sortir ce week-end

8 et j'ai le choix entre un concours hippique,

9 une exposition d'horticulture ou une exposition canine. **(10)**

10 Faites attention ! L'eau dans les trains n'est pas potable. **(11)**

11 J'ai acheté un service de couteaux en acier inoxydable. **(12)**

12 La police a relevé des empreintes digitales sur les lieux du crime.

13 C'est un pays qui doit se situer quelque part en Afrique australe. **(13)**

14 Tous ces mots peuvent vous paraître bien compliqués

15 mais ne vous en faites pas : rappelez-vous ce qu'on dit :

16 « Ce n'est qu'une question de mots. Il n'y en a jamais eu d'autres en France. »

NOTES

(7) 'Rétro': back - 'vidéo': I see - *un rétroviseur:* a rear-view mirror. As you have probably noticed, a knowledge of Latin is a great help in deciphering unfamiliar words. Even if you don't know Latin, it is simple to learn a few prefixes and suffixes and the roots of many words are the same as in English.

5 When driving in snowy weather, don't forget to look often in the rear-view mirror

6 and to change down before braking; that will save you having slight accidents.

7 Talk about entertainment!   We are supposed to go out this week-end

8 and I have the choice between a horse-show,

9 a flower-show or a dog-show.

10 Watch out!   The water in trains is not drinkable.

11 I bought a set of stainless-steel knives.

12 The police took fingerprints at the scene of the crime.

13 It's a country which must be somewhere in southern Africa.

14 All these words may appear very complicated to you

15 but don't worry: remember what we say:

16 'It's only a question of words.   There have never been any others in France.'

NOTES

(8) 'Rétro': backward; 'gressus': to go (think of English, retrograde), to change (gears) downwards. *Une vitesse:* a gear. *La boîte de vitesses:* the gear-box. *Passer les vitesses:* to change gear.

(9) *Un accrochage* is a familiar word meaning a slight car accident.

(10) Look how English avoids the Latin and Greek compounds in everyday language: a horse-show, a flower-show, a dog show (although we have the words 'hippic', 'horticultural' and 'canine').

(11) Normally, for some adjectives, French has one where English has two (*illisible* means both unreadable and illegible). Here, we have the opposite: *potable:* which can be drunk safely, *eau potable:* drinking water and *buvable:* drinkable because it is good.

(12) Oxydation is the process of rusting (*la rouille:* rust); *inoxydable:* which cannot rust, i.e. stainless steel. (In everyday French, we say *l'inox:* stainless steel.)

(13) More Latin roots. We know *le Nord, le Sud, l'Ouest* and *l'Est* but their adjectives are *septentrional* (northern), *austral* (southern), *oriental* (eastern) and *occidental* (western). However, in place-names we would find the first set *L'Allemagne de l'Est:* East Germany, *L'Afrique du Sud:* South Africa.

EXERCICES

1. Malgré des améliorations, il y a encore beaucoup à faire. **2.** Tu parles d'une distraction ! La pièce était franchement ennuyeuse. **3.** Je devais sortir ce week-end, mais j'ai la grippe. **4.** Pourquoi portez-vous des lunettes ? Etes-vous myope ou presbyte ? **5.** Il faut être prudent en conduisant par temps pluvieux. **6.** Attention ! Cette eau n'est pas potable.

Mettez les mots qui manquent.
Fill in the blanks.

1   *Ils . . . . de sortir après vingt heures.*

They forbade him to go out after 8.00 p.m.

2   *Ça . . . . vous . . . . curieux, mais c'est vrai.*

It may appear curious to you, but it's true.

3   *Ne vous . . . . pas pour lui ; il se débrouillera.*

Don't worry about him; he'll get by.

4   *. . . . . -vous . . . . . je vous ai dit.*

Remember what I told you.

****

TRENTE-QUATRIEME (34e) LEÇON

Il n'y a pas toujours d'équivalent

1   Dans chaque langue, il existe des mots qui désignent des choses ou des coutumes **(1)**

*****

EXERCISES: 1. Despite some improvements, there is still a lot to do. **2.** Talk about entertainment! The play was frankly boring. **3.** I was supposed to go out this week-end, but I have the flu. **4.** Why do you wear glasses? Are you short- or long-sighted? **5.** You must be careful when driving in rainy weather. **6.** Watch out! That water is not drinkable.

5 *Il n' . . jamais . . de problèmes avec sa santé.*

There have never been any problems with his health.

Mots qui manquaient :

1. lui ont défendu **2.** peut - paraître **3.** en faites **4.** Rappelez - ce que **5.** 'y a - eu.

****

34th LESSON

There is not always an equivalent

1 In each language words exist which designate things or customs

NOTES

(1) French often uses a verb where the copula 'to be' is sufficient in English. *Paris est situé sur la Seine:* Paris is on the Seine.
The verb *exister* is also thus used. Notice that **before** the subject, the expression is singular: *Il existe des mots.* If it were placed after the subject, it would be governed by it and would agree: *Des mots existent.*

2 propres à chaque pays et pour lesquels il n'y a pas toujours d'équivalent. Regardez ces phrases : **(2)**

3 — Présentez-vous à la mairie avec votre carte d'identité, votre livret de famille et un extrait de casier judiciaire. **(3) (4)**

4 — Pour téléphoner, faut-il des jetons ou des pièces ? **(5)**

5 — N'oublie pas de t'arrêter à la charcuterie en revenant ; il nous faut des cochonnailles pour ce soir. **(6)**

6 — Pour acheter la vignette de votre voiture, vous devez vous rendre dans un bureau de tabac **(7) (8)**

7 avec la carte grise de votre véhicule. **(9)**

8 — Pouvez-vous mettre un peu de chauffage ? Je suis frileux. **(10)**

9 — L'entreprise sera fermée le vendredi 22 ; les employés font le pont. **(11)**

NOTES

(2) *Propre* is a word we find echoes of in English (property, proprietor, etc.). *Mon propre appartement:* My own flat. *Il a ses propres chaussures de ski:* He has his own ski-shoes. The expression *propre à* (which agrees) means: peculiar to, belonging especially to. *Il a un style propre à lui:* He has his own style. (There is no idea of 'strange' in the words 'peculiar to'.)

(3) France is a more bureaucratic society than England or the United States of America. For a start, every French person has *une carte d'identité* (foreign residents have *une carte de séjour);* when one marries, one is issued with *un livret* (a small book) *de famille* in which are registered births, childrens' marriages and deaths.

(4) From the verb *jeter* (to throw); *un jeton* was originally used for calculation, whence the English translation 'a counter' (we still find this usage where *jetons* are used in card or dice games). If you want to make a phone-call from a café it is often necessary to purchase a token at the bar. (In colloquial speech - and especially in Paris - the word is pronounced [un shtohn].) If you call someone a *faux-jeton* you mean he is a hypocrite.

*****

2   peculiar to each country and for which there is not always an equivalent.   Look at these sentences:

3 —   Present yourself at the town-hall with your identity card, your family record and an extract from your police record.

4 —   To telephone, do I need tokens or coins?

5 —   Don't forget to stop at the delicatessen on your way back; we need pork-products for this evening.

6 —   To buy a tax disc for your car, you must go to a 'tabac'

7   with the registration card of your vehicle.

8 —   Can you put the heating on a little?   I'm always cold.

9 —   The company will be closed on Friday 22nd; the employees are having a long week-end.

NOTES

(6) A wonderful institution, this shop is specialised in pork products (collectively called *des cochonnailles (f))* like *du pâté; des saucissons; du jambon de pays* (salted ham) and other delights.
The word comes from a corruption of *la chair* (flesh) *cuite* (cooked). We translate, for want of a better word - or a better shop - by 'delicatessen'.

(7) Every year French people have to buy a tax disc for their car. This is displayed on *le pare-brise* (the windscreen). It is called *une vignette*.

(8) We have already come across this establishment - more usually called *un tabac*; it is a bar-café with a special counter where one buys not only tobacco etc. but also postage stamps, fiscal stamps and other similar items. If the *tabac* is marked *P.M.U. (Pari Mutuel Urbain)* one may also place bets on the State-run *tiercé* or *quarté* (horse races).

(9) *La carte grise* is a card issued with each vehicle indicating the owner's name and address, the age of the car and other specifications (*un véhicule* is masculine).

(10) French has some adjectives which cannot be fully translated because they describe a permanent state. For example, we would say *J'ai froid* for I am cold, but if one feels the cold all the time, the adjective would be *frileux (-euse)*. Other examples: *Il a peur*: He's afraid but *Il est peureux*: He's a 'scaredy-cat', always afraid. *Il est famélique* rather than *Il a faim* for someone with hollow legs!

(11) Public holidays are called *des jours fériés*. If one of these falls on a Thursday or a Tuesday, it is quite common to take off the following or preceding day to add to the week-end. This is called - graphically - *un pont* (a bridge). To indulge in this agreeable pastime is called *faire le pont*.

10 — Surtout ne va pas voir ce dentiste ; il prend très cher et il n'est pas conventionné. **(12) (13)**

11 — Il ne gagne pas gros. Il est payé au SMIC, **(14)**

12 mais il fait des économies à la maison ; c'est un bricoleur-né. **(15)**

13 — Désirez-vous prendre l'apéritif ? — Non, merci. — Alors, nous passerons tout de suite aux hors-d'œuvre.

IL DOIT SE RENDRE À LA MAIRIE À TROIS HEURES

EXERCICES

1. J'ai acheté des jetons pour le téléphone mais il est en panne. **2.** N'oubliez pas de prendre le journal en revenant. **3.** Il doit se rendre à la mairie à trois heures. **4.** Ne lui racontez pas des histoires de fantômes. Elle est peureuse. **5.** Surtout ne lui dites pas que j'ai oublié d'acheter la vignette ! **6.** Ce sont des coutumes propres à son pays.

Mettez les mots qui manquent.
Fill in the blanks.

1 . . . . *trois modèles différents.*

There are three different models.

10 — Above all, don't go and see that dentist; he charges a lot and he is not 'conventionné'.

11 — He doesn't earn a lot. He's paid the minimum wage

12 but he saves money at home; he's a born handyman.

13 — Do you want a drink before the meal? — No thank you. — Then we'll go straight on to the starters.

NOTES

(12) There is no equivalent to the verb to charge in French. (Be careful: *charger* means to load.) We can use this sort of expression: *Il m'a pris cent francs pour la réparation:* He charged me 100F for the repair, or simply turn the sentence differently with the verb *coûter.* They charge a fortune for it: *Ça coûte une fortune.*

(13) *Une convention* is a type of contract. Most French doctors and dentists apply a list of charges established by the State. They are called *des médecins conventionnés.*

(14) *Le SMIC* is *le salaire minimum inter-professionnel de croissance,* the minimum industrial wage. We will see this in more detail in Lesson 41.

(15) A hallowed French pastime - some would say institution - is *le bricolage;* this consists in doing handiwork around the house. The nearest English equivalent would be do-it-yourself. *Un bricoleur* or *une bricoleuse* is the personal noun.
Notice the place of *né (née)* after the noun - usually attached by *un trait d'union:* a hyphen.

EXERCISES: **1.** I bought tokens for the telephone but it is not working. **2.** Don't forget to get the newspaper on the way back. **3.** He has to go to the town-hall at 3 o'clock. **4.** Don't tell her ghost stories. She's a scaredy-cat. **5.** Above all, don't tell him/her I forgot to buy the tax disc! **6.** They are customs peculiar to his country/region.

2 *Nous* . . . . *dans l'entreprise mais*

elle était fermée.

We went to the company but it was closed.

3 *Il* . . . . *pour son travail.*

He used to charge too much for his work.

4 *Pour téléphoner,* .... — .. *des* ...... *ou des*

...... ?

To telephone, do you need tokens or coins?

5 ....-.... *à la* ...... *avec votre*

..... *de* ......

Present yourself at the town-hall with your resident's card.

****

TRENTE-CINQUIEME (35ᵉ) LEÇON

REVISION ET NOTES

1 This is the last major tense we have to learn. We have left it until now because not only is it not used in spoken French or in letters but its use in modern written French tends to be less frequent. It is a past tense and has several names *(le prétérit, le passé simple, le passé défini)* but the name we think will best sum up its use in the Past Historic.

First of all, how is it formed?
Verbs like *donner*

*je donn***ai**	*nous donn***âmes**
*tu donn***as**	*vous donn***âtes**
*il donn***a**	*ils donn***èrent**

a) There are no exceptions.
b) Notice the circumflex on the first and second persons plural.
c) If the stem ends in 'g' (e.g. *manger*) we place an 'e' before the 'a' to retain the 'zh' sound: *je mangeai, il mangea;* if the stem ends in 'c' (e.g. *commencer*) we retain the 's' sound by writing a cedilla under the 'c': *il commença, nous commençâmes* etc.

Mots qui manquaient :

1. Il existe 2. nous sommes rendus 3. prenait trop cher 4. faut-il - jetons - pièces 5. Présentez-vous - mairie - carte - séjour.

*****

We are not trying to drown you with words but to 'surround' you, to create an atmosphere where French represents the life in France and not a set of translations from English.   We hope you are enjoying it!

****

35th LESSON

Verbs like *vendre* and *finir* add - *is* - *is* - *it* - *îmes* - *îtes* - *irent* to the stems

je fin**is**	nous fin**îmes**
tu fin**is**	vous fin**îtes**
il fin**it**	ils fin**irent**

a) some exceptions: *lire, mourir, se faire, connaître, courir,* these take the endings of the third group.
b) Again, notice the cedillas.
c) Check the verb list at the back of the book for irregular verbs and *venir*.

Irregular verbs like *vouloir* or *boire:*

je b**us**	je voul**us**
tu b**us**	tu voul**us**
il b**ut**	il voul**ut**
nous b**ûmes**	nous voul**ûmes**
vous b**ûtes**	vous voul**ûtes**
ils b**urent**	ils voul**urent**

Exceptions: *s'asseoir* and *voir* take the endings of the second group.
(We apologise for this rather formal approach, but since this is a tense you will probably not come across often we do not wish to spend too many lessons developing the usage of the different verb groups.)
When is it used?

A simple answer would be: 'When writing, it replaces the *passé composé*'. True enough, but above all it is a literary tense which carries the narrative forward by describing actions or events in the past.

Il se leva, prit la bouteille, se versa un verre et le but: He got up, took the bottle, poured himself a glass and drank it.

It's as 'simple' as that! Be careful, however, because we don't use the past historic when setting the scene. *Il faisait froid et une légère bruine tombait sur la ville.* Look carefully at the two ideas: 'It **was** cold...' not for one moment but for quite a while - 'and a light drizzle **was** falling' - continually.

To give you a better idea of how the different tenses come together, read the following extract from a detective novel:

Il faisait noir. Legrand attendait impatiemment l'arrivée de l'inspecteur. Il était caché derrière une armoire. Soudain, il entendit des bruits - une voiture s'arrêta, une porte claqua et quelqu'un vint* vers la maison. Legrand voulut crier mais il retint son souffle.** La porte de la chambre s'ouvrit et le truand entendit la voix du policier. « Legrand » cria-t-il « j'ai reçu ton message et je suis venu te voir. Que veux-tu ? »

* *venir: je vins; tu vins; il vint; nous vînmes; vous vîntes; ils vinrent*
** *retenir son souffle:* to hold one's breath

Read the passage again to make sure you understand it. Now read it once more. Notice those verbs which set the scene (imperfect), those which carry the narrative along (past historic) and those used in dialogue *(passé composé)*.

Remember that a simple past in English often expresses a description, not an action.

****

*****

La fenêtre donnait sur la cour: The window looked on to the courtyard.

Remember, you will not use this tense yourself (except in exercises) and you will not hear it spoken except in old expressions like *Il fut un temps...:* One upon a time. However, for some obscure reason, foreign films dubbed into French often have characters speaking with the past historic. This can lead to a Chicago gangster speaking like Châteaubriand. Se be on your guard!

2 The correct preposition to use with place names. Here are a few easy rules.

a) *Elle va / il habite en Allemagne / en Suisse / en Australie* in front of feminine gender countries (those ending in 'e' except *le Mexique*) we use **en**;
b) *Elle va / il habite au Japon / au Portugal / aux Etats-Unis* in front of masculine gender countries (those not ending in 'e') and plural-groups we use **aux**.
c) The notion of the article applies to the regions of France.
We would say *habiter/aller en Normandie, en Provence* but *dans le Jura, dans les Vosges.* This notion also applies to the administrative *départements,* which all begin with articles *dans la Nièvre, dans l'Aisne.* If the *département* name is composed, however, we use **en** - *en Seine-et-Marne.*
d) For islands, there is no real rule, just usage. Try and memorise some of these examples:
en Corse (Corsica), *en Sardaigne* (Sardinia), *à la Martinique, à la Réunion, à St-Barthélémy, à Malte, à Chypre.*

At this advanced stage many a French person would correct a mistake without being able to say why it was wrong. Constant reading and listening will help you assimilate this sort of detail gradually.

****

*****

TRENTE-SIXIEME (36e) LEÇON

Pas un grand succès... (1)

1   Laurent amena Anne-Marie dans un restaurant qu'il ne connaissait pas

2   mais dont il avait lu une critique élogieuse une semaine auparavant. (2)

3 — Dites-moi, que veut dire : « Homard S.G. » ? demanda Anne-Marie. — Ça veut dire que le prix dépend de la grosseur ; (3)

4   plus il est gros, plus il est cher, mais dis-moi « tu », je t'en prie. — Si vous... si tu veux. (N.1)

5   A ce moment, le garçon arriva. — Que prenez-vous ? — Un homard à l'armoricaine pour mademoiselle (4)

6   et une langouste pour moi. Rien avant.

NOTES

(1) *Grand* covers many different aspects where English would use other adjectives than 'big'. *Un homme grand:* a tall man (if there is another adjective with it, *grand* comes before the noun - *un grand homme blond); des grandes jambes:* long legs. *Les grandes vacances:* the long holiday. *Les yeux grands ouverts:* wide open eyes. *Un objectif grand angle:* a wide-angled lens. *Un grand bruit:* a loud noise. *Les grandes pluies:* heavy rains. *Grand* also means great: *un grand homme:* a great man (notice the position of the adjective). *A son grand regret:* to his/her great regret. This makes life easier, doesn't it?

36th LESSON

Not a great success

1   Laurent took Anne-Marie to a restaurant which he didn't know

2   but about which he had read a very flattering review a week before.

3 — Tell me, what does 'Lobster S.G.' mean? asked Anne-Marie. — It means that the price depends on the size;

4   the larger it is, the more expensive it is, but call me 'tu' please. — O.K.

5   At the moment, the waiter arrived. — What will you have? — A lobster 'armoricaine' for the lady

6   and a crayfish for me. Nothing before.

NOTES

(2) We have already seen some nouns which change their meaning according to their gender. *Une critique:* a criticism or an review; *un critique:* a critic; *critiquer:* to criticise; *faire une critique:* to review.

(3) *Gros* literally means 'fat' but it also indicates bulk as well as size. *Un gros salaire:* a high salary. *Un gros morceau:* a large piece. *Un gros pullover:* a thick sweater. *Acheter en gros:* to buy in bulk. (*Un gros mot:* a swear word).
So *la grosseur* is the size of something, rather than its dimensions. We use *la taille* for the size in clothes, etc., *la grosseur* for the bulk. Other words for the dimensions are *la longueur:* length, *la largeur:* width, *l'épaisseur:* thickness (*épais:* thick). S.G. stands for *selon* (according to) *grosseur.*

(4) *L'Armorique:* is the old name for Brittany (Chaucer spoke of Armorica). Some restaurants try to attribute this speciality to the New World by calling it *homard à l'américaine!* The French have a habit of making an adjective (or noun) from a region - for example *un Girondin:* is someone from the region of Bordeaux... in the *département* of the *Gironde; un Cévenol* is from the *Cévennes; un Savoyard* from the *Savoie.* Don't be afraid to ask which *département* is referred to as not everybody is that good with Geography!
It can be even more disconcerting when the same is done with towns. *Un Stéphanois* is from *St-Etienne, un Palois* from *Pau.* Although we can do this in English, it is much less frequent than in a language which has set rules governing the formation of words. You will often hear such usage on television and radio when the announcers are speaking of sporting teams: *les Bitterois ont gagné hier:* Béziers (!) won yesterday.

7 — Bien, monsieur. Et que boirez-vous ? — Montrez-moi la carte des vins s'il vous plaît.

8 (Une demi-heure plus tard le repas arriva... et il était froid.) Laurent s'énerva :

9 — Monsieur, s'il vous plaît. Voulez-vous bien ramener ceci à la cuisine. Les deux plats sont froids.

10 Pour un restaurant de cette catégorie, ce n'est franchement pas très sérieux ! **(5)**

11 Le repas se termina dans un silence glacial...

12 jusqu'au moment où arriva l'addition. **(6)**

13 — Garçon ! Je crois qu'il doit y avoir une erreur. — Vraiment ?

14 — Ou bien c'est une erreur ou vous avez inscrit ma date de naissance.

15 Veuillez vérifier s'il vous plaît. **(7)**

EXERCICES

1. Ce manteau est trop petit. Avez-vous la taille au-dessus ? **2.** La boîte fait six centimètres de longueur et cinq d'épaisseur. **3.** Tu peux leur faire confiance ; c'est une firme très sérieuse. **4.** Il y a un grand bruit dans le moteur. **5.** C'est une période où on est très calme : ce sont les grandes vacances. **6.** Veuillez vérifier votre monnaie à la caisse.

Mettez les mots qui manquent.
Fill in the blanks.

1 *Il a de . . . . . . bras, d'énormes mains et de . . . . doigts.*

He has long arms, enormous hands and thick fingers.

2 *Napoléon était un . . . . . homme mais il n'était pas . . . . . !*

Napoléon was a great man but he wasn't very tall!

7 — Very good, sir. And what will you have to drink? — Let me see the wine list, please.

8 (Half an hour later, the meal arrived and it was cold.) Laurent got angry:

9 — Excuse me, please. Will you please take this back to the kitchen. Both dishes are cold.

10 For a restaurant of this category, it's frankly not good enough!

11 The meal finished in a glacial silence...

12 until the moment when the bill arrived.

13 — Waiter! I think there must be a mistake. — Really?

14 — Either it's a mistake or you've written down my date of birth.

15 Please check it.

NOTES

(5) An adjective which is 'typically French'. The literal meaning is 'serious' but it is found everywhere with meanings like 'business-like', 'reliable', 'responsible'; *une école sérieuse:* a good, studious school; *une firme sérieuse:* a dependable, reliable firm; *un homme sérieux:* a thorough, business-like (etc.) man. It is much easier to understand the context than to translate it. Here, Laurent says *Ce n'est pas sérieux!* when complaining. An English equivalent would be 'It's just not good enough!'; *garder son sérieux:* to keep a straight face.

(6) Watch out for relative pronouns with time and place. *L'endroit où il est né:* the place **where** he was born; *le jour où elle passa l'examen:* the day **when** she took the examination.

(7) Look back through the story and notice the different expressions Laurent uses to address the waiter. He starts politely: *Voulez-vous bien...* and finishes rather abruptly: *Veuillez...* Try and picture different situations where each expression would be appropriate.

EXERCISES: 1. This coat is too small. Do you have the next size up? **2.** The box is 6 centimetres long and 5 centimetres deep. **3.** You can trust them; it's a very dependable firm. **4.** There is a loud noise in the engine. **5.** It is a period when we are very quiet: it's the long holiday. **6.** Please check your change at the cash desk.

3 *Il l'* . . . . . . *à dîner, et l'* . . . . . *dans un*

restaurant

He invited her to dinner and took her to a restaurant

Leçon 36

4 . . . . *il* . . . . *une critique une semaine*

. . . .

about which he had read a review one week before.

****

TRENTE-SEPTIEME (37e) LEÇON

Les râleurs (1)

1 Malheureusement, il n'y avait pas d'erreur dans l'addition et Laurent était furieux.

2 C'était se payer la tête du monde ! Un guet-apens pareil ! (2) (3)

3 Non seulement leur cuisine était froide, mais en plus c'était le coup de fusil ! (4)

4 Anne-Marie était, elle aussi, en colère, mais pour une toute autre raison : (5)

ILS SE SONT BATTUS À COUPS DE POING ET À COUPS DE PIED

NOTES

(1) This noun, and its verb *râler*, are superbly French! They mean to complain, to gripe, to be in a bad temper, a bad-tempered person, etc. (The usage is familiar.)
Remember that French is more flexible with adjectives used as nouns: we say *les riches* (the rich) but we can also say *un riche* (a rich person). Similarly *les aveugles, un aveugle* (the blind, a blind person).

5 *Qu'est-ce que c'est ?* . . . . -t- . . . .

   — *Un homard* . . . . - . .

   What is it? she asked. — A lobster, he replied.

Mots qui manquaient :

1. grands - gros 2. grand - grand 3. invita - amena 4. dont - avait lu - auparavant 5. demanda - elle - répondit - il.

****

37th LESSON

Bad-tempered people

1 Unfortunately, there was no mistake in the bill and Laurent was furious.

2 It was really being taken for a fool! Such a tourist-trap!

3 Not only was their cooking cold, but on top of that we were charged through the nose!

4 Anne-Marie was, too, angry but for a totally different reason:

NOTES

(2) An idiomatic expression *se payer la tête de quelqu'un* is to mock somebody. *Les passants se sont payé la tête de l'agent:* The passers-by laughed at the policeman. If we replace *quelqu'un* (or a proper noun) by *... du monde,* it means that the person in question is taking you for a ride, treating you outrageously.

(3) Pronounced [get-apohn], this noun means, literally, an ambush, but it is often used to mean an extortionate shop, restaurant, etc. The plural is *des guets-apens*. A similar expression is *un attrape-nigaud* (plural: *des attrape-nigauds.* Notice the position of the *s*).

(4) A very expressive idiom. *Un coup de fusil* is a gunshot; *tirer (un coup de fusil):* to fire (a shot); *un coup* is very widely used. Look at these examples: *Un coup de téléphone* or *de fil:* a phone-call; *un coup de soleil:* sunstroke; *un coup de pied:* a kick; *un coup de poing:* a punch (*un poing:* a fist). Notice in each example we are looking at one movement of an object (a fist, a foot, etc). There are so many uses that it will take time to learn them all.

Here are two idioms: *donner un coup de main:* to give someone a hand and *faire les 400 coups:* to paint the town red. We also know *un coup d'Etat.* Incidentally, the expression does not describe the bill itself but the restaurant, shop, etc. which is extortionate.

(5) Notice the word order in the sentence.

5   — Comment ? Tu m'invites à dîner et tu passes toute la soirée à râler comme ça ?

6   Quel mufle ! Raccompagne-moi s'il te plaît.

7   Soudain Laurent éclata de rire et lui dit : — Ça fait deux fois qu'on se dispute

8   et on se connaît depuis deux jours seulement ! Un bon début, n'est-ce pas ?

9   Anne-Marie se permit un sourire et répondit : — Je boirais bien un café... **(6)**

10   Dans un bar très chic, un client commande un magnum de champagne. **(7)**

11   Une demi-heure après, il commande quelque chose de plus petit et on lui apporte une bouteille. **(8)**

12   L'ayant terminée, il demande qu'on lui apporte une demi-bouteille. **(9) (10)**

13   Tout à coup, d'une voix furieuse, il crie : — Mais c'est un scandale !

14   Garçon ! Expliquez comment cela se fait **(11)**

15   que moins je bois, plus je suis saoul ? **(12)**

NOTES

(6) *Je mangerais bien quelque chose:* I could do with something to eat. *Je fumerais bien un bon cigare:* I'd love a good cigar. *J'irais bien voir ce film:* I'd love to go and see that film. Instead of using the conditional *J'aimerais bien...* with an infinitive: *J'aimerais bien aller,* we can simply put the verb itself into the conditional form.

(7) *Un magnum* is the equivalent of two bottles; it is sometimes possible to find *un jéroboam* which holds three litres, or even *un mathusalem* which holds about six quarts! Remember our rule about gender of proper nouns (see lesson 35 **(N.3)**). The region where this nectar originates is **La** *Champagne* but the wine *(le vin)* is **le** *champagne.*

(8) Contrast the use of *on* in these two sentences with that in sentences 7 and 8. In the spoken usage it often replaces *nous;* however, the correct usage is the impersonal form, as here, i.e. *on* refers to any of the staff of the bar.

*****

148

5 — What? You invite me to dinner and you spend the whole evening moaning like that?
6 What a boor! Take me home, please.
7 Suddenly Laurent burst out laughing and said to her: — That makes two times we have had an argument
8 and we've only known each other for two days! A good start, isn't it?
9 Anne-Marie allowed herself a smile and replied: — I'd love a coffee...

10 In a very chic bar, a customer orders a magnum of champagne.
11 Half an hour after, he orders something smaller and they bring him a bottle.
12 Having finished it, he asks them to bring him a half-bottle.
13 Suddenly, in a furious voice, he shouts: — This is a scandal!
14 Waiter! Explain how come
15 the less I drink, the drunker I get?

NOTES

(9) Remember, the subjunctive is used when the action described has not yet taken place and is dependent on someone else's will (lesson 35 (N.1). *Elle lui a demandé son nom:* She asked his name. *Elle a demandé que nous arrivions de bonne heure:* She asked that we be there early (notice the subjunctive in English - we would tend to say: She asked us to be there... etc.).
Nous avons demandé qu'on nous réveille tôt: We have asked that we be (to be) woken up early. Note: *demander que...* must always be followed by a pronoun (or a proper noun).

(10) Since *demi* comes before the noun, there is no agreement. *Une demi-heure* but *une heure et demie* (after the noun). We also find *mi-* which only exists when joined to another word by a hyphen and is invariable. *La mi-août:* mid-August; *la mi-été:* mid-summer and, in sport, *la mi-temps:* half-time.

(11) *Comment cela (ça) se fait que...?* is similar to our idiom How come...? *Comment se fait-il qu'il n'ait pas le dossier?:* How come he doesn't have the file? It must be followed by the subjunctive. *Comment se faisait-il qu'ils soient armés?:* How come they were armed?

(12) *Plus j'essaie, moins je réussis:* The harder I try, the less I succeed. Do not place definite articles before *plus* or *moins*. Remembering this proverb may help fix the rule: *Plus on est de fous, plus on rit:* The more, the merrier.

Leçon 37

EXERCICES

1. — J'ai faim ! Je mangerais bien un sandwich. — Comment ? Tu viens de déjeuner ! **2.** J'avais perdu mon permis - ils se sont payé ma tête au commissariat. **3.** Ne mange pas au nouveau restaurant chinois... c'est le coup de fusil ! **4.** Quel mufle de m'emmener dans un attrape-nigaud pareil. **5.** Nous nous connaissons depuis deux ans et nous nous sommes disputés une fois seulement. **6.** Ils se sont battus à coups de poing et à coups de pied.

Mettez les mots qui manquent.
Fill in the blanks.

1   *J'ai demandé . . . vous . . . . la réponse tout de suite.*

I have asked that you have the answer immediately.

2   *J' . . . . la pièce.*

I'd like to go and see the play again.

3   *. . . . vous insistez . . . . . vous avez de chances de*

. . . .

The more you insist the less chance you have of succeeding.

****

TRENTE-HUITIEME (38ᵉ) LEÇON

Il faut s'y faire (1)

1   Nous connaissons bien ce verbe faire ; mais nous allons en apprendre d'autres utilisations. Lisez plutôt :

*****

4 *Jean était, ... , furieux : c'était un scandale.*

John, too, was furious: it was a scandal.

5 *. ' . . . . , il . . . . une*

autre bouteille.

Having finished it, he asked for another bottle.

EXERCISES: 1. — I'm hungry! I'd love a sandwich. — What! You've just had lunch! **2.** I had lost my licence - they laughed at me at the police station. **3.** Don't eat at the new Chinese restaurant... it's a rip-off! **4.** What a boor to take me to such a tourist trap. **5.** We have known each other for two years and we have argued only once. **6.** They punched and kicked one another.

Mots qui manquaient :

1. que - ayez **2.** irais bien revoir **3.** Plus - moins - réussir **4.** lui aussi **5.** L'ayant terminée - demanda.

*****

Do you notice how, little by little, you are picking up French sentence-structure? You are learning all the little nuances almost without noticing them.

****
38th LESSON

You have to get used to it

1 We know this verb to do/make well; but we're going to learn new uses. Read on:

NOTES

(1) Indeed, the verb *faire* has over one hundred and twenty uses. They are actually quite easy to rember - or work out - once you have grasped a few basic principles, hence this lesson.
Our first usage is idiomatic: it means You have to get used to it. The verb *se faire à* (notice the postposition and contrast it with the ordinary reflexive use in line 3 means to get used to something. *C'était diffile au début mais je m'y suis fait petit à petit:* It was difficult at the beginning but, little by little, I got used to it.

2   Quand il fait beau, Paul se lève tôt et va faire un tennis au parc à côté. **(2) (3)**

3   Après avoir fait sa toilette, il se fait un café et il s'en va.

4   Comme il fait un peu frais aujourd'hui, Paul prend sa voiture

5   pour faire les deux kilomètres jusqu'aux courts de tennis.

6   Malheureusement, aujourd'hui il y a beaucoup de monde et Paul n'a pas fait de réservation.

7   Il va voir le préposé qui, lui, fait le sourd et ne répond pas. **(4) (5) (6)**

8   Alors Paul n'a qu'à attendre - il n'y a rien à faire. **(7) (8)**

9   Enfin il peut jouer. Il fait un bon match et rentre chez lui, content.

10   Sa femme l'attend à la porte. Elle fait la tête. **(9)**

NOTES

(2) *Faire* is used for almost all expressions concerning the weather. We know the most important ones - here are a few more.
Il fait frisquet: It's nippy.
Il fait maussade: It's gloomy.
Il fait du brouillard: It's foggy.

(3) Most sports vocabulary comes from English and although we usually use the verb *jouer* for to play, French easily uses a

2   When it's fine, Paul gets up early and goes to play tennis in a nearby park.

3   After having washed and shaved, he makes himself a coffee and goes off.

4   As it's a little cooler today, Paul takes his car

5   to do the two kilometres to the tennis-courts.

6   Bad luck! Today there are a lot of people and Paul hasn't made a reservation.

7   He goes to see the person in charge who turns a deaf ear and doesn't answer.

8   So Paul can only wait - nothing can be done.

9   At last he can play. He has a good match and returns home happy.

10   His wife is waiting for him at the door. She's in a mood.

NOTES

'franglais' word with *faire: Je vais faire un footing (!):* I'm going for a run. *Nous allons faire un bridge; Il fait un sprint tous les jours.* Try, where possible, to use *jouer!*

(4) *Le préposé* is a minor official in a administration and the word is often used in job titles. *Le préposé des postes* is the official title for a postman (the common word is *le facteur*); the name for *le préposé des douanes* (commonly *un douanier*): a customs officer. *Un préposé* is a useful word to know if you need to address - or find - the official in charge of a particular function.

(5) Notice this very common emphatic use of the pronoun to avoid any ambiguity. A very common trait of both the written and the spoken language.

(6) *Faire le sourd:* to turn a deaf ear to. The verb here means: to act like. *Ne faites pas l'idiot:* Don't act like an idiot; - or to look like: *Elle ne fait pas ses vingt ans/son âge:* She doesn't look twenty/her age.

(7) *Vous n'avez qu'à attendre:* You can only wait. *Je n'ai qu'à lui demander; il m'aidera:* I have only to ask him and he will help me. *Vous êtes fatigué? Vous n'avez qu'à vous coucher de bonne heure!:* You're tired? You only have to go to bed earlier! In fact this turn of phrase is very common when admonishing someone.

(8) *Il n'y a rien à faire; c'est déjà trop tard:* There's nothing to be done, it's already too late. *Je lui ai demandé; il n'y a rien à faire:* I asked him/her but it's useless. *Il n'y a rien à faire; vous devez payer l'amende:* You can do nothing; you have to pay the fine.

(9) *Faire la tête:* to sulk, to brood, to be in a bad mood. *Ne faites pas la tête!:* Don't sulk!
The more 'correct' verb is *bouder* (from which we get 'the boudoir' - a room where young girls would go and mope). We use this verb meaning to shun, to avoid. *Pourquoi boude-t-il tes cours?:* Why won't he come to your lessons?

11 — Fais-moi plaisir, chéri, lui dit-elle. La prochaine fois,
12 ne pars pas sans avoir fait un peu de
ménage.

13 Jacques Prévert ne fut pas seulement un
poète sublime ; il avait un sens de l'humour
très développé : **(10)**
14 voici un de ses conseils : Si quelqu'un vous
dit: « Je me tue à vous dire... »
15 laissez-le faire ! **(11)**

EXERCICES

1. J'ai fait vite parce qu'il fait frisquet ce soir. **2.** Il ne fait pas du tout son âge. Il fait beaucoup plus vieux. **3.** Vous êtes fauché ? Vous n'avez qu'à sortir moins souvent. **4.** Faites-moi plaisir. Aidez-moi à faire le ménage. **5.** Vous n'y arriverez pas comme ça. Laissez-moi faire. **6.** Prévert est né en 1900 à Neuilly.

Mettez les mots qui manquent.
Fill in the blanks.

1 *C'était dur mais elle . . . . son travail.*

It was difficult, but she got used to her job.

2 *Vous . . . . venir plus tôt ; ça sera plus facile.*

All you have to do is come earlier, it will be easier.

3 *. . . . - . . . . aussi . . . . . demain . . . aujourd'hui?*

Will it be as cool tomorrow as today?

4 *. . . . . fait le lit, il . . . .*

un café.

After having made the bed, he made himself a coffee.

154

11 — Make me happy, darling, she says to him. The next time

12 don't leave without having done a little house-work.

13 Jacques Prévert was not only a sublime poet; he also had a highly developed sense of humour:

14 here is some of his advice: If someone says to you 'I'm killing myself telling you...'

15 let him do it!

NOTES

(10) Jacques Prévert (1900-1977) is one of the finest of modern poets and screen-writers; he is also very easy to read. Try reading his best known collection *Paroles*. Putting your knowledge into action is the most worthwhile exercise in language-learning.

(11) *Laissez-moi faire:* Let me do it (in my own way). *Elle veut aider. Laissez-la faire:* She wants to help. Let her do it. Notice that the pronoun refers to the person, not the action - for which there is no definite article.

EXERCISES: 1. I was quick because it's chilly tonight.   2. He doesn't look his age at all.   He looks much older.   3 . You're broke?   All you have to do is go out less often.   4. Do me a favour.   Help me do the housework.   5. You won't manage like that. Let me do it.   6. Prévert was born in Neuilly in 1900.

5 *Ne . . . . . . pas . . . . Je vous aiderai.*

Laissez- . . . .

Don't sulk. I'll help you. Let me do it.

Mots qui manquaient :

1. s'est faite à 2. n'avez qu'à 3. Fera-t-il - frais - qu' 4. Après avoir - s'est fait 5. faites - la tête - moi faire.

TRENTE-NEUVIEME (39ᵉ) LEÇON

Et encore « faire »

1　Nous avons surpris cette conversation entre deux boxeurs à propos d'un ami. **(1)**

2　— Dis donc ! Tu sais que Bébert a fait fortune et a pris sa retraite. **(2)**

3　— Quoi, Bébert ? Ce grand bon à rien qui ne faisait que perdre ? Il était toujours K.O. ! Ne me fais pas rire. **(3) (4)**

4　— C'est bien lui. Il a fait graver des slogans publicitaires sur les semelles de ses chaussures ! **(N.2)**

5　— Ne range pas la lettre de Michel. Ta fille ne l'a pas encore lue.

6　— Je la lui ferai lire demain ; je l'ai fait lire à tout le monde sauf à elle. **(5)**

7　A propos, quelle heure est-il ? — Qu'est-ce qu'elle a, ta montre ?

8　— Je ne sais pas. Je l'ai fait réparer, mais elle ne marche toujours pas.

NOTES

(1) A useful expression *Je voulais vous parler.* — *A propos de quoi?:* I want to talk to you. — What about? *A propos de votre prêt, avez-vous reçu la réponse?:* About your loan, have you received the answer? (But we would say: *Elle m'a parlé* **de** *vous:* She told me about you.)

39th LESSON

And again 'faire'

1 We overheard this conversation between two boxers about a friend.

2 — Hey! You know that Bébert has made his fortune and has retired.

3 — What, Bébert? That big good-for-nothing who only lost? He was always out for the count. Don't make me laugh.

4 — That's him alright. He had advertising slogans engraved on the soles of his shoes!

5 — Don't put Michel's letter away. Your daughter hasn't read it yet.

6 — I'll let her read it tomorrow; I let everybody read it except her.

7 By the way, what time is it? — What's the matter with your watch?

8 — I don't know. I had it repaired, but it still doesn't work.

NOTES

The expression can also be used apostrophically. See line 7.
Un propos: a remark, or in the plural, talk; *des propos de table:* table talk; *des propos méchants:* unpleasant gossip. At the end of a printed interview we often find the credit: *Propos recueillis par...* lit.: Remarks collected by...

(2) *Se retirer* is to withdraw from or to retreat. To retire is *prendre sa retraite:* a person in retirement is *un(e) retraité(e).*

(3) *Il n'a qu'un frère:* He has only one brother. We know the negation *ne... que* (only) with nouns. If we want to use it with a verb, we must use *faire: Je ne fais que travailler:* All I do is work. *Il ne fait que passer:* He's only passing through. *Nous ne faisons qu'essayer:* We're only trying.

(4) As we said in the last lesson, most sporting vocabulary comes directly from English: if the pronunciation can be Gallicised, so much the better *(un court de tennis).* If not we end up with *le ring; le round; l'uppercut* (!) and... *K.O.* [ka oh]. Figuratively it means to be dead tired. Interestingly enough, a punch is not the same word but *le coup de poing; la boxe:* boxing.

(5) *Je lui ferai lire la lettre:* I will have her/let her read the letter **but** if the second infinitive (here, *lire*) has a direct object, the object of *faire* becomes indirect. *Je la lui ferai lire. Je fais remplir le formulaire par l'intéressé:* I have the form filled in by the person concerned. But, *Je lui fais remplir le formulaire.*

9 — Jean-Jacques fait installer une piscine dans
son salon, tu sais ?

10 — Mais il n'aime pas nager. Il est vraiment sot,
ce garçon ! **(6)**

11 — Du tout ! C'est beaucoup moins cher que de
faire réparer le toit. **(7)**

12 Et connaissez-vous ce joli jeu de mots du
grand gourmet Curnonsky ?

13 Il a dit que le bifteck peut être de la viande
que les restaurateurs font cuire -

14 ou du cuir que les restaurateurs font viande !
(9)

EXERCICES

1. Dites donc ! Avez-vous lu le journal aujourd'hui ? **2.** A
propos de votre femme, va-t-elle mieux ? **3.** J'aime la
viande saignante. Faites cuire mon bifteck très peu, s'il
vous plaît. **4.** Il est d'une sottise incroyable. — Pas du
tout ! **5.** Qu'est-ce qu'elle a, votre montre ? **6.** Il a pris sa
retraite le mois dernier.

Mettez les mots qui manquent.
Fill in the blanks.

1 *Je ne . . . . répéter . . . . . j'ai entendu.*

I'm only repeating what I've heard.

2 *Qu'il est drôle! Il . . . .*

How funny he is! He makes us laugh.

3 *J' . . . . le toit. On n'aura plus de problèmes.*

I've had the roof repaired. We'll have no more problems.

4 *Cette histoire est passionnante. Je . . . .*

. . . . demain.

This story is fascinating. I'll have them read it tomorrow.

9 — Jean-Jacques is having a swimming-pool installed in his living-room, did you know?

10 — But he doesn't like swimming. He's really idiotic,
that boy!

11 — Not at all! It's much cheaper that having the
roof repaired.

12 And do you know this pretty pun by the great
gourmet Curnonsky?

13 He said that a steak was either a piece of meat
that restaurant-owners have cooked

14 or a piece of leather which restaurant-owners
make (into) meat! (Obviously the pun cannot
translate!)

NOTES

(6) A rather elegant word (feminine *sotte*) meaning foolish, idiotic or just
plain silly, it gives us the noun *une sottise:* foolishness. *Un sot
à bientôt vidé son sac:* A fool's fate is soon sealed.

(7) An elided form of *Pas du tout!* Slightly more emphatic.

(8) Yes, a beef steak! This is the official spelling of the French word,
though you will certainly see others on menus etc. In popular
language *gagner son bifteck* means to earn one's living.
Other cuts of steak are *une entrecôte* (lit. between ribs): a ribsteak;
un faux-filet: not a fillet, but a prime cut none-the-less.
Un pavé: a thick cut, the most celebrated of which is the one
named after the author whose favourite cut it was: *un
chateaubriand (ou un châteaubriant).*
Since ways of cutting meat differ among countries, you will just
have to experiment.

(9) It is pointless to explain puns *(un jeu de mots):* but when one starts
to understand them - and later, to make them - it is a sign of real
mastery of the language; *cuire:* to cook - *le cuir:* leather.

EXERCISES: 1. I say! Have you read the paper today? **2.** And your
wife, is she better? **3.** I like rare meat. Have the steak cooked very
little, please. **4.** He's so incredibly stupid. — Not at all! **5.** What's
the matter with your watch? **6.** He retired last month.

5 *Où est la lettre? Je ne . .' . . pas . . . .*

Where is the letter? I haven't read it yet.

Mots qui manquaient :

1. fais que - ce que **2.** nous fait rire **3.** ai fait réparer **4.** la leur ferai lire **5.**
l'ai - encore lue.

QUARANTIEME (40e) LEÇON

S.V.P.

1 Les sigles et les initiales sont très usités en français parlé et écrit ; regardez ces exemples : **(1)**

2 Il a une belle situation ; il est P.-D.G. d'une grosse société qui s'appelle SOFACOM S.A. **(2) (3)**

3 Aux abords de la ville, il y avait des cités d'H.L.M. et de tristes villes-dortoirs.`**(4)**

4 — Zut ! Il y a la grève des P.T.T. Le télégramme n'arrivera jamais à temps. **(5)**

5 Le taxi l'a déposée devant la gare S.N.C.F. deux minutes avant que le train ne parte. **(6) (7) (N.3)**

6 Seul le S.M.I.C. n'est pas touché par le blocage des prix et des salaires. **(8)**

7 La R.A.T.P. annonce l'ouverture d'une nouvelle ligne R.E.R. entre Châtelet et Roissy. **(9)**

NOTES

(1) A rather annoying feature of modern French is the tendency in the media to speak 'initialese'; this habit has passed into everyday speech at all levels. The aim of this lesson is to present the most frequently-used and simply to transpose them. Don't hesitate to check a dictionary - or to ask someone - should you come across a new set of initials.
Incidentally *un sigle* is translated by a rather pompous English word, an acronym, but it really means: a set of initials.

(2) *Un P.-D.G.: un président-directeur général:* a chairman and managing director. *Le président:* is either the Chairman or the President. *Un directeur:* a manager. *La direction:* the management. If you should see *Changement de direction* on a sign outside a shop or restaurant, it just means that the management has changed!

(3) *Une S.A.: Société anonyme:* limited company.
Une S.A.R.L.: une société anonyme à responsabilité limitée: a limited liability company. Remember, since laws differ from country to country, business structures may not be exactly the same.

40th LESSON

Please...

1 Acronyms and initials are very widely used in spoken and written French; look at these examples:

2 He has an excellent job; he is Charmain and Managing Director of a large company called SOFACOM Ltd.

3 On the outskirts of the town, there were complexes of subsidised flats and sad dormitory towns.

4 — Damn! There is a postal strike. The telegram will never arrive on time.

5 The taxi dropped her off in front of the station two minutes before the train left.

6 Only the minimum salary is untouched by the price and wage freeze.

7 The Paris Transport Authority announces the opening of a new Regional Express line between Châtelet et Roissy.

NOTES

(4) *Une H.L.M.: une habitation à loyer modéré:* housing which is subsidised by the Government or the local authority (*un loyer:* a rent); *un locataire:* a tenant, *un propriétaire:* literally is the owner of the property, but the word often represents the English landlord.

(5) *Les P.T.T.: les postes, télégraphes et téléphones:* the Post Office. The new title is: *P.T.T. Télécommunications.*

(6) *La S.N.C.F.: la Société Nationale des Chemins de fer Français:* the French state railway company.

(7) An expletive *ne* is where the word has no negative meaning. We find it with the expression of time *avant que* and with a comparative followed by a verb: So, we would say *Il est plus grand que moi* but *il est plus grand que tu* **ne** *penses* (He is taller than you think). *Ils gagnent moins que vous* **ne** *croyez:* They earn less than you think. See also lines 15 and 16.

(8) *Le S.M.I.C.: le salaire minimum interprofessionnel de croissance:* is sometimes calles the *S.M.I.G.,* G standing for *garanti.* See also note 18.

(9) *La R.A.T.P.: la Régie autonome des transports parisiens:* the Parisian Transport Authority. *Une régie* is a legal term and is often applied to organisations under state control. Another famous example is the state-run *Régie Renault. Le R.E.R.* is the fast suburban train network: *le réseau express régional. Un réseau:* a network.

8   Les négociations P.S.-P.C. sont arrivées aujourd'hui au point mort, un porte-parole du P.S. l'a fait savoir. **(10) (11) (12)**

9   Après les émeutes de la semaine dernière, le ministre des DOM-TOM est arrivé ce matin dans l'île **(13) (14)**

10   où une compagnie de C.R.S. est déjà en place. **(15)**

11   — Monsieur Richard vous appelle en P.C.V. de Bordeaux ; acceptez-vous de payer ? **(16)**

12   Visites des égouts de Paris. R.V. à 10 heures, pont de l'Alma.

13   A partir de certains sigles, nous fabriquons même des noms. **(17)**

14   Bien qu'il soit smicard, il n'est pas syndiqué, mais son grand-père est cégétiste depuis belle lurette. **(N.3) (18) (19) 20) (21)**

15   Un énarque est un homme qui utilise plus de mots qu'il ne faut **(22) (7)**

16   pour en dire plus long qu'il ne sait.

NOTES

(10) *Le P.S.: le Parti Socialiste - le P.C.(F.): le Parti communiste (français).* Political parties are almost always referred to by their initials.

(11) *Un porte-parole:* a spokesman. The plural is the same: *des porte-parole.* There are many compound nouns with *porte-*, usually meaning carrier, holder, support, etc. They are usually (1) masculine and (2) invariable but you should always check in a dictionary. Here are a few examples: *un porte-documents* (singular masculine invariable): a document case; *un porte-conteneurs* (singular masculine invariable): a container ship; *un porte-cigarettes* (singular masculine invariable): a cigarette-holder.

(12) *Faire savoir:* to let (someone) know. *Faites-le moi savoir au plus vite:* Let me know (it) as soon as possible. Without a direct object, the expression means: let it be known or to announce.
Le ministre a fait savoir que les augmentations de prix ne touchaient pas les plus défavorisés: The minister announced the price increases did not affect the under-privileged.

(13) Be careful: *un ministre:* a minister; *un ministère:* a ministry.

8   Negotiations between the Socialist and the Communist parties reached deadlock today, a Socialist Party spokesman announced.

9   After last week's riots, the minister for Overseas Territories arrived on the island today

10   where a company of riot police is already in place.

11 — Monsieur Richard is calling you collect from Bordeaux.   Do you accept the charges?

12   Visits of Paris sewers.   Meeting at 10.00 a.m. at the Alma bridge.

13   From certain acronyms, we even make up nouns.

14   Although he earns the minimum salary, he's not a member of a trade union, but his grandfather has been a member of the C.G.T. for donkey's years.

15   A person from the E.N.A. is a man who uses more words than necessary

16   to say more than he knows.

NOTES

(14) *Les DOM-TOM: les Départements d'outre-mer et les Territoires d'outre-mer.* These are French overseas *(outre-mer)* possessions such as Guadeloupe, Martinique, St-Pierre et Miquelon etc. The press often talks of events which take place *outre-Manche* (across the Channel) i.e. in Britain, *outre-Rhin* (across the Rhine) i.e. in Germany or *outre-Atlantique* (across the Atlantic) i.e. in the U.S.A.

(15) *Les C.R.S.: les Compagnies républicaines de sécurité.* These are special police, used especially in riots and crowd-control situations. *Un C.R.S.:* a member of the C.R.S.

(16) *Appeler en P.C.V.:* to call collect. The call is *payable à l'arrivée.*

(17) *Un nom* is both a name and, in grammar, a noun.

(18) There are several proper nouns made up from initials. We already know *le S.M.I.C.* so a person who earns the minimum salary is often referred to as *un smicard.*

(19) *Un syndicat:* a trade-union; *un syndicaliste:* a trade unionist; *se syndiquer:* to form **OR** to join a trade-union. *Etre syndiqué(e):* to belong to a trade union.

(20) *La C.G.T.: Confédération Générale du Travail* (the General Confederation of Labour) is one of the three major trade-unions; a member of the C.G.T. is thus called *un cégétiste.*

(21) *Depuis belle lurette:* for ages, for donkey's years. A rather elegant way of saying *depuis très longtemps.*

(22) *L'E.N.A.* is *l'Ecole Nationale d'Administration,* a special school which trains most of France's top politicians and senior civil servants who, while at school and after, are called *les énarques.* They tend to have a reputation for being long-winded...

EXERCICES

1. Dépêchez-vous ; il est plus tard que vous ne pensez. **2.** Je voudrais vous parler avant que vous ne partiez. **3.** Ils me l'ont fait savoir par télégramme. **4.** Les prix vont augmenter à la sortie du blocage des prix et des salaires. **5.** Quel est le nom du ministre de l'Intérieur ? **6.** A partir de demain, vous ne pourrez plus appeler en P.C.V. d'ici.

Mettez les mots qui manquent.
Fill in the blanks.

1   *Il ne fait pas . . . . , ...'il . . . .*

   syndiqué.

   He is not striking, even though he belongs to a trade-union.

2   *Visitons les . . . . nous . .*

   . . . .

   Let's visit the sewers before we leave.

3   *Nous . . . . depuis . . . .*

   We have been friends for donkey's years.

4   *Ne . . . donnez pas plus . .'. . . .'. . . . .*

   Don't give him/her more than is necessary.

****

QUARANTE ET UNIEME (41ᵉ) LEÇON

La conjoncture (1)

1   Le dossier qui défraye la chronique cette semaine est celui du débat à l'Assemblée sur le budget. (2)

NOTES
(1) *La conjoncture* is a modish word meaning: the current situation. *Etant donné la conjoncture économique...:* Because of the economic situation at the moment...

EXERCISES: 1. Hurry up; it's later than you think. **2.** I'd like to talk to you before you leave. **3.** They let me know by telegram. **4.** Prices are going to rise at the end of the price and wage freeze. **5.** What's the name of the minister of the Interior? **6.** From tomorrow, you will no longer be able to call collect from here.

5 Les . . . . . . - . . . . . . des partis l' . . . .

. . . . . . hier.

The spokesman for the parties announced it yesterday.

Mots qui manquaient :

1. la grève, bien qu' - soit **2.** égouts avant que - ne partions **3.** sommes amis - belle lurette **4.** lui - qu'il n'en faut **5.** porte-parole - ont fait savoir.

****

41st LESSON

The current situation

1   The story making headline news this week is the debate at the Assembly about the budget.

NOTES

(2) *Défrayer la chronique:* to make headline news. We also find *... qui fait la une,* i.e. which makes page one news.

2 Monsieur Salin, député de la Marne, a accusé le gouvernement d'avoir mis la charrue avant les bœufs avec les nouvelles mesures contre le chômage. **(3)**

3 — Le ministre, a-t-il dit, a voulu dorer la pilule en annonçant de nouvelles indemnités, **(4)**

4 mais ce sont les contribuables qui en feront les frais. **(5) (6)**

5 Le premier projet gouvernemental est tombé à l'eau, faute de préparation et maintenant nous attendons impatiemment des solutions concrètes. **(7) (8)**

6 Je sais bien, a continué le député, que les parlementaires ont du pain sur la planche mais, après tout, **(9)**

7 n'est-ce pas pour cela qu'ils ont été élus ?

8 Ses remarques, semble-t-il, ont fait mouche car c'est le ministre du Budget lui-même qui, étonné, a répondu : **(10) (11)**

NOTES

(3) Notice the pronunciation of the plural [beu] (remember *un œuf* [euf], *des œufs* [eu]). In English it's the horse, and not the oxen, which are mistakenly placed before a cart, not a plough *(une charrue)*.

(4) *L'or* (masculine): gold; *dorer:* to gild; *dorer la pilule:* to put a pleasant exterior on an unpleasant fact; *une pilule:* a pill; *prendre la pilule:* to be on the pill. Another very common word for a pill is *un cachet.*

(5) After the revolution of 1789, the name *l'impôt* was subtly changed to *la contribution* (which didn't make it any easier to pay!). The word is used in official documents but otherwise we speak of *les impôts.* (However, a tax-payer is still called *un(e) contribuable*). *L'impôt* is used for income tax and high revenues but *une taxe* is used for duties, sales taxes, etc.
La T.V.A.: la taxe à la valeur ajoutée: value added tax (incidentally a French invention).

* * * * *

2 Monsieur Salin, député for the Marne, accused the government of having put the cart before the horse with its new measures against unemployment.

3 — The minister, he said, wanted to gild the lily by announcing new benefits,

4 but it is the tax-payers who will suffer the expense.

5 The first government plan fell flat due to lack of preparation and now we are waiting impatiently for concrete solutions.

6 I know very well, said the député, that the parliamentarians have their hands full but, after all,

7 isn't it for that that they were elected?

8 It would seem that his remarks hit home because it was the minister of the Budget himself, who replied in a rather astonished way:

NOTES

(6) *Faire les frais de quelque chose* means to suffer the consequences of something, be these financial or otherwise; (*les frais* = expenses). *C'est nous qui avons fait les frais de son idée:* We suffered the consequences of his/her idea.

(7) *Faute de* (and its opposite *grâce à*) are very useful expressions. *Il a dû abandonner, faute de provisions:* He had to give up, due to lack of provisions. *Faute de beurre, j'ai utilisé de la margarine:* For want of butter, I used margarine. *Prenez ceci, faute de mieux:* Take this, for want of something better. *Grâce à lui, nous avons pu finir:* Thanks to him, we were able to finish.

(8) We know that, to form adverbs, we usually add *-ment* to the feminine form of the adjective *(heureux - heureusement)*. If the adverb ends with a vowel (e.g. *vrai*) we just add *-ment (vraiment)*. However, if the adjective ends with *-ent*, *-ant*, we add *-emment* or *amment* (note the double consonant), *constant - constamment; impatient - impatiemment*. Exceptions are: *énorme - énormément; précis - précisément; profond - profondément; aveugle - aveuglément* (blindly), also *lent - lentement* and *gentil - gentiment*.

(9) *Avoir du pain sur la planche:* to have one's work cut ou⁺

(10) *Faire mouche* is to hit the bull's eye - to hit home. In the olden days, ladies would paint black beauty spots on their faces to emphasise the whiteness of their skins; these spots were called *les mouches galantes*. They resembled the black spot in the centre of a target.

(11) Notice the elegant way we can avoid using a phrase. *Confus, il ne savait que dire:* He was so confused he didn't know what to say. *Surpris, il se mit à bégayer:* He was so surprised he began to stutter.

9 — Monsieur le député, vos critiques à notre égard sont quelque peu tirées par les cheveux et manquent d'honnêteté. **(12)**

10   On vous pose une question et vous, vous sautez du coq à l'âne pour éviter de donner des réponses exactes, n'est-ce pas vrai ? **(13)**

11   Car, vous le savez pertinemment, c'est le gouvernement qui veille au grain, **(14)**

12   c'est votre gouvernement qui vous fera sortir de l'ornière

13   et c'est pour cela que je dis aux Françaises et aux Français de soutenir le gouvernement dans son action. Il faut nous soutenir ! **(15)**

14 — Mais, monsieur le Ministre, n'avez-vous pas oublié le dicton qui dit

15   qu'un gouvernement que l'on soutient est un gouvernement qui tombe ?

EXERCICES

1. Non seulement il saute du coq à l'âne mais ses arguments sont tirés par les cheveux. **2.** Faute de crème vous pouvez utiliser du lait. **3.** Ce sont eux qui ont raison et vous le savez pertinemment. **4.** Fatigué, il s'est couché dès son retour. **5.** C'est vous qui êtes le coupable n'est-ce pas vrai ? **6.** Ce n'est pas important ! Ne mettez pas la charrue avant les bœufs.

9 — Mister député, your criticisms against us are rather far-fetched and lack honesty.

10 You are asked a question and you change subject rapidly to avoid giving exact answers, isn't that so?

11 Because, you know for a fact, that it is the government which is keeping its eyes open,

12 that it's your government which will get you out of the rut

13 and that is why I say to French women and men to support the government in its action. You must support us!

14 — But Mr minister, haven't you forgotten the saying which goes :

15 a government which one supports is a government which is falling?

NOTES

(12) *Etre tiré par les cheveux* is used to describe an argument or an explanation which is far-fetched. The explanation of the expression is an example itself: apparently, Moslems would shave their skulls, leaving only one lock of hair so that Mohamed could seize it and drag them to Paradise... Far-fetched? *Tiré par les cheveux...!*

(13) *Sauter du coq à l'âne* is to jump from one subject to another seemingly unrelated. The origin is obscure and the explanations indelicate but English has a similar expression: a cock and bull story!

(14) *Veiller au grain* is to keep a look-out, to be watchful, to keep an eye on. It was originally a maritime expression, *le grain* being a gust of wind. *Veiller* is not just to keep watch (*un veilleur de nuit:* a night watchman) but to stay up late. *J'ai veillé jusqu'à trois heures:* I stayed up till 3.00 a.m. *Veillez à ce que vos outils soient en bon état:* Check that your tools are in good condition. *La veille de....:* the day before, the eve. *La veille de mon anniversaire:* the day before my birthday.

(15) *Françaises, Français!* The most famous exponent of this rhetorical device in modern times was Général de Gaulle but he has, even today, many imitators!

EXERCISES: 1. Not only does he jump from one subject to another but his arguments are far-fetched. **2.** If you don't have cream, you can use milk. **3.** It's they who are right and you know that for a fact. **4.** He was tired so he went to bed as soon as he got back. **5.** It's you who are guilty, isn't that true? **6.** That's not important! Don't put the cart before the horse.

Mettez les mots qui manquent.
Fill in the blanks.

1 *Ça . . . . . suffire, ...*

That will have to do for want of something better.

2 *Veillez . . . . . . tout . . . . bien fermé à clé.*

Check that everything is closed and locked.

3 *. ´ . . . . oublié quelque chose ?*

Haven't you forgotten something?

****

QUARANTE-DEUXIEME (42ᵉ) LEÇON

REVISION ET NOTES

1 *Vous - tu:* when to use which, and when to change from the first to the second, can be delicate and correct usage takes some time to 'get the feel of'.

The simplest basic rule is: use *vous* with everyone except young children. If you use *vous* with French friends of your age, they will probably ask you to use the *tu* form. Wait until they do so, with expressions like: *Tu peux me tutoyer* or *Dis-moi tu,* rather than taking the initiative yourself.

Older people often find it hard to use *tu;* for them, the *vous* form is a way of showing respect, rather than denying intimacy. Conversely, among teenagers, it is almost *de rigueur* to use the familiar form.

Never use *tu* with an official, a policeman or a public employee (even if you like them...) since it is considered

4 *L'avocat a* . . . . *son client de prison.*

The lawyer got his client out of prison.

5 *Formez les adverbes à partir de ces adjectifs.*

impatient . . . . *constant* . . . .

indépendant . . . . *énorme* . . . .

gentil . . . . *vite* . . . .

Mots qui manquaient :

1. devra - faute de mieux 2. à ce que - soit 3. N'avez-vous pas 4. fait sortir 5. impatiemment, indépendamment, gentiment, constamment, énormément, vite*.

* Of course, *vite* is already an adverb!

****

42nd LESSON

very insulting. Normally it is the older of two people who will suggest to the other the use of the familiar form.

The verbs are *tutoyer* and *vouvoyer* (notice the spelling). These few rules will help you not to offend people - remember that the French are more formalistic than the Anglo-Saxons. However, being a foreigner is to one's advantage if one puts an indelicate foot in it!

2 *Faire* with an infinitive. English distinguishes two types of situation:

(I) You **make** me **laugh** (i.e. one person does something to another).
(II) I'm **having** a suit **made** (i.e. the action is performed by someone else). French uses *faire* and the infinitive for both cases. So:

(I) *Vous me faites rire.*
(II) *Je fais faire un costume.*
Notice the word order very carefully.

This makes life easier, *n'est-ce pas?* Look at these examples:

Cela me fait penser à mon enfance: It makes me think of my childhood.

Le vent faisait claquer les volets: The wind made the shutters slam.

Voilà la maison qu'il fait construire: There is the house he's having built (*fait* does not 'agree').

Il fera faire des travaux quand il aura de l'argent: He will have work done when he has money.

Remember this important construction (see Lesson 1, Note 4):

Il se fait comprendre: He makes himself understood.

Elle se fait respecter: She makes herself respected.

Je les ai fait photocopier: I had them photocopied.

Remember: *faire* + **infinitive**

When we have a construction with make + an adjective: It makes me happy/sad etc., we use the verb *rendre.*

Cela me rend très heureux/triste, etc.

****

QUARANTE-TROISIEME (43e) LEÇON

Ah, les vacances...

1 Décidément, nos amis Laurent et Anne-Marie n'ont pas de chance ! Ou peut-être Laurent aime-t-il se plaindre.

2 Toujours est-il qu'ils s'en allèrent en vacances dans un grand hôtel sur la Côte-d'Azur **(1)**

3 où ils restèrent trois semaines. Quand ils furent repartis, Laurent adressa cette lettre au directeur de l'établissement : **(N.1)**

NOTES

(1) *Je ne sais pas si elle est Anglaise ou Allemande, toujours est-il qu'elle parle un excellent français:* I don't know whether she's English or German, in any case, she speaks excellent French. This

3 A further use of the subjunctive is that with certain conjunctions, temporal and otherwise. Look at these examples:

(a) *Ils resteront* **jusqu'à ce que** *nous arrivions* (until)

(b) **D'ici à ce qu'***il dise la vérité, nous avons le temps* (before)

OR

(c) *Il parle fort* **de façon qu'***on le comprenne* (so that)

(d) *Prenez un verre,* **à moins que** *vous ne soyez pressé* (unless)

(e) *Elle est arrivée* **sans que** *je le sache* (without).

Other common expressions after which the subjunctive is used are: *afin que* (in order that); *ce n'est pas que* (it's not that); *pour que* (so that). We will see two others during the next week.

Notice that in all cases the action referred to is not **definite**: hypothetical, doubtful, intentional - each is 'sub-joined' to the first, indicative, verb.

Note: *avant que, de peur que* and *de crainte que* (the latter two meaning: for fear that) are all constructed with an expletive **NE**.

****

43rd LESSON

Ah, the holidays...

1 Decidedly, our friends Laurent and Anne-Marie have no luck! Or perhaps Laurent likes to complain.

2 In any case, they went off on holiday to a large hotel on the Côte-d'Azur

3 where they stayed three weeks. When they had left, Laurent sent this letter to the manager of the establishment:

NOTES (suite)

rather elegant expression, *toujours est-il que* is equivalent to *en tout cas,* in any case.

Another use is equivalent to the English: be that as it may. *Il m'a dit qu'il a envoyé le chèque; toujours est-il que je n'ai rien reçu:* He told me that he has sent the cheque; be that as it may, I haven't received anything.

4 Monsieur le Directeur, Je voudrais vous faire part des conditions dans lesquelles s'est déroulé notre séjour dans votre hôtel. **(N.2) (2) (3)**

5 D'abord, j'ai fait une réservation par lettre pour une chambre double avec salle de bains ;

6 quand mon amie et moi, nous sommes arrivés, on nous a dit qu'on n'avait pas reçu la lettre et qu'il ne restait que des chambres simples.

7 Nous avons dû accepter, mais ces chambres - exiguës de surcroît - se trouvaient à côté de la cage de l'ascenseur.

8 Pis encore, les portes ne fermaient pas à clé. **(4) (5)**

9 Quant à la cuisine gastronomique dont vous vous enorgueillissiez dans votre brochure, **(6)**

10 il suffit de dire que les prestations apportées ne valaient même pas ce que l'on peut trouver dans des restaurants self-service. **(7) (8)**

11 Le sous-directeur, à qui je me suis adressé, nous a accordé une réduction sur le prix des chambres

12 mais il n'en reste pas moins que nous avons payé fort cher pour un désastre ! **(9)**

NOTES (suite)

(2) This rather formal expression is another way of saying *informer* or, simpler still, *parler de*. Its literal meaning - to make someone a part of - is fairly clear.
Elle m'a fait part de ses projets: She told me about her plans. *Un faire-part* (masculine and invariable, although *une part* is feminine) is an announcement of a wedding or a death, in the form of a card sent to those concerned by the family.
Remember, on the phone, *C'est de la part de qui?* means: Who's speaking?

(3) *La manifestation s'est déroulée dans le calme:* The demonstration took place in calm conditions. Literally, to unroll or to unwind, the verb is often used to describe the unfolding of events.

(4) *Pis* is an alternative form of *pire* found in expressions like *de mal en pis:* from bad to worse. *Pis encore...:* What is worse... (*pire* can be used in both these expressions). We also know *Tant pis!:* Hard luck!

4 Dear Sir, I would like to let you know about the conditions in which our stay in your hotel took place.

5 Firstly, I made a reservation by letter for a double room with bath;

6 when my friend and I arrived we were told that the letter had not been received and that there were only single rooms left.

7 We had to accept but these rooms - which, moreover, were tiny - were located next to the lift-shaft.

8 Worse still, the doors did not lock.

9 As for the gastronomic cooking on which you prided yourself so much in your brochure,

10 suffice it to say that what was served was not even worth what one can find in self-service restaurants.

11 The Assistant Manager, to whom I spoke, granted us a reduction on the price of the rooms

12 but nonetheless we paid highly for a disaster!

NOTES (suite)

(5) The verb to lock is *fermer à clé(f)*; to unlock, simply *ouvrir*. A lock: *une serrure*.

(6) The infinitive is *s'enorgueillir*. Well-placed pride is *la fierté. Il est fier de sa situation:* He is proud of his job. Exaggerated pride is *l'orgueil* (masculine) which could almost be translated as arrogance, the verb is often translated: to boast.

(7) *Une prestation:* is the act of providing a service and is often found in 'officialese'. For example, a travel agency offering a package tour is responsible for *les prestations terrestres:* i.e. the services on the ground (hotel, tours, guides, etc.). It would take up too much space to give all the possible uses of the word. Suffice it to say that it refers to the services provided - in this case the cooking offered by the hotel.

(8) Purists are trying to eradicate this barbaric expression, replacing it with *libre-service*. Much work will have to be done before the French stop using *le self* and start saying *un restaurant libre-service*. We hope they make it!

(9) *Il nous a fait une réduction mais il n'en reste pas moins que nous avons payé trop cher:* He granted us a reduction, nevertheless we still paid too much. The expression avoids using *bien que* with a subjunctive. *Bien qu'il nous ait fait une réduction, nous avons payé trop cher:* Even though he granted us a reduction, etc.

13 J'espère que vous jugerez bon de me dédommager et, dans cette attente, je vous prie d'agréer, Monsieur le Directeur, l'expression de mes sentiments distingués. **(10)**

14 Dès qu'il eut pris connaissance des commentaires de Laurent, le directeur envoya la réponse suivante : **(N.1)**

15 Monsieur, suite à votre courrier du 20 courant, je me suis renseigné auprès de mes employés **(11)**

16 et il semble qu'il y a eu effectivement quelques difficultés.

17 Entre autres, notre Chef de cuisine était malade et son remplaçant n'était pas encore rodé. **(12)**

18 Je vous envoie avec la présente un chèque de trois cents francs et j'espère, malgré ces incidents, vous revoir dans notre établissement. **(13)**

19 Je vous prie d'agréer, Monsieur, l'expression de mes sentiments distingués.

20 Comme quoi, tout est bien qui finit bien.

EXERCICES

1. Ils s'en sont allés en vacances sur la Côte-d'Azur. 2. Je me suis adressé au sous-directeur qui m'a accordé une réduction. 3. Oui, mais il n'en reste pas moins que nos vacances ont été gâchées. 4. Je vous aiderais volontiers mais c'est que je n'ai pas le temps. 5. Ils s'enorgueillissent de leur bel appartement. 6. Comme quoi, tout est bien qui finit bien.

Mettez les mots qui manquent.
Fill in the blanks.

1 . . . . . 'il . . . reçu la réclamation, il envoya un chèque.

As soon as he received the complaint, he sent off a cheque.

13 I hope you will consider it right to make me some compensation and, while waiting for this, I remain Yours faithfully.

14 As soon as he learned of Laurent's comments, the Manager sent the following reply:

15 Dear Sir, further to your letter of the 20th of this month, I made enquiries among my staff

16 and it does in fact seem that there were a few difficulties.

17 Among others, our Head Cook was sick and his replacement was not yet experienced enough.

18 I am sending a cheque for 300F with this letter and I hope, despite these incidents, to see you again in our establishment.

19 Yours faithfully.

20 Which goes to show, that all's well that ends well.

NOTES (suite)

(10) *Les dommages et intérêts:* financial damages. *Dédommager* is to make financial compensation. Physical damage is *les dégâts* (usually in the plural - see Lesson 46).
Quel dommage!: What a pity!

(11) *Du mois courant:* of the current month. This is similar to the English '... of the 20th inst.' and is making way for a less stilted form like *le 20 de ce mois.*

(12) *Roder* means to break in (a horse or a car). *En rodage:* running in. The manager means that the chef's replacement had not yet had enough experience on the job.

(13) i.e. *la présente lettre* - this letter.

EXERCISES: 1. They went off on holiday to the Côte-d'Azur. **2.** I spoke to the Assistant Manager who granted me a reduction. **3.** Yes, but nevertheless, our holidays were ruined. **4.** I'd willingly help you; the thing is, I haven't got the time. **5.** They boast about their beautiful flat. **6.** Which goes to show that all's well that ends well.

2 *Quand il* . . . . *l'histoire, tout le*

monde éclata de rire.

When he had told the story, everybody burst out laughing.

3 *Après* . . *'ils* . . . . . . *fini leur travail, ils*

   s' . . . . *en vacances.*

   After they had finished their work, they went off on holiday.

4 *Ils craignaient de la violence, mais* . . . . *s'est*

   bien . . . .

   They feared violence, but everything went off well.

5 *Je vais* . . . .

   mes employés.

   I'm going to make enquiries among my staff.

****

QUARANTE-QUATRIEME (44e) LEÇON

L'humour

1 Les Français ont une longue tradition humoris-
   tique qui remonte aux œuvres paillardes de
   Rabelais **(1)**
2 et qui a continué au fil des années pour
   produire des esprits tels qu'Alphonse Allais ou
   Sacha Guitry **(2) (3)**
3 pour ne citer que deux des plus sémillants.
   Allais était un spécialiste de l'humour noir
4 (l'argent aide à supporter la pauvreté) et de
   l'observation pointue, par exemple :

NOTES

(1) François Rabelais was a fifteenth century monk and doctor who
remains famous for his books *Gargantua* and *Pantagruel:* his name
is synonymous with licence and ribaldry which often make one
forget the philosophical nature of his satires.

AH, LES VACANCES

Mots qui manquaient :

1. Dès qu - eut 2. eut raconté 3. qu - eurent - en allèrent 4. tout - déroulé 5. me renseigner auprès de.

****

44th LESSON

Humour

1 The French have a long humorous tradition which goes back to the bawdy works of Rabelais

2 and has continued down through the years to produce such wits as Alphonse Allais or Sacha Guitry

3 to name only two of the most sparkling. Allais was a specialist of black humour

4 (money helps one put up with poverty) and of pointed observation, for example:

NOTES (suite)

(2) Alphonse Allais (1855-1901) is best known for his anecdotal style of rather black humour in which he develops the logic of the absurd.

(3) Born in Russia towards the end of the nineteenth century, Sacha Guitry, whose father Lucien was an illustrious actor, remains the quintessential observer of bourgeois life and morals. Both in his plays and his films, his acid wit and verbal elegance sparkle so much that they tend often to hide the rather sad side of his observations.

Leçon 44

5 « Plus les galets ont roulé, plus ils sont polis. Pour les conducteurs, c'est le contraire... » **(4)**

6 Guitry maniait un humour corrosif, souvent aux dépens de la femme.

7 Il disait : « Le meilleur moyen de faire tourner la tête à une femme, c'est de lui dire qu'elle a un beau profil ». **(5)**

8 Mais il était aussi un peu philosophe dans son genre : quelqu'un qui peut dire :

9 « Quand on donne un baiser à quelqu'un, c'est qu'on a envie d'être embrassé soi-même »

10 est sans doute moins cynique qu'il n'en a l'air. **(6)**

11 La littérature française est parsemée d'auteurs humoristiques et l'un des plus grands plaisirs qu'il y a à parler une langue

12 est de pouvoir rire avec les gens du pays... et à la fin, faire quelque plaisanterie soi-même. **(N.3)**

PLUS, VOUS INSISTEZ PLUS IL VOUS DIRA NON

13 Mais cet humour ne se borne pas aux belles lettres, il est présent aussi dans la vie quotidienne. **(7)**

14 Tout amusant qu'il est, il comporte toujours une pointe de réalisme qui lui est propre. **(8)**

5   'The more pebbles roll, the more polished they become. With drivers, it's the opposite...'

6   Guitry wielded corrosive humour, often at women's expense.

7   He said: 'The best way to turn a woman's head is to tell her she has a beautiful profile'.

8   But he was also a bit of a philosopher in his own way: anyone who can say:

9   'When we give someone a kiss it's because we want to be kissed ourselves'

10   is doubtless less cynical than he seems.

11   French literature is studded with humorous authors and one of the greatest pleasures of speaking a language

12   is to be able to laugh with the people of the country... and finally to make some joke oneself.

13   But this humour doesn't restrict itself to literature, it is also present in daily life.

14   As amusing as it is, it always contains an edge of realism which is peculiar to it.

NOTES (suite)

(4) One of the most difficult things to appreciate in a foreign language is the pun - but once you do begin to pick up on wordplay, you're well on the way to total possession of the language. Did you get this one? If not, work it out for yourself:
rouler: to roll **AND** to drive
polir: to polish - *poli:* polished **OR** polite.

(5) Notice how we have to use *faire* before *tourner,* i.e. to make the woman turn her own head rather than to grab it oneself and twist. English is ambiguous here. *J'ai tourné la tête pour ne pas voir:* I turned my head (away) so as not to see. *Je lui ai fait tourner la tête quand je lui ai dit qu'elle était belle:* I turned her head when I told her she was beautiful (using 'make' would indicate force or obligation).

(6) Remember that with *plus* and *moins* in expressions like *Il est plus intelligent qu'on ne pense:* He is more intelligent than one thinks. *Ils sont moins riches qu'on ne dit:* They are less rich than people say, we must use the *ne explétif* which has no negative force at all.

(7) *Les belles lettres* is a synonym for literature.

(8) *Tout* before an adjective may be used in the sense of however...
Tout intelligents qu'ils sont, ils ne réussiront jamais l'examen: However intelligent they are, they will never pass the exam. Notice that *tout* remains invariable.

15 J'ai entendu un jour le propos d'un plombier qui répondait à une cliente qui chantait les louanges de la vie parisienne.

16 Il lui répliqua : « Paris, c'est la seule ville en France où on est réveillé par le bruit des oiseaux qui toussent ».

17 Ou bien cette enseigne qui orne la plupart des cafés se trouvant devant les cimetières :

18 « Quoi qu'on dise, quoi qu'on fasse, on est mieux ici qu'en face » !

19 Parfois on rit jaune, mais au moins on rit. **(9)**

EXERCICES

1. Plus vous insistez, plus il vous dira non. **2.** Je ne vous citerai que les plus connus. **3.** Elle est un peu artiste dans son genre. **4.** Ne vous bornez pas à vos études ; essayez de faire autre chose en plus. **5.** Quoi qu'on en dise, je trouve qu'il écrit très bien. **6.** Qu'est-ce qu'il a ri jaune quand il a lu le rapport.

Mettez les mots qui manquent.
Fill in the blanks.

1 *Il n'est pas . . . . . méchant qu' . . . ' . . .*

l' . . .

He's not as unpleasant as he seems.

2 *. . . . amusants . . ' . . . . ,*

ils travaillent sérieusement.

However amusing they may be, they work seriously.

3 *. . . . . . ' . . . . , c'est voué à*

l'échec.

Whatever we do, it's doomed to failure.

15 One day I heard the remark of a plumber who was answering a customer who was singing the praises of Parisian life.

16 He replied: 'Paris is the only city in France where one is woken up by the sound of the birds coughing'.

17 Or else that sign which decorates most cafés located in front of cemeteries:

18 'Whatever you say, whatever you do, you're better off here than over the road'.

19 Sometimes you laugh despite yourself, but at least you laugh.

NOTES (suite)

(9) *Rire jaune* is to laugh in a forced, sickly way, often at one's own expense or because of the grimness of a situation. *On s'est bien amusés, mais j'ai ri jaune quand j'ai reçu la facture:* We had a good time, but I laughed on the other side of my face when I got the bill.

EXERCICES

1. The more you insist, the more he will say no.   **2.** I will only quote the best known.   **3.** She's a bit of an artist in her own way.   **4.** Don't restrict yourself to your studies; try and do something else as well.   **5.** Whatever people say, I find he writes very well.   **6.** Didn't he laugh on the other side of his face when he read the report!

4 *Il* . . . . *une pointe d'humour qui*

. . . .

It contains its own peculiar edge of humour.

5 *L'argent* . . . *a* . . . . *la tête.*

Money turned his/her head.

Mots qui manquaient :

1. aussi - il n'en a - air **2.** Tout - qu'ils sont **3.** Quoi qu'on fasse **4.** comporte - lui est propre **5.** lui - fait tourner.

QUARANTE-CINQUIEME (45ᵉ) LEÇON

Il ou elle ? (N.4)

1 Sous un beau soleil printanier un touriste anglais s'assit à une terrasse de café, commanda un thé et se mit à lire son journal. **(1)**

2 Quelques minutes plus tard, le garçon lui apporta la consommation ; l'Anglais s'apprêtait à la boire quand il se rendit compte **(2) (3)**

3 qu'un insecte flottait à la surface. Il héla le serveur : « Garçon, s'il vous plaît, fit-il avec un fort accent,

4 il y a **un** mouche dans mon thé ! » Un Français assis à une table voisine, voulut aider l'étranger qui semblait ignorer la langue de Racine. **(4) (5)**

5 Il se pencha, tapota l'Anglais sur l'épaule et lui dit : « Monsieur, je vous prie de m'excuser, mais c'est **une** mouche ». **(4)**

6 L'autre était éberlué. Il regarda son voisin d'un air admiratif et s'exclama : « Monsieur, quelle vue extraordinaire ! » **(6)**

7 Il s'agit là, bien sûr, d'une plaisanterie, mais vous qui parlez bien le français, vous vous rendez compte de l'importance des genres.

NOTES

(1) *Printanier* is the adjective from *printemps;* the other formations are: *été - estival; automne - automnal* and *hiver - hivernal.*

(2) Remember, nationalities (be they nouns or adjectives) only take a capital letter when referring to an inhabitant of the country. *Le français:* the French language - *un Français:* a Frenchman.

(3) *Il s'apprêtait à partir quand le téléphone a sonné:* He was getting ready to leave when the phone rang. Coming from the adjective *prêt* (ready), *s'apprêter à* means to get ready to, or to be about to, depending on the context and the proximity of the two events. *Je m'apprêtais à le boire, quand j'ai vu un insecte:* I was about to drink it when I saw an insect.

(4) Of course, the joke here is that 'fly' is a feminine noun, so the Englishman should say *une mouche* (*un mouche* does not exist).

(5) *La langue de Racine* i.e. French, rather like we may say 'the language of Shakespeare' for English.

45th LESSON

He or she (i.e. masculine or feminine)?

1 In beautiful spring sunshine, an English tourist sat down at a café terrace, ordered a tea and began to read his paper.

2 A few minutes later, the waiter brought the drink, the Englishman was about to drink it when he realised

3 that an insect was floating on the surface. He hailed the server: 'Waiter, please! he said, in a strong accent,

4 there is a fly [but mistaken gender] in my tea!' A Frenchman sitting at a neighbouring table, wanted to help the foreigner who seemed to be unaware of the language of Racine.

5 He leant forward, tapped the Englishman on the shoulder and said to him: 'Sir, please excuse me, but it's a (using the correct feminine article) fly'.

6 The other man was flabbergasted. He looked at his neighbour in an admiring way and exclaimed: 'Sir, what extraordinary eyesight!'

7 Of course, this is a joke, but you who speak French well realise the importance of genders.

NOTES (suite)

(6) *La vue* can mean view. *Il y a une très belle vue à partir de cette chambre:* There is a beautiful view from this bedroom. *Quel est son point de vue?:* What is his/her point of view?
Sight: *à première vue:* at first sight.
Je l'ai perdu de vue: I lost sight of her.
OR eyesight: *J'ai une très bonne vue:* I have very good eyesight.

Leçon 45

8 Certes, vous ne croyez plus que « l'ascenseur » est féminin mais c'est d'autant plus important **(7)**

9 qu'il y a des mots qui changent de sens selon qu'ils sont au masculin ou au féminin.

10 Vous en connaissez déjà certains, mais regardez bien les exemples suivants :

11 Passez-moi **le mode** d'emploi pour le lave-vaisselle, MAIS : Elle suit toujours **la mode** pour s'habiller. **(8)**

12 Elle ne craint pas **la mort,** MAIS : L'accident a fait **un mort** et deux blessés. **(9)**

13 Il a **un** beau **physique,** MAIS : **La physique** nucléaire est la science de l'avenir. **(10)**

14 Ils habitent **une** grande **tour** Place d'Italie à Paris, MAIS : Qui a gagné **le Tour** de France cette année ? **(11)**

15 Ces **moules** sont-elles fraîches ? MAIS : Elle a besoin d'**un moule** à tarte pour faire le gâteau. **(12)**

16 Donnez-moi **une livre** de betteraves, MAIS : Son nouveau **livre** vient de paraître. **(13)**

17 Vous voyez que ce n'est pas bien compliqué - il faut simplement faire un petit peu attention.

NOTES (suite)

(7) A problem many learners have - and to which you must pay attention - is to learn the gender of nouns beginning with 'a' because of the *l'* apostrophe which precedes them. An untrained ear will hear *la censeur* and take the noun as being feminine - it is, of course, masculine. Pay special attention to this problem and remember: learn the gender with the noun.

EXERCICES

1. Ils s'apprêtaient à téléphoner quand leurs amis arrivèrent. **2.** Ne te penche pas par la fenêtre ! **3.** Ne vous énervez pas ! Il s'agit d'une plaisanterie. **4.** Le mot est différent selon qu'il est au masculin ou au féminin. **5.** Il faut le lui rendre ; c'est d'autant plus important que ce n'est pas à moi. **6.** Il m'a regardé d'un air éberlué.

8 Of course, you no longer believe that *l'ascenseur* (the lift) is feminine, but it is all the more important

9 since there are words which change meaning depending on whether they are masculine or feminine.

10 You already know some, but look carefully at the following examples:

11 Pass me the instruction-book for the dishwasher BUT: In dressing, she always follows the fashion.

12 She is not afraid of death BUT: The accident killed one person and injured two others.

13 He is handsome BUT: Nuclear physics is the science of the future.

14 They live in a large tower-building at the Place d'Italie in Paris BUT: Who won the Tour de France this year?

15 Are these mussels fresh? BUT: She needs a cake-tin to make the cake.

16 Give me a pound of beetroot BUT: His (or her) new book has just come out.

17 You see, it's not really complicated - you just have to be a little careful.

NOTES (suite)

(8) *Le mode:* a mode, a way of doing something; *Le mode de vie:* The way of life. *Un mode d'emploi:* a mode of employment, i.e., an instruction book. *La mode:* fashion. *C'est à la mode:* It's fashionable.

(9) *La mort:* death. *Un mort:* a dead person (male or female!). Notice the sentence construction.

(10) *Un physique:* physique, external appearances.
La physique: physics, the science.

(11) *Une tour:* a tower, or a tower-block.
Un tour: a tour, a circuit.

(12) *Une moule:* a mussel - *un moule:* a mould, something into which a liquid is poured to form a shape when it solidifies.

(13) *Une livre, (500 g)* = half a kilo.
Un livre = a book.

EXERCISES: 1. They were about to telephone when their friends arrived. **2.** Don't lean out of the window! **3.** Don't get angry! It's only a joke. **4.** The word is different depending on whether it's masculine or feminine. **5.** We must give it back to him/her; it's all the more important because it's not mine. **6.** He looked at me flabbergasted.

Mettez l'article défini

1 . . *mode de vie.*

2 . . *physique expérimentale.*

3 . . *tour du monde.*

4 . . *moule à gâteau.*

5 . . *livre de grammaire.*

Traduisez

1 Paris fashion.

2 Accidental death.

3 The Eiffel Tower.

4 An adventure book.

5 The Post Office.

****

QUARANTE-SIXIEME (46ᵉ) LEÇON

Singulier ou pluriel ? (1)

1 — As-tu entendu la nouvelle ? Jean-Pierre s'est marié avec une Anglaise ! (2)

2 — Parle-t-elle français ? — Oui, elle a fait d'énormes progrès depuis deux mois.

3 Et elle a une chance inouïe : c'est son mari qui lui fait la cuisine. Une bonne cuisine française ! (3) (4)

NOTES

(1) Notice, in the following dialogues, how some nouns are singular whereas in English they would be plural, and vice versa. Since this is arbitrary, our explanations have been kept to the minimum: I'm afraid they just have to be memorised!

(2) *Une nouvelle:* an item of news. Whereas English would say: Have you heard the news?, French will make the distinction between one or several items of news *(la / les nouvelle(s)). Pas de nouvelles, bonnes nouvelles:* No news is good news. Notice this idiomatic usage: *J'ai un cognac dont vous me direz des nouvelles:* I've got a cognac that you'll love (literally: which you'll give me news of after you have drunk it) - a pure and picturesque Gallicism.

The news broadcast is called either *les actualités* or *les informations* (see line 8). As with *nouvelle(s)* we can say *J'ai une information pour vous,* which means one item of information but which English would translate as: I have some information for you.

Mots qui manquaient :

1. Le 2. La 3. Le 4. Le 5. Le.

Translation:

1. La mode parisienne. 2. La mort accidentelle. 3. La Tour Eiffel. 4. Un livre d'aventures. 5. La poste.

*****

****

46th LESSON

Singular or plural?

1 — Have you heard the news? Jean-Pierre has married an English girl!

2 — Does she speak French? — Yes, she's made enormous progress over the last two months.

3 — And she is incredibly lucky: her husband cooks for her. Good French cooking!

NOTES (suite)

(3) We saw that *la vue* was the eyesight (lesson 45, note 6); hearing is *l'ouïe* [lwee] (feminine). (There is a defective verb *ouïr* which is hardly used, but whose present imperative is familiar to those who know the shout of the English Town Crier: *Oyez! Oyez!* - pronounced [wayay] in French.) So, *inouï* [inwee] means: unheard-of, incredible.

(4) To cook: *faire la cuisine*. Most cookery operations take the verb *faire;* to fry: *faire frire;* to boil: *faire bouillir;* to bake: *faire cuire au four*. French cookery terms and descriptions are far more colourful than their English counterparts: compare the pragmatic boiled egg with the poetic *œuf à la coque* or even *des œufs au plat* with... fried eggs.

Bilingual menus are a wealth of examples where English just doesn't have the evocative power of French. I remember seeing *un navarin d'agneau printanier* called: boiled lamb with vegetables. Ah well...

4 — Mais comment cela se fait-il ? Autrefois, il brûlait même les œufs au plat ! **(5)**

5 — Je vais te donner un conseil : ton mari ferait pareil si tu avais fait comme elle. — Ah bon ?

6 — Oui. Le premier soir elle lui a dit : Viens, chéri, je vais te faire bouillir un steak. Et depuis lors... ! **(6)**

7 — J'ai un travail pour toi. Peux-tu déplacer ce meuble pour le mettre derrière la porte ? **(7)**

8 — N'éteins pas la télévision après les informations : je voudrais voir la météo. **(2) (8)**

9 — A quoi bon ? Tu sais bien que, quoi qu'ils disent, il fera un temps de chien ce weekend. **(9)**

NOTES (suite)

(5) *Comment cela se fait-il* or, more common in spoken French, *comment ça se fait?*: an invariable idiom comparable to the English: How come? How did that happen?

(6) *Lors:* this adverb is another form of *alors* and is mainly used in the following ways: *Lors de leur déménagement, ils ont perdu beaucoup de choses:* During their move, they lost a lot of things. *(Lors de* can be replaced by *pendant.) Depuis lors, je ne les ai*

4 — But how come? In the past, he even used to burn fried eggs!

5 — I'll give you some advice: your husband would do the same if you had done what she did. — Really?

6 — Yes. The first evening, she said to him: Come on, darling, I'm going to boil you a steak. And since then...!

7 — I have a job for you. Can you move this piece of furniture to put it behind the door ?

8 — Don't turn off the television after the news: I'd like to watch the weather forecast.

9 — What for? You know very well that whatever they say, the weather will be terrible this week-end.

NOTES (suite)

jamais revus: Since then, I have never seen them again. *(Depuis lors* can be replaced by *Depuis ce temps.)*

A similar form is *dès lors* which means: from that time on. *Il s'est caché et dès lors il est devenu suspect:* He went into hiding; since then he has been a suspect.

(7) *Les meubles:* furniture - the collective noun. We also say *un meuble* which literally translates as: a piece of furniture but, in regular usage, English would be more specific:

Déplacez ce meuble: Move that table/chair/cupboard, etc.

Un appartement meublé: a furnished flat. Be careful of the 'false friend' *fournir* which means to supply.

(8) A (fortunate) abbreviation of *les prévisions météorologiques.*

(9) We also saw in an earlier lesson the expression *quoi que,* the concessive expression followed by a subjunctive. *Quoi qu'il dise:* Whatever he says. *Quoi qu'il arrive:* Whatever happens... (Also, note the expression: *Quoi qu'il en soit:* Whatever the case may be.)

We also find other relatives used in such a way: *Qui que vous soyez, vous ne pouvez entrer:* Whoever you are, you can't go in. *Où que vous alliez, gardez ceci sur vous:* Wherever you go, keep this with you.

Be careful not to confuse *quoi que* with the conjunction *quoique,* in one word, also followed by the subjunctive, which means: although. *Quoiqu'ils soient pauvres, ils sont très heureux:* Although they are poor, they are very happy. A synonym for this is *Bien que.*

Leçon 46

10 — Quelle belle chanson ! — Oui, c'est une
vieille poésie française mais sur une musique
très moderne. **(10)**

11 — Il a un comportement bizarre depuis quelque
temps, notre Michel. Il doit travailler trop.
12 — Tu sais, il essaie de gagner plus d'argent que
sa femme n'en dépense. **(11)**

EXERCICES

1. Si tu as faim, je vais te faire cuire des œufs au plat. **2.**
Depuis quelque temps, il a une chance inouïe au casino : il
gagne tout le temps. **3.** Si j'avais su cela, j'aurais fait
pareil. **4.** Je vais m'expliquer avec le policier. - A quoi
bon ? Tu devras toujours payer l'amende. **5.** Quoi qu'il en
soit, je vais essayer: on ne sait jamais. **6.** Tu vois, je n'ai
pas eu d'amende ! - Comment ça se fait ? - Non, je vais
en prison !

Mettez les mots qui manquent.
Fill in the blanks.

1 *Pas de* . . . . , ...

No news is good news.

2 *Quand* . ' . . . . . *terminé* . . . . ,

je t'aiderai.

When I have finished this job, I'll help you.

3 *Il* . . . . *de* . . . . . *le*

week-end dernier.

The weather was terrible last week-end.

10 — What a beautiful song! — Yes, it's an old French poem but set to very modern music.

11 — He's been behaving strangely for some time, our Michel. He must be working too hard.

12 — You know, he's trying to earn more money than his wife spends.

NOTES (suite)

(10) *La poésie:* poetry; *une poésie:* a poem (we also have the word *un poème*). *La musique:* music; *une musique:* a tune (we also have the word *un air*).

(11) See Lesson 44, Note 6.

EXERCISES: 1. If you're hungry, I'll make you some fried eggs. **2.** For some time, he's been having incredible luck at the casino: he wins all the time. **3.** If I had known that, I would have done the same. **4.** I'm going to have things out with the policeman. - What for? You will still get a fine. **5.** Whatever happens, I'll try: you never know. **6.** You see, I didn't get a fine! - How come? - No, I'm going to prison!

4 *Elle a pris des cours et,* . . . . ,

elle a fait d' . . . .

She took some lessons, and since then, she has made enormous

progress.

5 . . . .' . . . . , *sa femme dépense*

plus . . .' . . . .

Whatever he does, his wife spends more than he earns.

Mots qui manquaient :

1. nouvelles bonnes nouvelles **2.** j'aurai - ce travail **3.** a fait un temps - chien **4.** depuis lors - énormes progrès **5.** Quoi qu'il fasse - qu'il ne gagne.

QUARANTE-SEPTIEME (47ᵉ) LEÇON

Les critiques

1 Un peintre abstrait invita un critique d'art à sa maison de campagne pour le week-end. (1)

2 Quand il fut rentré, sa femme lui demanda comment il avait passé son temps.

3 — C'était fort agréable : calme, détendu mais quand même stimulant intellectuellement.

4 Vois-tu, lui passait ses journées à peindre et sa femme était toujours fourrée à la cuisine. (2) (3) (4)

5 Le soir, ils se mettaient à table dans l'atelier et chacun essayait de deviner ce qu'avait fait l'autre. (5)

C'EST À CROIRE QU'IL LE FAIT EXPRÈS

6 Il semblerait que les critiques passent leur temps à démolir des pauvres artistes :

7 — La première pièce qu'on ait joué dans le Théâtre de la Ville à Paris en 1950 était une pièce de Jean Dupont.

8 ... et pourtant le théâtre est toujours là !

47th LESSON

Critics

1   An abstract painter invited an art critic to his country house for the week-end.

2   When he had returned, his wife asked him how he had spent his time.

3 — It was very agreeable: calm, relaxed but all the same, intellectually stimulating.

4   You see, he spent his days painting and his wife was never out of the kitchen.

5   In the evenings, they would sit down at table in the studio and each would try and guess what the other had made.

6   It would appear that critics spend their time demolishing poor artists:

7 — The first play acted in 'Le Théâtre de la Ville' in Paris in 1950 was a play by Jean Dupont

8   ... and yet the theatre is still there!

NOTES

(1) See Lesson 45. *Un critique* is the person who reviews plays, books etc. What he or she writes is *une critique:* a review.

(2) When we are going to compare two different people's actions, we use this form to separate clearly, the two people. *Anne-Marie aime le jazz mais Laurent, lui, préfère le rock:* Anne-Marie likes jazz whereas Laurent likes rock music. *A la maison, lui fait la cuisine et elle fait la vaisselle.* It is, of course, perfectly correct to use the nominative *il* (or, in the case of: *Eux sont Allemands, les autres sont Anglais,* we can use *ils*); the pronoun increases the distinction.

(3) *Je passe mon temps à lire:* I spend my time reading. *Ils passent leur temps à critiquer les artistes:* They spend their time criticising artists.
In the same way as we have learned to memorise a noun together with its gender, we must get into the habit of learning the prepositions taken by each verb. Once memorised, do the exercises, invent your own sentences until what you have memorised becomes fully assimilated.

(4) A familiar term *Il est toujours fourré chez nous:* He's always hanging round our place.

(5) Read the last two sentences again. Notice how the critic is talking, not about one specific evening, but several such evenings. In English we use what we call the past frequentative (they used to..., they would..., etc.) to express this repetition of the same actions. French uses the imperfect to exactly the same effect.

Leçon 47

9   A propos d'un barbier qui s'était converti en acteur - d'un talent et d'une sensibilité discutables - **(6)**

10   un critique écrivit : Cet acteur minaudier se permet maintenant

11   d'écorcher les auteurs qu'il rasait autrefois ! **(7)**

12   C'est à croire parfois que ces malotrus sont inspirés du diable, selon les artistes. **(8)**

13   Un auteur dont l'œuvre avait été ridiculisée par un critique particulièrement acide, l'invita à dîner pour s'expliquer avec lui. **(9) (10)**

14 — Mais vous n'avez donc aucune âme, aucun sens de la religion si vous critiquez mes pièces.

15   Ne croyez-vous pas dans l'au-delà ? **(11)**

16   Le critique regarda autour de lui le beau décor du restaurant somptueux

17   et répondit : — Non, je crois que je préfère le vin d'ici. **(12)**

NOTES (suite)

(6) The adjective applies to both nouns so it therefore must agree. *La langue et la littérature françaises:* French language and literature.

(7) *L'écorce* (f.): the bark of a tree, the skin from an orange.
Ecorcher means to flay, to remove the skin from. It is therefore very vivid when used as a metaphor. *L'épicier écorchait ses clients:* The grocer used to swindle his clients (compare this with the English slang: to fleece, or the American: to rip off).
Raser means both to shave **and** to bore. Bear the double sense of each word in mind, then read the line again. Not bad for concentrated meanness? Since *raser* means both to shave and to bore *une barbe* is a beard, but the exclamation *La barbe!* means: What a bore!

EXERCICES

1. Une fois rentré, il a raconté son week-end à sa femme.
2. On ne le trouve jamais, celui-là : il est toujours fourré chez ses amis. 3. Lui passait son temps à écrire, elle à peindre. 4. Il n'a pas deviné ce qu'avait fait sa femme. 5. Ses photos de vacances ! La barbe ! 6. C'est à croire qu'il le fait exprès.

9   Concerning a barber who had become an actor - of debatable sensitivity and talent -

10   one critic wrote: This simpering actor now allows himself

11   to murder the authors whom in other times he used to shave!

12   It's enough to make one believe that these oafs are inspired by the devil - according to artists.

13   An author whose work had been ridiculed by a particularly acid critic, invited him to dinner to have it out with him.

14 — But you have no soul, no sense of religion if you criticise my plays.

15   Don't you believe in the beyond?

16   The critic looked around him at the beautiful decor of the sumptuous restaurant

17   and replied: — No, I prefer to drink wine right here.

NOTES (suite)

(8) A delightful word meaning a boor, an oaf, one with no manners. It originally meant someone who was born under an unlucky star.

(9) See Lesson 45. *Une œuvre:* a work of art; *l'œuvre* (m.): the complete works of an artist.

(10) *Je voudrais m'expliquer:* I'd like to make myself clear.
Expliquez-vous!: Explain yourself!
But *s'expliquer avec quelqu'un* means to make things clear on both sides, to have things out. *Il s'est expliqué avec l'agent:* He had it out with the policeman.

(11) As you know, *au-delà* is a preposition meaning beyond. *Leur maison est au-delà de la colline:* Their house is beyond the hill. So, used as a noun, *l'au-delà* means The Beyond, i.e., the infinite.

(12) Do you get the pun? No? Read line 15 aloud and pronounce the last word very slowly: it sounds like *l'eau de là...* The critic prefers *le vin d'ici!*

EXERCISES: 1. Once he had returned, he told his wife about his week-end. **2.** We can never find him: he's always hanging around his friend's place. **3.** He used to spend his time writing, and she spent hers painting. **4.** He didn't guess what his wife had made. **5.** His holiday photos! What a bore! **6.** You'd think he did it deliberately.

Mettez les mots qui manquent.
Fill in the blanks.

1 *C'est la seule* . . . . . . *que vous* . . . . *de vous*

en sortir.

It's the only chance you have to get out of it.

2 *La première femme que* . .' . . . . *était*

Française.

The first woman I ever knew was French.

3 *Il* . . . . *tout son temps* .

. . . . *les autres.*

He used to spend all his time criticising others.

****

QUARANTE-HUITIEME (48e) LEÇON

L'inspecteur mène l'enquête

1   La scène était bien sinistre. Dans la cuisine
     d'un pavillon vétuste, un homme était affalé
     sur la table, mort. **(1)**

2   Un revolver était à côté de sa main. Il y avait
     en plus un couvert, une assiette et une
     salière renversée. **(2)**

NOTES

(1) Most people in French towns live in flats. Many dream of moving
    out to the suburbs and living in *un pavillon* - a detached house.
    The word describes the building only, not the idea of a home.
    Even if you live in a flat, you could say: *Venez à la maison ce soir:*
    Come home this evening. *Ils se font construire un pavillon en
    banlieue:* They are having a house built in the suburbs.

4 *Nous enseignons la langue et la*

. . . .

We teach French language and literature.

5 *Il* . . . . *lui;*

son ami l'attendait . . - . . . . . . *la porte.*

He looked around him; his friend was waiting for him beyond the

door.

Mots qui manquaient :

1. chance - ayez 2. j'aie connue 3. passait - à critiquer 4. littérature
françaises 5. regarde autour de - au-delà de.

*The puns and jokes serve a purpose other than just to
entertain you: they teach you to manipulate the language,
to play with the words in order to find other meanings. But we hope you smile as well!*

****

48th LESSON

The inspector leads the investigation

1 The scene was really sinister. In the kitchen of a
decrepit house, a man lay sprawled on the table,
dead.

2 A revolver was next to his hand. There was also
one place-setting, a plate and an overturned salt-
cellar.

NOTES (suite)

(2) *Le couvert.* From the verb *couvrir, le couvert* is what covers the
table, i.e. knife, fork, spoon, etc. *Mettre le couvert:* To lay the table.
When preceded by a number, the word means a place-setting. *Il y
avait deux couverts de préparés:* Two places were set. When
reserving at a restaurant, you may be asked: *Combien de
couverts?* Understand: How many people?

3 Le sergent de police faisait son rapport à un inspecteur en civil : « Il s'agit d'un certain Paul Houssard, âgé de cinquante ans.

4 Il était peintre, mais sans grande réussite, d'après ce que j'ai pu apprendre. **(3)**

5 Il y a deux mois environ, il a eu une crise cardiaque et il s'est retiré dans cette maison.

6 J'en ai conclu qu'il n'avait plus de raison de vivre ; il s'est fait un dernier repas et ensuite, il s'est donné la mort. **(4)**

7 Mourir comme ça, quelle horreur ! Qu'en pensez-vous, monsieur l'inspecteur ? » **(5)** **(6)**

8 Les deux policiers étaient en manches de chemise car il faisait une chaleur torride.

9 — C'est la seule hypothèse que vous ayez pu retenir ? répondit l'inspecteur. Peut-être y a-t-il des indices que vous avez négligés. **(N.5)**

10 Bien qu'il ait été dans la misère pendant longtemps une galerie venait de lui commander vingt tableaux.

11 Regardons cette pièce à présent. Voyons voir, un couvert. **(7)**

12 Il s'approcha de l'évier où il trouva une assiette, un verre et une fourchette propres.

13 — Regardez ; ici on a jeté les restes du repas, mais il n'y a pas trop longtemps, vu la chaleur.

3 The police sergeant was making his report to a plain-clothes inspector: 'The person in question is a certain Paul Housard, aged 50.

4 He was a painter, but without great success, from what I have been able to gather.

5 About two months ago, he had a heart attack and he withdrew to this house.

6 I have concluded that he no longer had a reason to live; he made himself a last meal and, afterwards, killed himself.

7 Dying like that, how horrible! What do you think, inspector?'

8 The two policemen were in shirt sleeves because it was unbearably hot.

9 — Is that the only hypothesis you have been able to retain? replied the inspector. Perhaps there are other clues which you have overlooked.

10 Although he had lived in poverty for a long time, a gallery had just ordered twenty pictures from him.

11 Now, let's look at this room... Let's see: one place-setting.

12 He went over to the sink where he found a plate, a glass and a fork - all clean.

13 — Look; here's where someone threw away the remains of the meal - but not too long ago, given the heat.

NOTES (suite)

(3) *D'après ce que:* from what... *D'après ce qu'il m'a dit, la maison serait déjà louée:* From what he told me, it seems the house has already been let.
D'après ce que j'ai pu comprendre... From what I was able to gather.
The partitive *d'* is very important, otherwise the phrase is a simple temporal clause. *Après ce qu'il m'a dit, je n'y remettrai plus les pieds:* After what he said to me, I'll never set foot there again.

(4) *Se donner la mort* is a synonym for *se suicider.*

(5) The infinitive may be used in exclamations. *Fumer comme ça! Mais c'est dangereux!:* Smoking like that! It's dangerous! *Conduire si vite! C'est stupide:* Driving that fast! It's stupid.

(6) (See also note on letter-writing in Lesson 49 N.2.) In formal situations, when addressing a person who has a title (e.g. *commissaire, directeur, ministre,* etc.) you would use the title prefaced by *Monsieur le...* or *Madame la...* The correct form of address to a policeman is *Monsieur l'Agent.*

(7) *A présent,* now, at this very moment. *Vous êtes prêts? Partons à présent:* Are you ready? Let's go right now.

Leçon 48

14 — Là-dessus, j'ai une théorie, dit le sergent. C'était un homme méticuleux et il ne voulait pas laisser sa maison sale.

15 — Pensez-vous ! Il débarrasse la table, fait la vaisselle et ensuite il se tire une balle dans le crâne ? **(8)**

16 Quelles que fussent ses habitudes, il ne serait pas allé jusqu'à ce point. **(9)**

17 Non, regardez bien. Il avait invité quelqu'un à déjeuner et c'est cet invité qui l'a tué !

18 Ensuite, il a voulu effacer les traces de sa visite. Non, il ne s'agit pas d'un suicide... mais d'un meurtre ! **(10)**

19 Comment l'inspecteur a-t-il pu déduire la présence d'une autre personne ? Relisez les indices.

(Vous trouverez la solution à la leçon 49 !)

NOTES (suite)

(8) A gentle rebuke in reply to a question or a statement indicating that the opposite is true. *Tu as passé de bonnes vacances? Penses-tu! Il a plu tout le temps:* Did you have a good holiday? You're joking! It rained all the time.
Elle m'a dit qu'elle serait là à neuf heures. Pensez-vous! Elle est toujours en retard: She said she would be here at nine. That's what you think! She's always late.
English equivalents are: What? No fear! You must be joking! That's what you think.

(9) (See lesson 46, Note 9.) Another concessive expression followed by the subjunctive is *Quel que...* Whatever. Unlike *qui que* or *quoi que, Quel* must agree with the noun. *Quelles que soient vos opinions:* Whatever your opinions may be. *Réveillez-moi quelle*

EXERCICES

1. De quoi s'agit-il ? **2.** D'après ce qu'on me dit, il est parti sans laisser d'adresse. **3.** Fumer une pipe ! Quelle horreur ! **4.** Il faisait tellement chaud qu'ils étaient en manches de chemise. **5.** Voici le seul indice que j'aie pu trouver. **6.** Alors, c'est un vrai play-boy ? Penses-tu ! Il est marié avec quatre enfants !

14 — I've got a theory about that, said the sergeant. He was a meticulous man and he didn't want to leave his house dirty.

15 — Think again! He clears the table, does the washing-up and then he fires a bullet into his skull?

16 Whatever his habits, he would not have gone that far.

17 No, look carefully. He had invited someone to dinner and it's that guest who killed him!

18 Afterwards, he wanted to wipe out the traces of his visit. No, it's not a suicide... but a murder!

19 How did the inspector deduce the presence of another person? Re-read the clues.
(You will find the solution in Lesson 49!)

NOTES (suite)

que soit l'heure quand il arrivera: Wake me up whatever time it is when he arrives. *Quels que soient ses espoirs:* Whatever his/her hopes may be.
Let's recapitulate:
Qui que vous soyez: Whoever you are/may be.
Quoi qu'ils disent: Whatever they say.
Où que vous alliez: Wherever you go.
Quel que soit votre nom: Whatever your name is.
There are a couple of other, less common, constructions which we will see later.
Quelles que soient ses habitudes: Whatever his habits may be... but in the text, the person is dead, so we can no longer use a present subjunctive. *Fussent* is the imperfect subjunctive of *être* BUT, before you give up in despair thinking: Oh no! Another tense! Let us point out that (a) it is very rarely used in modern written French and almost never when speaking, (b) there are ways around the problem which the French themselves use. Enough for the time being - we will touch again on the imperfect subjunctive later.

(10) The verb *s'agir de* is awkward. It often appears to mean nothing more than 'to be'. The dictionary definitions are numerous: 'to be a question of', 'to be about', 'to concern', etc. The best way to assimilate it is to take note of the examples you have seen so far and wait until the use of the expression falls into place. Look again at lines 3 and 18.

EXERCISES: 1. What's this all about? **2.** From what I was told, he left without leaving an address. **3.** How horrible to smoke a pipe! **4.** It was so hot that they were in their shirt-sleeves. **5.** Here is the only clue I was able to find. **6.** So, he's a real play-boy? You're joking! He's married with four children.

Mettez les mots qui manquent.
Fill in the blanks.

1 *Je le* . . . . . *quand même,* . . . .

. . . . . . *vos opinions.*

I will do it all the same, whatever your opinions may be.

2 *Il doit essayer* . . . . *ses*

problèmes.

He must try whatever his problems.

****

QUARANTE-NEUVIEME (49ᵉ) LEÇON

REVISION ET NOTES

This is the last real grammar lesson we will have to deal
with: there are certain rules concerned with what is called
la concordance des temps (tense sequences) which are
very important, especially since they involve certain
notions which do not exist in English tense structure. It is
also at this level that we shall see more clearly the
differences between the written and the spoken languages, the latter dropping several of the more complex
forms and replacing them with equivalents which purists
would reprove, but which make life much easier.

1 This tense is called *le passé antérieur* and is now only
used in written French.
First of all, let's look at the pluperfect tense again. *Je lui
avais donné un cadeau l'année précédente:* I had given her
a present the year before.
But if this pluperfect idea is expressed in a compound

3 *Je l'aime bien,* . . . . *nous* . . . .

des idées différentes.

I like him/her a lot, even though we have different ideas.

4 . . . . *j'ai appris à son sujet, je ne le reverrai plus.*

After what I learned about him, I don't want to see him any longer.

5 . . . . . . *'on vous* . . . . , . . *s'* . . . . . *'un meurtre.*

Whatever they tell you, it really is a murder.

Mots qui manquaient :

1. ferai - quelles que soient **2.** quels que soient **3.** bien que - ayons **4.** Après ce que **5.** Quoi qu' - dise, il - agit d'.

****

49th LESSON

sentence, where the connection is made by a conjunction of time - like *quand, après que, dès que,* etc., the verb which would normally go into the pluperfect is put into the *passé antérieur* and the other verb(s) into the *passé simple.* English has no equivalent for this, translating both *simple* and *antérieur* by the pluperfect. Look at these examples:

Quand il eut fini de parler, il regagna sa place: When he had finished speaking, he went back to his place.

Dès qu'ils eurent raconté leur histoire, tout le monde applaudit: When they had finished telling their story, everyone applauded.

The tense is formed with the *passé simple* of *avoir: j'eus; tu eus; il/elle eut; nous eûmes; vous eûtes; ils eurent;* and the past participle of the verb.

(Remember that, if the verb is conjugated with *être,* we will use *je fus; tu fus; il fut; nous fûmes; vous fûtes; ils furent.*)

We know that the *passé simple* is not used in spoken

French, which poses a problem also for the *passé antérieur*. We get round this by using, of course, the *passé composé* for the second verb and a sort of *passé surcomposé* after the conjunction of time. This uses the past participle of *avoir* and the past participle of the verb in question so our examples would 'sound' like this:

Quand il a eu fini de parler, il a regagné sa place and:

Dès qu'ils ont eu raconté leur histoire, tout le monde a applaudi.

Look at these examples of transposition from written to spoken

Dès qu'il eut terminé le livre. - Dès qu'il a eu terminé le livre. - A peine fut-elle partie. - A peine a-t-elle été partie. (Notice this inversion after *à peine*.)

Après que nous fûmes rentrés. - Après que nous soyons rentrés.

This form is only used when there is a conjunction of time, so watch out for *après que; à peine; dès que; aussitôt que; lorsque;* and approach the construction of a sentence with care. After a few tries, it will seem logical. (When there is no conjunction of time, we simply use the imperfect. *A cinq heures, il avait déjà fini:* At 5.00 he had already finished.)

2 *Letter-writing.* A whole book could be devoted to the writing of official letters in French. The first thing that strikes an Anglo-Saxon is the seeming 'floweriness' of the language and the elaborate salutations and complimentary closes.

It takes much practice to achieve the 'correct' style and our direct way of writing, if translated literally, sounds abrupt to a French ear.

Let's content ourselves with making the following observations:

(i) The salutation. The usual opening is: *Monsieur*, (or *Madame, Mademoiselle*, etc.). The use of *Chèr(e)* is restricted to cases where the correspondents know one another fairly well. When writing to an official, his or her title is brought into the salutation: *Monsieur le Directeur, Monsieur le Ministre,* etc.

(ii) The complimentary close is always elaborate, along

the lines of: *Je vous prie de bien vouloir agréer, Monsieur, l'expression de mes sentiments les meilleurs.*

If, as mentioned above, we use a title in the salutation, it is re-iterated in the close: *Veuillez agréer, Monsieur le Directeur, l'expression de mes sentiments respectueux.*

How simple our 'Yours faithfully' seems!

Such conventions do not, of course, apply to correspondence between friends.

Read Laurent's letter again and notice the rather elaborate language. If you ever have to write official letters, it is worthwhile buying a special book which sets out all the conventions. (Most French offices have at least one!)

3 *Quelque:* We have seen, over this week, several different uses of this word. Here is another nuance.

We know the simple form: *Donnez-moi quelques prunes:* Give me a few plums. When written, as in our example (Lesson 44, line 12) without an *s* either on *quelque* or on the noun, it is equivalent to the English usage: some... or other.

Faire quelque plaisanterie: to make some joke or other.

Avez-vous quelque ami qui puisse vous aider?: Do you have some friend or other who could help you?

Elle gagne quelque cinq mille francs: She earns some five thousand francs.

4 Gender is always a problem for the Anglo-Saxon learner. Here are some rules to be used as reference:

MASCULINE

Endings: *-age -ail -eau -ège - eil -ier -oir -our*

Nouns: names of trees, metals, months, days and seasons, languages, towns - and countries not ending in *e.*

FEMININE

Endings: *-ade -aille -aison -ance -ée -eille -ence -esse -ette -ie -ière -ille -ion -ise -té -tié -tion -tude -ue -ure*

Nouns: flowers, fruits and sciences and those countries ending in *e.*

There are, of course, exceptions - especially to the endings rule - but these are best learned by making mistakes rather than trying to learn lists which could easily get mixed up anyway!

- Because of the arbitrary nature of gender, some nouns have one form but, if applied to a person of a different gender - i.e. sex, may change the article. Thus *un élève* is masculine but, if applied to a girl pupil, we way say *une élève*. The same is true of *un(e) enfant*. Other examples are *artiste, esclave* and *hypocrite*.

We have already seen the problem when a woman occupies a job or position for which the noun is masculine (*médecin, écrivain, professeur,* etc.). Inventiveness is necessary to bring out the fact that the person is a woman. *Elle est un excellent médecin. Vous voyez cette dame? C'est le professeur de français de ma fille.* It would be too easy if there were rules for everything!

5 Another use of the subjunctive which sometimes catches us unawares is that after superlative adjectives and the words *le premier, le dernier* and *le seul.*
La première chanson que j'aie entendue en français était "A la Claire Fontaine": The first song I heard in French was 'A la Claire Fontaine'.

****

CINQUANTIEME (50e) LEÇON

De l'histoire de la langue

1 Que savons-nous de cette langue que nous parlons tous les jours ? Quelles sont ses origines, d'où viennent sa grammaire et ses mots ?

2 Pendant les premiers siècles après Jésus-Christ, les envahisseurs romains, les colons et les marchands apportèrent une langue latine **(1)**

*****

C'est la dernière voiture qui soit sortie de l'usine avant qu'elle ne ferme: It was the last car to leave the factory before it closed.

C'était le plus beau film que j'aie jamais vu: It was the most beautiful film I have ever seen.

La seule personne qui sache quelque chose de l'affaire est Monsieur Blanc: The only person who knows anything about the affair is Mr Blanc.

Not difficult, as you can see, but requires attention.

Your knowledge of grammar and vocabulary is by now far and away sufficient to allow you to enjoy the pleasure of reading French literature. In the coming lessons, we will present you with some of the classics and we hope this will encourage you to read more - and more modern authors - for your own enjoyment.

Answer to the puzzle in Lesson 48: *Quelqu'un ayant souffert d'une crise cardiaque n'aurait jamais mis du sel à table pour lui-même; c'était donc pour son invité - qui l'a assassiné.*

****

50th LESSON

About the history of the language

1 What do we know about this language we speak every day? What are its origins, where do its grammar and its words come from?

2 During the first centuries after Jesus Christ, Roman invaders, colonists and merchants brought a Latin language

NOTES

(1) Notice the pronunciation [zhayzoo kree]. B.C. = *avant Jésus-Christ.* A.D. = *après Jésus-Christ.* A Christian is *un chrétien* but Christianity is *le christianisme.*

3 bien différente de celle des poètes et penseurs de l'Empire romain, étant plus populaire. **(2) (3)**

4 Elle supplanta petit à petit les langues régionales gauloises et devint le gallo-romain. **(4)**

5 Plus tard, vers le Xe siècle, on retrouve deux groupes de langues à peu près séparés par le cours de la Loire : **(5)**

6 la langue d'oc dans le sud du pays et la langue d'oïl dans le nord, ces deux mots correspondant aux différentes façons de dire ''oui''. **(6) (N.1)**

7 Lentement mais sûrement, ce fut la langue d'oïl - celle parlée en Ile-de-France et par la famille royale qui prit le dessus.

8 Mais le français n'était pas encore fixé, il n'y avait pas d'orthographe officielle, le même mot étant orthographié de plusieurs façons. **(7)**

NOTES (suite)

(2) To be different from: *être différent de. Nous sommes très différents l'un de l'autre:* We're very different one from the other. When the adjective is in the plural, it is usually placed **before** the noun: *différentes personnes ont dit que... ... correspondant aux différentes façons de dire ''oui''* (line 6). Although the verb *différer* does exist, meaning to differ, French prefers a paraphrase: *Ils ne s'accordent pas sur ce point:* They differ about this point.
Be careful *différer* also means to defer, to put off. *Une émission en différé:* a recorded programme, as opposed to *une émission en direct:* a live programme.

(3) A word which can lead to confusion; its etymology is the Latin word for 'the people' and *populaire* retains some of the feeling of being close to the people. For example: *les classes populaires* are the working classes, *une manifestation populaire* is a mass demonstration, *une chanson populaire* is a folk song, etc. The notion of popular in English is rendered by *succès* in French: a popular novel would be *un roman à succès* or a popular song *une chanson à la mode* (pop music is *la musique 'pop'!*). Sometimes, the idea of success and of being with or from the people is the same: to make onself popular: *se rendre populaire*. In opinion polls, so beloved of the French, the speak of: *la cote de popularité:* the popularity rating.

3   very different from that of the poets and thinkers of the Roman Empire, being more uneducated.

4   It supplanted the regional Gallic languages and became Gallo-Roman.

5   Later, towards the 10th century, we come across two groups of languages, almost separated by the flow of the Loire river:

6   the 'langue d'oc' in the south of the country and the 'langue d'oïl' in the north, these two words corresponding to the different ways of saying 'yes'.

7   Slowly but surely, it was the 'langue d'oïl' - that spoken in the Isle de France and by the royal family which gained the upper hand.

8   But French was not yet fixed, there was no official spelling, the same word being spelled in different ways.

NOTES (suite)

(4) *Romain* designates anything appertaining to the Roman Empire: *l'année romaine, l'empereur romain,* etc. There is another adjective, *roman(-ane)* which describes peoples and civilisations conquered by the Romans.
Les langues romanes sont écrites en caractères romains: Romance languages are written in Roman characters.

(5) Remember the different meanings of *un cours ?! Le cours du Rhône:* the flow (or course) of the Rhône, *un cours particulier:* a private lesson, *l'examen est en cours:* the examination is in progress, *au cours de l'été:* during summer.
Don't confuse it with the feminine noun *la cour* (see line 13), which means a court, either royal or legal - or simply a courtyard. Remember, always, to learn your genders.

(6) Although it was the 'langue d'oïl' which became French as we know it, *le Languedoc* (and the *Roussillon*) is a province covering five *départements* in the south and south west. The regional language, which still exists, is called *l'occitan.*

(7) We know the verb *épeler* whence we get 'to spell'; we now meet another verb which has the same translation but a different, more complex, sense: *orthographier. Epeler* means to read out, one by one, the letters of a word, to spell out. An official would say: *Voulez-vous m'épeler votre nom s'il vous plaît ?* But *orthographier* contains the idea of convention and correctness: it is the **only correct** way to spell a word. *Une faute d'orthographe* is more than just a spelling mistake - it is a mistake that breaks grammatical conventions. One's handwriting is *l'écriture* (f) and *un autographe* is either an autograph or a hand-written letter. The latter is most often expressed by *une lettre manuscrite.*

9 Enfin, au XVIe siècle, Malherbe vint ; ce poète et auteur commença l'œuvre de la fixation de la langue. **(8)**

10 Un autre grand événement fut la fondation de l'Académie française en 1635 : le français était en train de devenir la langue que nous connaissons aujourd'hui.

11 Justement, on parle aujourd'hui d'une ''crise du français'', d'invasion de mots étrangers :

12 il n'en est rien, sinon peut-être un manque de souplesse de la part de ceux qui décident de ce qui est ''bon'' et de ce qui est ''mauvais''. **(N.2)**

13 Cette langue qui fut celle des cours royales étrangères reste de nos jours celle de la diplomatie, de la mode, de la cuisine, des arts... certains diraient de l'amour ! **(5)**

14 Elle est précise, juste et claire - un auteur célèbre a écrit : ce qui n'est pas clair n'est pas français, **(9)**

15 mais elle est aussi une langue littéraire magnifique, souple et sensuelle. Nous allons vous présenter quelques-uns des meilleurs auteurs avec des extraits de leur œuvre. **(10)**

NOTES (suite)

(8) The expression *'Enfin Malherbe vint'* is an old chestnut in French *lycées* where schoolchildren are taught that it was largely due to the influence of this sixteenth century poet that verse-forms were tightened and the language itself was codified. This is to some extent true. The founding of *l'Académie française* by Richelieu,

EXERCICES

1. Parlons de l'affaire des diamants : qu'en savez-vous ? 2. Ces deux étudiants sont à peu près au même niveau. 3. Lentement mais sûrement, c'est le plus petit qui a pris le dessus. 4. Ils ont prétendu que les diamants avaient été volés. Il n'en est rien. 5. Ce fut la langue des cours royales, maintenant c'est celle de la diplomatie. 6. Certains diraient que c'est une langue très sensuelle.

9 Finally, in the sixteenth century, Malherbe arrived; this poet and author began the work of fixing the language.

10 Another great event was the founding of the French Academy in 1635; French was becoming the language we know today.

11 Indeed, people talk today of a 'crisis of French', of an invasion of foreign words:

12 nothing of the sort unless there is a lack of flexibility on the side of those who decide what is 'right' and what is 'wrong'.

13 This language, which was the one spoken in foreign royal courts, remains nowadays the one used in diplomacy, fashion, cooking, arts... some people would say in love!

14 It is precise, accurate and clear - a famous author wrote: what is not clear is not French

15 but it is also a magnificent literary language, flexible and sensual. We are going to introduce you to some of the best authors with extracts from their works.

NOTES (suite)

seven years after Malherbe's death, institutionalized the French language. The *Académie,* whose members are called *les Immortels* exists today. The presence of such an official body has, in recent years, made it difficult for French to adapt to modern demands, especially in technical fields.

The quotation, incidentally, is from Boileau.

(9) *Juste* (the adjective is both masculine and feminine) has the English meaning of just, i.e. fair, and also the sense of accurate, exacte: *Quelle est l'heure juste ?:* What's the right time? *Le mot juste:* the right word for the situation.

Cette guitare n'est pas juste: This guitar is out of tune.

On m'a dit que vous l'avez vue. Est-ce juste ?: I was told you had seen her. Is that correct?

Juste is also an adverb. *Frapper juste:* to strike an accurate blow. *Ça tombe juste:* that happened at just the right moment.

(10) Remember: *une œuvre:* a work - *un œuvre:* the complete works of an artist, etc.

EXERCISES: 1. Let's talk about the affair of the diamonds: what do you know about it? **2.** These two students are at almost the same level. **3.** Slowly but surely, the smaller one gained the upper hand. **4.** They insisted that the diamonds had been stolen? Nothing of the sort. **5.** It was the language of the Royal Courts, now it's that of diplomacy. **6.** Certain people would say it's a very sensual language.

213

Mettez les mots qui manquent.
Fill in the blanks.

1 . . . . *il* . . . . *les langues*

régionales.

Little by little it will supplant regional languages.

2 . . *la langue française, Boileau* . . . .

"Enfin Malherbe . . . ."

Of the French language, Boileau wrote: 'Finally, Malherbe came'.

3 *Les langues gauloises* . . . . . . *remplacées par le Gallo-*

romain.

The Gallic languages were replaced by Gallo-Roman.

4 . . . *élève fait beaucoup de* . . . . . .

. . . .

This pupil makes a lot of spelling mistakes.

****

CINQUANTE ET UNIEME (51ᵉ) LEÇON

La vie de Victor Hugo (1)

1 Victor Hugo fut la plus grande figure de la
littérature française du XIXᵉ siècle ; son œuvre
était très diversifiée - romans, drames, poésie,
(2)

NOTES

(1) We are now going to introduce you to some of the major figures
of French literature and their works. We will give you biographi -
cal sketches - as here - written in 'text-book' style (revise the
different forms of the *passé simple*) to acquaint you with a formal
register still very prevalent in reference books. On the other hand,
so as not to burden you with too much information, and to
encourage your own powers of assimilation our text-notes will

5 . . . . *d'une crise du français ; il* . . ' . .

. . . .

People speak of a crisis of French; nothing of the sort!

Mots qui manquaient :

1. Petit à petit - supplantera - **2.** De - écrivit - vint **3.** - furent - **4.** Cet - fautes d'orthographe **5.** On parle - n'en est rien!

****

51st LESSON

The life of Victor Hugo

1 Victor Hugo was the greatest figure in French literature of the nineteenth century; his work was very varied - novels, plays, poetry

NOTES (suite)

contain the minimum of information necessary. We hope this will encourage you to use dictionaries and read other works of reference.

(2) In a literary sense *le drame* is drama and *un drame* a serious play; by extension, it can be used, as in line 13 to mean a catastrophic event (less strong than *une tragédie;* compare lines 13 and 17). Hyperbole has brought it into the realm of familiar speech. *Il ne faut pas en faire un drame !:* Don't make a scene about it!

2 et il réussit dans tous ces genres, étant un homme à la fois politique, populaire et le témoin de son temps.

3 Sa vie oscillait entre la gloire publique et la tragédie personnelle - et tout fut reflété dans une production artistique prodigieuse.

4 Hugo naquit à Besançon en 1802 et eut une enfance heureuse. Il effectua plusieurs séjours à l'étranger - en Italie et en Espagne - en suivant son père qui était général et comte de l'Empire. **(3)**

5 Il montra très jeune non seulement sa vocation littéraire mais aussi cette vision de l'homme et de l'artiste qui allait diriger sa vie. **(N.3)**

6 ''Je veux être Chateaubriand ou rien !'' écrivit-il en 1816. **(4)**

7 Deux années plus tard, il publia son premier roman dont le succès convainquit son père de son talent alors que celui-ci le destinait à une carrière académique.

8 En 1819, avec ses frères, il fonda un journal et, en même temps, il tomba amoureux d'Adèle Foucher, qu'il épousa en 1823.

9 Sa carrière de poète débuta la même année, et il publia aussi deux autres romans. C'était l'époque du schisme entre le classicisme et le romantisme.

10 Hugo se déclara d'abord conciliateur entre ces deux tendances, mais il était en fait plus tourné vers le romantisme.

11 Entre 1827 et 1830, il publia trois pièces de théâtre dont la dernière - Hernani - provoqua une vraie bataille entre le monde littéraire traditionnel et une nouvelle vague de jeunes écrivains.

2 and he succeeded in all these genres, being at the same time a politician, a man of the people and the witness of his time.

3 His life swung between public glory and personal tragedy - and everything was reflected in a prodigious artistic production.

4 Hugo was born in Besançon in 1802 and had a happy childhood. He made several trips abroad - to Italy and to Spain - following his father who was a general and a count of the Empire.

5 Very young, he showed not only his literary vocation but also that vision of the man and the artist which was to direct his life.

6 'I want to be Chateaubriand or nothing' he wrote in 1816.

7 Two years later he published his first novel, the success of which convinced his father of his talent, whereas the latter had destined him for an academic career.

8 In 1819, with his brothers, he founded a newspaper and, at the same time, he fell in love with Adèle Foucher, whom he married in 1823.

9 His career as a poet began in the same year, and he also published two other novels. It was the time of the schism between classicism and romanticism.

10 Hugo declared himself first of all the conciliator between these two schools but he was, in fact, more orientated towards romanticism.

11 Between 1827 and 1830 he published three plays, the last of which - Hernani - provoked a real battle between the literary Establishment and a new wave of young writers.

NOTES (suite)

(3) *Effectuer:* to carry out, to execute, etc., is often used in compounds where English would use 'to make'. *Effectuer un paiement:* to make a payment. *Le savant effectua plusieurs expériences:* The scientist made/carried out several experiments.

(4) François-René Chateaubriand (1768-1848) was the model for a lot of Hugo's ideals: writer, politician and man of action, his life was guided by a sense of honour and duty.

12 Ces derniers, en soutenant la pièce, en assurèrent le succès et, enfin, le triomphe du romantisme et de l'art nouveau. **(5)**

13 Hugo commença alors à connaître la gloire artistique - et le drame personnel ; son salon était devenu le rendez-vous du ''Tout Paris'' littéraire, **(6)**

14 mais sa femme Adèle commença à avoir une liaison avec l'auteur - et l'ami d'Hugo - Sainte-Beuve.

15 Hugo, à son tour, s'éprit de Juliette Drouet, qui devint sa maîtresse et sa compagne fidèle. **(7)**

16 Ce fut à cette époque qu'il écrivit l'un de ses chefs-d'œuvre : Notre-Dame de Paris.

17 Sa vie - toujours partagée entre la célébrité et la souffrance - connut une nouvelle tragédie en 1843 lorsque le premier de ses quatre enfants - Léopoldine - se noya dans un accident de bateau.

18 Peut-être fut-ce à cause de cette perte cruelle qu'il se lança dans la vie politique. **(8)**

NOTES (suite)

(5) *Soutenir:* apart from its physical sense of to hold up - *Cette colonne soutient le bâtiment:* This column holds up the whole building -, there is a metaphorical sense of to support, to giving one's backing to. *Les députés de l'opposition ont soutenu la motion:* The opposition Members of Parliament supported the motion.

12   These latter, by supporting the play, assured its success and, finally, the triumph of romanticism and the new art.

13   Hugo then began to enjoy artistic glory - and personal crisis; his salon had become the meeting-place of the Tout-Paris literati

14   but his wife Adèle began to have an affair with the author - and friend of Hugo's - Sainte-Beuve.

15   Hugo, in turn, became enamoured of Juliette Drouet, who became his mistress and his faithful companion.

16   It was at this time that he wrote one of his masterpieces: Notre-Dame de Paris.

17   His life - always split between celebrity and suffering - underwent a new tragedy in 1843 when the first of his four children - Léopoldine - drowned in a boating accident.

18   Perhaps it was because of this cruel loss that he launched himself into political life.

NOTES (suite)

The similar verb *supporter* is more often used to mean to tolerate: *Je ne supporte plus ses actions:* I can no longer stand his actions. Be careful, however: *un supporteur:* a supporter (or, simply, *un supporter!*). *Un souteneur:* a pimp!

(6) A pecularity in the use of *tout* in front of the name of a city which is in the feminine. We would write *Toute Rome est paralysée par la grève:* The whole of Rome is paralysed by the strike. Here we are considering the city. But if we are talking about the people of the city, we would say: *Tout Rome attend l'arrivée du Président français:* The whole of Rome is waiting for the arrival of the French president.

So, when hyphenated *le Tout-Rome, le Tout-Paris,* we are talking about 'the upper crust' of these cities. We can qualify them by adding different adjectives: *le Tout-Paris littéraire, le Tout-Londres musical.*

(7) *S'éprendre de quelqu'un* is a more fanciful way of saying *tomber amoureux de quelqu'un; s'éprendre de quelque chose:* to take a liking to something. The past participle is *épris(e).*

(8) *Il viendra peut-être:* Perhaps he will come. The hyphen is very important when writing this adverb. Look at this sentence: *Il peut être admis:* He (it) may be admitted. Here we are dealing with a verbal group (plural: *peuvent être*).

Peut-être (adverb) carries the notion of possibility - or speculation. The latter shade of meaning may be enhanced by inverting the auxiliary. *Peut-être est-elle malade* is more speculative than *Elle est peut-être malade.* This nuance concerns written French much more than the spoken language.

19 Nommé pair de France en 1845, il combattit en libéral pour les droits des peuples. Il essaya de soulever le peuple de Paris contre le prince Louis-Napoléon

20 mais en vain, et, craignant l'arrestation, il fuit le pays en décembre 1851.

21 Hugo l'exilé, d'abord à Bruxelles, se réfugia enfin dans les îles anglo-normandes ; du haut des falaises de Guernesey, il put contempler les côtes de France **(9)**

22 et il ressentit le besoin de s'expliquer - de se venger.

23 Il publia une série de pamphlets et d'écrits sur la situation politique dans son pays - et c'est à Guernesey aussi

24 qu'il acheva son roman peut-être le plus célèbre : Les Misérables. **(10)**

25 En 1870, Victor Hugo put regagner Paris, mais la tristesse guettait toujours son bonheur : sa femme mourut en 1868 et son fils, Charles, trois ans après.

26 Toujours actif en littérature et en politique, Hugo décéda en 1885, écrivain du siècle et écho de son époque.

27 ''Ce siècle est à la barre et je suis son témoin.'' **(11)**

NOTES (suite)

(9) *L'exil* (m): exile, the state of being excluded from one's country; *l'exilé(e):* the person who is exiled.

EXERCICES

1. Un drame s'est produit hier dans la capitale : un homme a été assassiné. **2.** Il l'ignorait mais cette jeune fille allait devenir sa femme. **3.** Il a écrit trois pièces dont la dernière était une grande réussite. **4.** Monsieur, je vous assure de mon soutien entier. **5.** Il fut nommé directeur de la société. **6.** Ils ont effectué plusieurs séjours à l'étranger pendant leur enfance.

19 Appointed Peer of France in 1845 he fought as a liberal for the rights of peoples. He tried to raise the people of Paris against Prince Louis Napoleon

20 but in vain and, fearing arrest, he fled the country in December 1851.

21 Hugo the exile, first in Brussels, found refuge finally in the Channel Islands; from the top of the cliffs of Guernsey, he was able to contemplate the French coast

22 and he felt the need to explain himself - and to avenge himself.

23 He published a series of pamphlets and writings on the political situation in his country - and it was in Guernsey, too,

24 that he finished perhaps his most famous novel: Les Misérables.

25 In 1870, Victor Hugo was able to go back to Paris, but sadness always dogged his happiness: his wife died in 1868 and his son, Charles, three years after.

26 Still active in literature and politics, Hugo died in 1885, writer of the century and echo of his time.

27 'This century is appearing in court and I am its witness.'

NOTES (suite)

(10) *Achever:* to conclude, to finish off a piece of work. *Aussitôt que j'aurai achevé ce travail, je vous enverrai la facture:* As soon as I have finished off this piece of work, I'll send you the bill.

(11) The quotation is from *'l'Année Terrible'* (1872).

EXERCISES: 1. A terrible incident occurred yesterday in the capital: a man was murdered. **2.** He was unaware of it, but this young girl was to become his wife. **3.** He wrote three plays, the last of which was a great success. **4.** Sir, I assure you of my entire support. **5.** He was appointed director of the company. **6.** They made several trips abroad during their childhood.

Mettez les mots qui manquent.
Fill in the blanks.

1 . . . . . - . . . . - . . *à cause de cela qu'il a quitté*

le pays.

Perhaps it was because of that that he left the country.

2 *Au bout de vingt ans, il avait* . . . . . . *trois*

. . . . . - ' . . . . . .

At the end of twenty years, he had finished three masterpieces.

3 *Nous allons* . . . . *un certain nombre*

d' . . . .

We are going to carry out a certain number of experiments.

4 *Il ne le savait pas, mais ses professeurs* . . . .

. . . . . *une grande influence sur son œuvre.*

He did not know it, but his teachers were to have a great influence

on his work.

****

CINQUANTE-DEUXIEME (52ᵉ) LEÇON

Les Misérables (1)

1 (Gavroche, panier à la main, va chercher des munitions sur les cadavres gisant devant la barricade - en pleine vue des soldats.) (2)

2 ''Il rampait à plat ventre, galopait à quatre pattes, prenait son panier aux dents, se tordait, glissait, serpentait d'un mort à l'autre

NOTES

(1) This vast masterpiece is perhaps Hugo's best known work abroad. It is both an epic novel - with majestically described scenes like the battle of Waterloo - and a humanitarian novel which advances education, social justice and charity as the only weapons against ignorance and poverty. (Remember *la misère* means poverty.) This particular scene - the death of Gavroche - is one of the best-known parts of the book: how the impudent, courageous *gamin* scales the barricades under fire to collect up ammunition from the

5 *Il . . . . un roman . . . . le succès*

. . . . son père de son talent.

He wrote a novel the success of which convinced his father of his

talent.

Mots qui manquaient :

1. Peut-être (notice the hyphen) - était-ce - **2.** - achevé - chefs-
d'œuvre **3.** - effectuer - expériences **4.** - allaient avoir **5.** - écrivit - dont
- convainquit.

****

52nd LESSON

Les Misérables

1 (Gavroche, basket in hand, goes to take ammunition
   from the corpses lying in front of the barricade - in
   full view of the soldiers.)
2 'He crawled flat on his stomach, scampered on all
   fours, took his basket between his teeth, twisted
   around, slid and snaked from one corpse to another

NOTES (suite)

dead soldiers' cartridge belts. (Raymond Bernard's 1933 film
adaptation of the book made this a memorable moment of cinema
as well.) We have abridged it very slightly for reasons of space.
(2) There are several verbs in French which only exist in certain forms.
We called these 'defective verbs' (in English 'can' and 'must' are
defective). The infinitive of this verb is *gésir* but the only forms
commonly found are the present participle *gisant,* the third person
singular in the expression *ci-gît:* (here lies...) - found on
tombstones - and, sometimes, the imperfect. The idea is of lying
helpless or dead. (*Un gisant* is a recumbent stone figure on a
tomb.)

3   et vidait la giberne ou la cartouchière comme un singe ouvre une noix. **(3)**

4   De la barricade, dont il était encore assez près, on n'osait lui crier de revenir, de peur d'appeler l'attention sur lui. **(4)**

5   A force d'aller en avant, il parvint au point où le brouillard de la fusillade devenait transparent, **(5)**

6   si bien que les tirailleurs, massés à l'angle de la rue, se montrèrent soudainement quelque chose qui remuait dans la fumée.

7   Au moment où Gavroche débarrassait de ses cartouches un sergent gisant près d'une borne, une balle frappa le cadavre. **(6)**

8   — Fichtre ! fit Gavroche. Voilà qu'on me tue mes morts.

9   Une deuxième balle fit étinceler le pavé à côté de lui. Une troisième renversa son panier. Gavroche regarda et vit que cela venait des tirailleurs de la banlieue. **(7) (8) (9)**

LE BROUILLARD ÉTAIT DEVENU TRANSPARENT SI BIEN QUE NOUS AVONS PU RETROUVER LA ROUTE

NOTES (suite)

(3) Notice the way the different verbs in the imperfect build up a picture not act by act, but by describing the movements and their cumulative effect. This effect, like brush strokes on a canvas, is used several times in the extract - e.g. line 15 - and is difficult to render exactly because the imperfect gives the idea of continuity not translated by our past tenses. We have used the frequentative (... would go, etc.).

3 and emptied the cartridge pouch or belt like a monkey opening a nut.

4 From the barricade, which he was still fairly close to, nobody dared call him to come back, for fear of drawing attention to him.

5 By constantly going forward, he reached a point where the smoke of the firing had become transparent,

6 so that the riflemen, in a bunch at the corner of the street, were suddenly able to point out to each other something moving around in the smoke.

7 At the very moment that Gavroche was removing the cartridges from a sergeant lying dead near a post, a bullet struck the corpse.

8 — Good heavens! said Gavroche, now they're starting to kill my corpses.

9 A second bullet struck sparks from the paving beside him. A third overturned his basket. Gavroche looked and saw that the firing was coming from the Suburban Guard riflemen.

NOTES (suite)

(4) *Dont* because we say *près de*.
Elle est près du mur or *Le mur dont elle est près*.

(5) *A force de:* by dint of, through the repetition of an action. *A force de demander, il a reçu la permission:* Through asking repeatedly, he received permission. *A force de trop travailler, il s'est rendu malade:* Through working too hard, he made himself sick. *A force de* contains the idea of repeated action.

(6) Notice the beautifully concise construction of this sentence.

(7) Literally: made spark; *une étincelle:* a spark. Remember French uses *faire* more extensively than any other auxiliary (some 300 uses are quoted). English: struck sparks.

(8) *Un pavé* is a paving-stone or a cobble-stone. It also means the paving itself. In 1968, one of the students' slogans was *'Sous les pavés, la plage'* : 'Under the cobbles is the beach' (i.e. freedom). In a restaurant, *un pavé* is a thick steak.

(9) The incident takes place between Republicans and the forces of Louis-Philippe during the first riots of 1832 (which were to be repeated in 1834). The soldiers used to put down the rebellion came from different regiments. The one referred to here was *Les Gardes Nationaux de la Banlieue de Paris*.

10 Il se dressa tout droit, debout, les cheveux au vent, les mains sur les hanches, l'œil fixé sur les gardes nationaux qui tiraient, et chanta :

11 ''On est laid à Nanterre, C'est la faute à Voltaire
Et bête à Palaiseau, C'est la faute à Rousseau.'' **(10)**

12 Puis il ramassa son panier, y remit, sans en perdre une seule, les cartouches qui en étaient tombées, et, avançant vers la fusillade, alla dépouiller une autre giberne. **(6)**

13 Là, une quatrième balle le manqua encore. Gavroche chanta [...]. Cela continua ainsi quelque temps.

14 Le spectacle était épouvantable et charmant. Gavroche, fusillé, taquinait la fusillade. Il avait l'air de s'amuser beaucoup [...]. On le visait sans succès, on le manquait toujours.

15 Il se couchait, puis se redressait, s'effaçait dans un coin de porte, puis bondissait, disparaissait, reparaissait, se sauvait, revenait, ripostait à la mitraille par des pieds de nez. [...] **(11)**

16 La barricade tremblait ; lui, il chantait. Ce n'était pas un enfant, ce n'était pas un homme ; c'était un étrange gamin fée. [...] **(12)**

17 Les balles couraient après lui, il était plus leste qu'elles. Il jouait on ne sait quel effrayant jeu de cache-cache avec la mort.

18 Une balle pourtant, mieux ajustée ou plus traître que les autres, finit par atteindre l'enfant feu follet. On vit Gavroche chanceler, puis il s'affaissa.

NOTES (suite)

(10) *C'est la faute à Voltaire et C'est la faute à Rousseau* were popular rallying cries of those against the 1789 Revolution: the other part of the song - mentioning two Parisian suburbs and casting aspersions on their inhabitants - was Gavroche's way of mocking his enemies.

10 He drew himself upright, on his feet, his hair blowing in the wind, hands on hips, staring at the National Guardsmen who were shooting at him and sang:

11 'They're ugly in Nanterre, and it's the fault of old Voltaire and dumb in Palaiseau, and it's the fault of Rousseau'.

12 Then he picked up his basket and, without dropping a single one, put back all the cartridges that had fallen out; advancing towards the gunfire, he went to empty another pouch.

13 There, yet a fourth bullet missed him. Gavroche sang. This continued in the same way for some time.

14 The sight was horrifying and charming. Gavroche was shot at and teased the fusillade. He seemed to be enjoying himself greatly. They aimed without success, and always missed him.

15 He would lie down, jump up, hide in a doorway, then he would leap around, disappearing and reappearing, running away and coming back, and cocking snooks in answer to the hail of shots.

16 Those on the barricade were trembling - and he would sing! This was not a child, this was not a man: it was a strange urchin fairy.

17 Bullets whistled after him, but he was the sprightlier. He was playing who knows what terrifying game of hide-and-seek with death.

18 However, one bullet - better aimed or more treacherous than the others - finally hit the young will-o'-the-wisp. Gavroche was seen to stagger then sink to the ground.

NOTES (suite)

(11) See note 3. *La mitraille* is a hail of bullets. In more modern French, we find *une mitrailleuse:* a machine-gun and *une mitraillette:* a sub-machine gun.
Notice, apart from the occasional archaic word (e.g. *giberne*) how 'modern' the language is.

(12) Here, and in the last line, are two examples of beautiful juxtaposition of words. *Un gamin* is a street urchin and *une fée,* a fairy. What a wonderful image. *Une grande âme:* a great soul. The use of *petite* in no way diminishes the second adjective, it simply indicates that although Gavroche was small, his soul was still great.

19 Toute la barricade poussa un cri ; mais Gavroche n'était tombé que pour se redresser ; [...] un long filet de sang rayait son visage,

20 il éleva ses deux bras en l'air, regarda du côté d'où était venu le coup, et se mit à chanter :

21 ''Je suis tombé par terre, C'est la faute à Voltaire
Le nez dans le ruisseau, C'est la faute à ...''

22 Il n'acheva point. Une seconde balle du même tireur l'arrêta court. Cette fois, il s'abattit la face contre le pavé, et ne remua plus.

23 Cette petite grande âme venait de s'envoler.'' (12)

We hope that this brief extract will encourage you to dip into more of Hugo's work, especially now you have seen that, for all his reputation as being a 'classic' author, he is extremely readable.

EXERCICES

1. Le club dont il est membre est très exclusif. 2. A force de pratiquer la langue tous les jours, vous la maîtriserez très vite. 3. Le brouillard était devenu transparent si bien que nous avons pu retrouver la route. 4. Ah ce bruit ! Voilà qu'on m'empêche de travailler ! 5. Ils habitent je ne sais quelle banlieue de Paris. 6. Une balle a fini par atteindre Gavroche en pleine figure.

*****

Essayer de reproduire ces deux phrases dont on vous donne les traductions... et quelques mots :

1 At the very moment that Gavroche was removing the cartridges

from a sergeant lying dead near a post, a bullet struck the corpse.

Au . . . . Gavroche . . . .

19 The whole barricade let out a cry, but Gavroche had only fallen to pick himself up once more; a long trickle of blood ran down his face,

20 he lifted his arms to the sky, looked over to where the shot had come from and began to sing:

21 'I fell to the ground, it's the fault of Voltaire
The nose in the gutter, and it's the fault of...'

22 He never finished. A second bullet from the same marksman stopped him dead. This time his face struck the cobbles and he no longer moved.

23 That young, great soul had just flown away.'

EXERCISES: 1. The club of which he is a member is very exclusive. **2.** Through practising the language every day, you will master it very quickly. **3.** The mist had cleared up so much so that we were able to find the road again. **4.** Oh, the noise! There they are, preventing me from working! **5.** They live in I don't know which suburb of Paris. **6.** A bullet finally struck Gavroche full in the face.

*****

de . . . . *un* . . . .

près d' . . . ., *une balle* . . . . . . *le* . . . .

2 Then he picked up his basket and, without dropping a single one,

put back all the cartridges that had fallen out.

Puis il . . . . *son* . . . ., ... ,

sans . . *perdre une* . . . . . ., *les* . . . . *qui*

. . . .

Mots qui manquaient :

1. - moment où - débarrassait - ses cartouches - sergent gisant - une borne - frappa - cadavre. 2. - ramassa - panier, y remit, - en - seule - cartouches - en étaient tombées.

The aim of the last two exercises is to give you the feel of the precise nature of French syntax.

CINQUANTE-TROISIEME (53ᵉ) LEÇON

Les Régions de France - Le Sud-Ouest

1 Nous continuons notre périple à travers la France et la Navarre en faisant un saut dans le Sud-Ouest. **(1) (2) (3)**

2 La région commence sur la côte de l'océan Atlantique (de Bordeaux à la frontière espagnole vers Biarritz)

3 et, en suivant les Pyrénées enneigées, elle atteint la mer Méditerranée et va presque jusqu'au port de Marseille.

LES GENG DU SUD-OUEST SONT FIERG, BAGARREURG ET TRÈS SYMPATHIQUES

4 Basques, Occitans, un peu Sarrasins, un peu Catalans, un peu Espagnols,

5 les habitants du Sud-Ouest sont fiers, bagarreurs et très sympathiques. (D'Artagnan, le héros des *Trois Mousquetaires,* était de ce pays.) **(4) (5)**

6 Les industries sont variées : vins à Bordeaux, technologie et avions à Toulouse, pruneaux à Agen, foie gras et truffes à Périgueux... **(6)**

53rd LESSON

The regions of France - The South-West

1　We are continuing our tour through France and Navarre with a quick trip to the south-west.

2　The region begins on the Atlantic coast (from Bordeaux to the Spanish border near Biarritz)

3　and, following the snow-capped Pyrenees, it reaches the Mediterranean Sea and runs almost to the port of Marseille.

4　Basques, Occitans, a little Saracen, a little Catalan, a little Spanish,

5　the inhabitants of the South-West are proud, pugnacious and very 'sympathiques'. (D'Artagnan, the hero of *The Three Musketeers,* was from this region.)

6　The industries are varied: wines in Bordeaux, technology and aeroplanes in Toulouse, prunes in Agen, liver pâté and truffles in Perigueux...

NOTES

(1) *Faire un tour:* to make a trip (although we can say *Je vais faire le tour du jardin/du pâté de maisons:* I'm going for a walk round the garden/the block.
Un périple is a much longer tour.
We also saw (Lesson 51 line 4) *faire* (or *effectuer) un séjour.* This gives us the idea that the traveller stays some time in the country - the case of Hugo makes this sense clear.

(2) The kingdom of Navarre (now part of Spain) was once annexed and joined to France. Later, in the sixteenth century it became part of Spain while the *basse Navarre* became French. The expression *de France et de Navarre* means: in every corner of France, high and low.

(3) *Faire un saut* (see also Note 1) means to take a quick trip. *Je ferai un saut en voiture pour venir te voir:* I'll pop over in the car to see you. *Faites un saut si vous avez le temps:* Drop in if you have time.

(4) *Se bagarrer* is a familiar way of saying *se battre. Les deux supporteurs se sont bagarrés. Une bagarre* is the noun. *Un bagarreur* is someone who likes fighting so, depending on your point of view, he/she is either pugnacious or rowdy. (Remember that the definition of an alcoholic is someone you don't like who drinks as much as you!) Everything is a question of context.

(5) As we have said before, there is just no equivalent for this wonderful word (and its diminutive *sympa*). Nice, kind, gentle, polite, O.K., etc. - none of them has enough descriptive power on its own. We'll leave it as... *sympathique.*

(6) Don't confuse *une prune:* a plum, with *un pruneau:* a prune. You may regret it...

7 Et tourisme partout : neige, plages, cheval, campagne, pêche sportive, surf et, si vous préférez, gastronomie. **(7)**

8 Goûtez les fameux cassoulets, le foie gras frais, les petits vins du pays ! **(8)**

9 Et, si vous ''sentez'' bien le pays, vous allez pouvoir parler de religion avec les gens du Sud-Ouest.

10 De leur religion évidemment : le Rugby ! **(9)**

11 Et ils le prennent au sérieux ! Lors d'un match de coupe entre Béziers et Narbonne,

12 l'ailier narbonnais réussit une percée spectaculaire et, prenant ses jambes à son cou, marqua un essai magnifique.

13 Un petit homme dans la foule applaudit très fort en criant : — Bravo ! Oh ! Bravo ! Mais son accent le trahit - il n'était pas du pays !

14 Un énorme supporteur biterrois se retourna vers l'intrus : — Vous êtes Narbonnais ? fit-il. **(10)**

15 — Euh... non, bredouilla l'autre. — Alors vous êtes peut-être Biterrois ? renchérit le malabar. **(11)**

16 — Mais, c'est-à-dire, je suis Parisien. Un moment de lourd silence et le colosse lui dit :

17 — Alors, taisez-vous et ne vous mêlez pas de choses qui ne vous concernent pas !

NOTES (suite)

(7) Leaving out the definite article in front of these nouns gives us the idea that the different activities are to be found in several different places (they are no longer definite but general).
Notice how *neige* then means snow, winter sports, etc., *cheval* horse-riding, pony trekking, etc. ...and *surf?* That's French for surfing!

(8) It is vital to understand the importance the French place on food, each region having its own specialities and different parts of these regions fiercely claiming their version the best. For example *le*

7   And tourism everywhere: snow, beaches, horse-riding, countryside, fishing competitions, surfing and, if you prefer, gastronomy.

8   Taste the famous cassoulets, the fresh liver pâté, the country wines!

9   And if you 'get the feel' of the region you will be able to discuss religion with the people of the South-West.

10   Their religion obviously: rugby!

11   And they take it very seriously! During a cup-match between Béziers and Narbonne,

12   the Narbonese winger broke away spectacularly and, taking to his heels scored a magnificent try.

13   A small man in the crowd applauded very loudly, shouting — Bravo! Oh bravo! But his accent betrayed him: he wasn't from the region!

14   An enormous Béziers supporter turned round to the intruder: — You're from Narbonne? he said.

15 — Er... no, stammered the other. — Then perhaps you're from Béziers? pursued the strapping fellow.

16 — But... that's to say, I'm Parisian. A moment of heavy silence and the giant said to him:

17 — Then shut up, and don't get mixed up in things that don't concern you!

NOTES (suite)

cassoulet, that divine mixture of preserved duck or goose, sausage and beans is the subject of rivalry between three towns: people say that the cassoulet of Castelnaudary is the king, that of Carcassone, the prince and that of Toulouse, the dauphin!

Le foie gras which we weakly translate as liver pâté is a luxurious speciality (whose preparation is rather disgusting) which is traditionally eaten at Christmas - and, in fact, at any other time an excuse can be found.

(9) Interestingly enough, rugby is hardly played at all in the north of France, where football is the traditional game.

(10) *Fit-il,* we came across this literary device in the preceding lesson (line 8); *fit* is, of course, the *passé simple* of *faire* but it is sometimes used instead of *dire* after a statement. - *"Fichtre" fit Gavroche. "Revenez ici" fit-il à haute voix.* It is not commonly used in spoken French.

(11) *Renchérir* literally means to make something more expensive *(cher)* but it is usually found in narratives when a speaker goes one step further in his statements (or goes one better than someone else). It is best understood as: to pursue, to insist.

EXERCICES: 1. La région commence à la côte, suit les Pyrénées et atteint la mer Méditerranée. **2.** Il y a énormément d'activités dans cette région : pêche, cheval, campagne, neige. **3.** Voyant la police arriver, le voleur prit ses jambes à son cou et se cacha. **4.** La firme a réussi une percée spectaculaire sur le marché américain. **5.** Veux-tu faire un saut à la boulangerie ? J'ai oublié le pain. **6.** Après le match les deux équipes de supporteurs se sont battues pendant une heure.

Mettez les mots qui manquent.
Fill in the blanks.

1 *"Taisez-vous"* . . . *le malabar. "Et ne vous mêlez pas de ces*

  choses" . . . . *son compagnon.*

  'Shut up' said the huge man. 'And don't get mixed up in that sort of

  thing' insisted his companion.

2 *Nous* . . . . *un* . . . . *partout en France*

  l'année dernière.

  We made a long trip throughout France last year.

3 *J'ai chaud. Je* . . . . *un* . . . . *dehors.*

  I'm hot. I'm going for a quick walk outside.

****

CINQUANTE-QUATRIEME (54ᵉ) LEÇON

Qu'est la France d'aujourd'hui ?

1 Qu'est-ce qui caractérise la France d'aujourd'hui ? Est-ce encore le commis-boulanger qui livre les baguettes croustillantes au jour levant,

EXERCISES: 1. The region begins at the coast, follows the Pyrenees and reaches the Mediterranean Sea. **2.** There are an enormous number of activities in this region: fishing, riding, country walks, skiing. **3.** Seeing the police arrive, the thief took to his heels and hid. **4.** The firm made a spectacular breakthrough on the American market. **5.** Will you pop out to the baker's? I've forgotten the bread. **6.** After the match the two teams of supporters fought for almost an hour.

4 *Ce . . 'est . . 'un jeu! Ne le . . . . . . pas . .*

. . . . !

It's only a game! Don't take it too seriously!

5 *Comment trouves-tu sa femme ! - Très . . . .*

How do you find his wife? - Nice, kind, gentle, amusing, intelligent,

etc.

Mots qui manquaient :

1. - fit - renchérit - **2.** - avons fait - périple - **3.** - vais faire - tour - **4.** - n - qu - prenez - au sérieux **5.** - sympathique.

This is what we mean by **la pratique du français** - *learning the language through learning about the people and the country.*

****

54th LESSON

What is today's France?

1 What characterises France today? Is it still the baker's-boy delivering crusty bread at day-break

Leçon 54

2   ou ces trains à grande vitesse, ces avions supersoniques, et ces ordinateurs qui sortent des nouveaux centres industriels ?

3   Est-ce la partie de pétanque sur la place du village, sous les platanes et avec les accents et visages de Pagnol, **(1) (2)**

4   ou les jeunes cadres dynamiques qui s'engouf-frent dans les bouches du métro tous les matins pour arriver à huit heures au bureau ? **(3)**

5   Dans cette France d'autoroutes, de voitures neuves, de gratte-ciel, trouve-t-on encore les sentiers paisibles qui mènent aux villages somnolents ? **(4)**

6   A toutes ces questions, l'étudiant peut répondre ''oui'' car, avant tout, la France est un pays de contradictions et de contrastes.

7   Le Général de Gaulle, dans une saillie exaspé-rée, a lancé : — Comment est-il possible de gouverner un pays où il y a trois cent soixante-cinq sortes de fromages ?

8   Depuis la deuxième guerre mondiale, le pays a connu des changements qui ont bouleversé l'édifice social.

9   Plus de quatre millions de personnes ont quitté la campagne pour chercher du travail dans les villes qui n'étaient pas équipées pour un tel afflux ;

2   or these high-speed trains, these supersonic planes and these computers that come out of the new industrial centres?

3   Is it the 'pétanque' game on the village square under the plane trees with the accents and faces of Pagnol,

4   or these young dynamic executives who surge into the métro every morning so as to arrive at 8.00 a.m. at the office?

5   In this France of motorways, of new cars and sky-scrapers, does one still find peaceful tracks leading to sleepy villages?

6   To all these questions, the student may answer 'yes' because, above all, France is a country of contradictions and contrasts.

7   General de Gaulle, in an exasperated sally, said — How is it possible to govern a country where there are three hundred and sixty five sorts of cheese?

8   Since the second world war, the country has undergone changes which have upset the fabric of society.

9   More than four million people left the countryside to look for work in towns which were not equipped for such an influx;

NOTES

(1) *La pétanque* is a game using metal balls *(des boules)* which are thrown at a smaller ball called *le cochonnet*. The game originated in the South (the name comes from two Provencal words meaning 'joined feet' - the feet must be together when the ball is thrown) and is an institution attracting crowds and comment.

(2) Perhaps the most famous game of *Pétanque* took place in the works of Marcel Pagnol (1895-1974) who enshrined the folklore of Provence and Marseilles in a series of books and plays.

(3) The entrances to *métro* stations are called *les bouches*.

(4) *Un gratte-ciel:* a sky-scraper. There is no plural form since the word is a translation from English. Another word often used to describe sky-scrapers, tower-blocks, etc., is *un building*. Needless to say, try to avoid it.

10   une économie artisanale est devenue une économie de grande consommation et les structures sociales et administratives n'étaient pas adaptées à ces changements. **(5)**

11   La modernisation s'est faite non seulement au niveau national mais aussi au niveau individuel.

12   L'introduction des congés payés avant la deuxième guerre a permis au gens d'élever, avec un flair tout ce qu'il y a de français, les loisirs au niveau d'un art. **(6) (7)**

13   Le "week-end" était devenu une institution. **(8)**

14   Avec plus de temps libre et avec une plus grande mobilité, les Français se sont aventurés au-delà de leurs frontières deux fois plus nombreux qu'avant 1939.

15   Le développement des médias - et surtout de la télévision - a ouvert de nouveaux horizons et a fourni matière au passe-temps national : le débat.

16   De nos jours, les habitants d'un Clochemerle se passionneraient pour des événements plus éloignés que ceux concernant leur propre village. **(9)**

17   Toutes ces transformations ne se sont pas faites dans l'unanimité, et peut-être les événements de mai 1968 étaient-ils une expression populaire de malaise. **(10)**

NOTES (suite)

(5) *Un artisan:* an artisan or a craftsman. The adjective *artisanal* is used in contrast to *industriel - la production artisanale:* small-scale skilled production.

(6) *Un congé* has, for principal meaning, leave of absence: (*congé de maladie:* sick leave) but it also has the sense of leaving one's job to go on holiday.
M. Dupont est en congé cette semaine: Mr Dupont is on holiday this week. This sounds more 'official' than *...est en vacances. Les congés payés:* paid holidays were introduced in France in 1936.

(7) *Il est tout ce qu'il y a de charmant:* He's charm itself (literally: everything there is of...) - *tout ce qu'il y a de* followed by an adjective means that the subject is the personification of that quality (or fault).

10   a craft-based economy became a mass consumption one and social and administrative structures were not adapted for these changes.

11   Modernisation happened not only at a national level but also at an individual level.

12   The introduction of paid holidays before the second war allowed people to elevate, with totally Gallic flair, leisure to the level of an art.

13   The 'week-end' had become an institution.

14   With more free time and with greater mobility, the French ventured out beyond their frontiers, twice as numerous as before 1939.

15   The development of the media - and especially television - opened new horizons and provided material for the national pastime: debating.

16   Today, the inhabitants of a Clochemerle would get passionately interested in events further away than those concerning their own village.

17   All these transformations did not take place unanimously, and perhaps the events of May 1968 were a popular expression of unease.

NOTES (suite)

(8) Years ago, when the French - like most other nations - worked on Saturdays, they would speak of *'la semaine anglaise'* i.e. five working days. When the same practice became common in France they simply imported the English word. Some vague attempt was made at Gallicising it: *la fin de semaine* but the import proved hard to uproot. Now offices and factories all over, on Fridays, ring to cries of *'Bon week-end!'*

(9) *Clochemerle,* written by Gabriel Chevallier in 1934, is the archetypal picture of village life in rural France with its rivalries, both political and amourous, its officials and craftsmen. The book, deliciously satirical, centres around a controversial decision to build a public toilet in the village square.

(10) The student riots of May 1968 spread to factories, shops and administrations, who went on the largest mass strike since the war, which almost brought down de Gaulle's government. Motives were varied, but at the base lay a frustration with the way in which economic changes had been pushed through over the heads of the man and woman in the street, further distancing him or her from the decision-making centres. The date remains a landmark in the French popular subconscious and any mention of *'les événements'* as they were coyly called, can still set off a furious debate.

18 Mais que l'on soit rassuré : la douce France restera ce foyer de contradictions, de diversités, de frustrations qui attire l'admiration - et parfois l'incompréhension - du reste du monde. **(11)**

19 Autant on verra les fruits d'une révolution technique et sociale radicale, **(N.5)**

20 autant on entendra le boucher et le notaire changer le monde autour d'un ''canon'' au Café du Commerce. **(12)**

EXERCICES

1. Tu veux faire une partie d'échecs? - Non merci, je n'aime pas les jeux intellectuels. **2.** Dans ces villes ultramodernes, trouve-t-on encore le Café du Commerce ? **3.** Depuis la guerre, la société a connu d'énormes changements qui ont bouleversé l'édifice social. **4.** Malheureusement, les artisans sont en voie de disparition. **5.** C'est une femme tout ce qu'il y a d'élégante. **6.** Le débat a fourni matière à discussion. **7.** Soyez rassuré, vous pourrez toujours partir en vacances.

Mettez les mots qui manquent.
Fill in the blanks.

1 *Ils . . . . le cinéma.*

They are passionately interested in cinema.

2 *. . . . . . vous gagnerez d'argent, ... vous*

payerez d'impôts.

The more you earn money, the more taxes you will pay.

3 *Les changements . . . .*

l'unanimité.

The changes were carried out unanimously.

18 But let us reassure ourselves: gentle France will remain this centre of contradictions, diversities and frustrations which attract the admiration - and sometimes the incomprehension - of the rest of the world.

19 As much as we will see the fruits of a radical technological and social revolution,

20 we will also hear the butcher and the notary changing the world over a glass of wine in the High Street café.

NOTES (suite)

(11) A word frequently come across: it comes from one of the Latin words for 'fire' - focus. So, basically, it means the hearth and, like in most cultures, where the fire burns, there is one's home, one's focal point. *Le foyer* means the home, or the centre of. *Le feu brûlait dans le foyer:* The fire was burning in the hearth. *Ils rentrent tard au foyer:* They come home late.
Ce que je veux, c'est un foyer, un vrai chez-moi: What I want is a home, a real place of my own. In such a context, the word has a more emotional meaning signifying home, family, etc.
Outside this context, it really is the focus, the centre of. *Cette université est un vrai foyer de contestation:* That university is a real centre of protest.

(12) *Le Café du Commerce* is a semi-mythical bar where people gather to discuss the issues of the day: politics, food, horse-racing, etc. *Les conversations du Café du Commerce* are a kind of public gossip-forum; often pejorative since the debaters are largely uninformed.
Un canon: is a familiar word for a glass of red wine.

EXERCISES: 1. Do you want a game of chess? No thankyou, I don't like intellectual games. **2.** In these ultra-modern cities can one still find the local café where everyone meets? **3.** Since the war, the society has undergone enormous changes which have upset the social fabric. **4.** Unfortunately, craftsmen are beginning to disappear. **5.** That woman is elegance itself. **6.** The debate provided discussion-matter. **7.** Reassure yourself, you will still be able to go on holiday.

4 *Le gouvernement a décidé* . . . . *de*

construire des . . . . - . . . .

The government decided above all to build sky-scrapers.

Most idiomatic phrases have more than one equivalent: where this is so, we try to give you one in the translation of the text and another one in the translation of the exercises, so you can see how, depending on the context, there may be a nuance of expression or a slightly different way of phrasing the same idea. Remember that, especially at this level, language is no longer a set of parallel expressions but a complete idiom in itself.

****

CINQUANTE-CINQUIEME (55e) LEÇON

La Presse écrite

1 Malgré l'opinion désobligeante de La Fontaine qui disait que ''tout faiseur de journaux doit tribut au Malin'', **(1) (2)**

2 la presse écrite en France est une industrie qui emploie 90.000 personnes, journalistes, photographes, rédacteurs et pigistes confondus, **(3)**

3 et qui consomme près d'un million de tonnes de papier par an !

4 Chaque jour, quelque douze millions d'exemplaires sont acheminés vers des points de vente, **(4)**

5 qu'il s'agisse de boutiques, de kiosques ou de ''crieurs'' qui vendent les journaux et les périodiques dans la rue.

NOTES

(1) Jean de La Fontaine is the seventeenth century poet best known for his adaptations of Aesop's Fables.

(2) The origin of this word is obviously *le mal* - evil and *Le Malin* was the name given to Satan (*le diable*). It has considerably softened from the time when *malin* meant someone who enjoyed evil (cf. malignant in English). It now has the meaning of smart, cunning; but the link with *mal* still remains and the shrewdness described is not always of divine inspiration.
Faites attention, il est très malin en affaires: Be careful, he's very shrewd in business.
Un sourire malin: a knowing smile.
It is often used sarcastically, when someone's action has the

5 *Ce village est hors des* . . . . *battus.*

This village is off the beaten track.

Mots qui manquaient :

1. - se passionnent pour - **2.** Autant - autant - **3.** - se sont faits dans -
4. - avant tout - gratte-ciel **5.** - sentiers -.

****

55th LESSON

The written press

1 Despite the unkind opinion of La Fontaine who said that 'all makers of newspapers owe tribute to the Devil',

2 the written press in France is an industry which employs 90,000 people, including journalists, photographers, editors and stringers,

3 and which consumes almost one million tonnes of paper per year.

4 Each day some twelve million copies are dispatched to sales points .

5 whether they be shops, kiosks or 'criers' who sell papers and periodicals in the street.

NOTES (suite)

opposite effect desired: *Tu as averti la police, c'est très malin:* You've alerted the police, that's **very** clever, isn't it!
Ne faites pas le malin: Don't try and be smart.
Elle prend un malin plaisir à le faire patienter: She takes a perverse pleasure in making him wait around.

(3) From the verb *confondre* which means to confuse or to confound, this idiom *tous... confondus* means everything taken together; *toutes tendances confondues:* all tendancies taken together; *tous journaux confondus:* all the newspapers as a whole.

(4) We know the noun *un chemin:* a way. *Acheminer vers* means to dispatch to, to direct towards. In the reflexive form we may find a sentence like this: *Ils s'acheminaient vers la maison quand ils rencontrèrent un auto-stoppeur:* They were on the way home when they met a hitch-hiker. As we have told you before, when you come across a new word which seems complex, look for a rootword that you know and, from the context, try and work out its meaning.

6 En moyenne, le Français consomme vingt kilos de journaux par an contre une cinquantaine pour un Américain. **(5)**

7 Mais que le choix est vaste ! Il y a, bien sûr, des grands quotidiens - à Paris on en compte vingt-cinq - **(6)**

8 et en province, il y a quatre fois ce chiffre ; mais on trouve aussi des hebdomadaires, des mensuels et des périodiques de toutes nuances.

9 Peut-on lire ce que l'on veut ? La liberté de la presse est inscrite dans la Constitution,

10 mais cette liberté n'exclut pas la responsabilité juridique : on peut, par exemple, critiquer les décisions, les choix du Président de la République,

11 mais on doit s'arrêter là où commence l'offense au Chef d'Etat.

12 Le Directeur d'un journal peut avoir à répondre de tout ce qui paraît dans sa publication, **(7) (8)**

13 mais ce sont quand même les journalistes et les rédacteurs qui sont responsables de leurs écrits.

6 On average, the French person consumes 20 kilogrammes of newspapers per year, against about fifty for an American.

7 But how vast the choice is! There are, of course, the major dailies - Paris has twenty-five

8 and in the provinces the figure is four times that; but one can also find weeklies, monthlies and periodicals of all shades of opinion.

9 Can one read what one wants ? Freedom of the press is written into the Constitution

10 but this freedom does not exclude judicial responsibility: one may, for example, criticise the decisions and the choices of the President of the Republic

11 but one must stop at the point where offence to the Head of State begins.

12 The Director of a newspaper may have to answer for everything which appears in his publication

13 but, all the same, the journalists and editors are responsible for what they write.

NOTES (suite)

(5) *Le Français moyen:* the average French person. *La moyenne:* the average. *En moyenne:* on average. *Au-dessus de la moyenne:* above average (opposite: *au-dessous*). *Le Moyen Age:* the Middle Ages.

(6) *Il y a trente aéroports en France ; Paris en compte quatre:* There are thirty airports in France; Paris has four.
Il compte parmi ses supporteurs, beaucoup de petits commerçants: Among his supporters, there are many small shopkeepers. This is a more elegant form than the simple verb *avoir* (which, of course, is perfectly correct).

(7) *Réponds au téléphone, s'il te plaît:* Answer the phone please. *Ils doivent répondre de leurs actions:* They have to answer for their actions.
Although on a lesser scale than English phrasal verbs, many French verbs change their meaning depending on the preposition which follows (the 'post position'). Here are a couple more:
Il a décidé de rester: He decided to stay.
Je me suis décidé à partir demain: I made up my mind to leave tomorrow.
Jean m'a demandé de lui prêter ma voiture: John asked me to lend him my car.
L'agent a demandé à voir mes papiers: The policeman asked to see my papers (the second *demander* is more authoritarian then the first).
We will point out any others as we come across them.

(8) Be careful of the following words: *publier:* to publish BUT *un éditeur:* a publisher - *un rédacteur:* an editor.

14 Le plus prestigieux de tous les journaux français est sans doute *Le Monde,* qui fut fondé en 1944.

15 Ce journal très sérieux, de présentation assez austère - il n'y a pas de photographies, par exemple -

16 est lu et en France et à l'étranger par les gens d'influence dans tous les milieux, qui respectent ses opinions

17 même s'ils ne les partagent pas (d'ailleurs *Le Monde* accorde une grande place aux tribunes libres de toutes tendances).

18 Que l'on achète un journal pour les petites annonces ou pour les informations politiques et sociales,

19 pour lire la critique du dernier film sorti ou pour faire les mots croisés,

20 le lecteur est sûr tous les jours de pouvoir choisir parmi un très large éventail d'opinions et d'orientations, qui, pour la plupart, ne doivent rien au diable ! **(9)**

EXERCICES

1. Chaque fois que nous sortons, il fait des réflexions désobligeantes. **2.** Nous avons plusieurs points de vente en région parisienne, **3.** et nos produits y sont acheminés tous les jours. **4.** Je n'ai pas à répondre de ce qu'écrit ce journaliste. **5.** On peut trouver des publications de toutes nuances. **6.** Ce journal, de présentation assez sévère, est très lu dans tous les milieux. **7.** Son style ne doit rien à personne.

Mettez les mots qui manquent.
Fill in the blanks.

1 *Le Monde* . . . . *après que la guerre* . . .

. . . . .

Le Monde was founded after the war had finished.

14 The most prestigious of all French papers is without doubt *Le Monde* which was founded in 1944.

15 This very serious newspaper, with a rather austere appearance - there are no photographs, for example -

16 is read, both in France and abroad, by people of influence in all circles, who respect its opinions

17 even if they don't share them (moreover, *Le Monde* grants a lot of space to open forums of all tendencies).

18 Whether one buys a paper for the small ads. or for the political and social information,

19 to read the review of the latest film out or to do the crossword,

20 the reader is sure every day of being able to choose from among a very wide range of opinions and orientations which, for the most part, owe nothing to the devil!

NOTES (suite)

(9) *Un éventail* is, in fact, a hand-held fan (for keeping one cool) but the idea of spreading has extended the word to mean: a range.
L'éventail des salaires: the range of salaries.

EXERCISES: 1. Each time we go out together, he makes unpleasant comments. **2.** We have several sales outlets in the Paris region, **3.** and our products are dispatched there every day. **4.** I don't have to answer for what this journalist writes. **5.** You can find publications of all shades of opinion. **6.** This newspaper, whose presentation is very stern, is widely read in all circles. **7.** His style owes nothing to anybody.

2 *Ce journal est très . . . . à Paris . . . .*

. . . .

This paper is widely read both in Paris and in the provinces.

3 *Il . .' . . . . devenir . . . .*

He decided to become an editor.

4 *Nous* . . . . *une grande place* . . . *idées de*

. . . .

We grant a lot of space to ideas of all shades of opinion.

****

CINQUANTE-SIXIEME (56ᵉ) LEÇON

REVISION ET NOTES

Now we have covered most of the grammar you will need, these notes will concentrate on points of detail and on broadening your knowledge of the use of expressions formed with words you already know.

1 We must be careful not to confuse the present participle with the present-participle-used-as-a-verbal-adjective.
The present participle always ends in *-ant* and is invariable; the verbal adjective usually ends in *-ant* but is not always the same as the participle, and it agrees with the noun. Look at this example:
A. *Sa mère, cette charmante femme, est souffrante:* His mother, that charming woman, is ill.
In both cases, we have the verbal adjective agreeing with a feminine noun.
B. *Il écrit des romans fascinants:* He writes fascinating novels.
Again, the agreement with the masculine plural. But the present participle remains invariable.
C. *Je les ai vus rentrant du travail:* I saw them returning from work.
D. *Ce sont deux mots correspondant aux différentes façons de dire "oui":* They are two words corresponding to the different ways of saying 'yes'.
It is especially important not to confuse the adjectival use (A and B) with the participial use (C and D) since some verbs - especially those ending in *-ger, -guer* and *-quer* have different spellings for each case.

5 *Vous êtes* . . . . *vos* . . . . . .

You are responsible for what you write.

Mots qui manquaient :

1. - fut fondé - fut finie **2.** - lu et - et en province **3.** - s'est décidé à - rédacteur **4.** - accordons - aux - toutes tendances **5.** - responsable de - écrits.

****

56th LESSON

Here are some of the more frequent ones:

Infinitive	Participle	Verbal adjective	
adhérer	*adhérant*	*adhérent*	to belong to
différer	*différant*	*différent*	to differ
fabriquer	*fabriquant*	*fabricant*	to make, manufacture
fatiguer	*fatiguant*	*fatigant*	to tire
naviguer	*naviguant*	*navigant*	to navigate, sail
négliger	*négligeant*	*négligent*	to neglect
provoquer	*provoquant*	*provocant*	to provoke

As you can see, the difference is in either the final vowel or the penultimate consonant.

Such details are important in **la pratique du français** !

2 *"Rien, rien de rien, non, je ne regrette rien..."* begins one of the most moving of all Edith Piaf's songs. Let's look more closely at the uses of **rien**.

First of all, notice how it changes place when used with a present tense:

Quand je ne comprends pas, je ne dis rien,

and with a compound tense:

Je n'ai pas compris, donc je n'ai rien dit.

Now look at these expressions:

Après son accident, il a continué comme si de rien n'était:

After his accident, he carried on as if nothing had happened.

Vous parlez d'un scandale, mais il n'en est rien: You talk of a scandal but it's nothing of the sort.

A le voir comme ça, il n'a rien d'un héros: Seeing him like that, he doesn't look at all like a hero.

Je ne comprends pas pourquoi, mais ses enfants n'ont rien de lui: I don't understand why, but his children are nothing like him,

and used with **que:**

Il faut y aller rien que pour la vue: You must go there, if only for the view.

Je me sens malade rien que d'y penser: I feel sick just thinking of it,

also as a noun:

Les réparations ont été faites en un rien de temps: The repairs were done in no time at all.

Il est un rien comédien: He's a bit of an actor.

In most cases, if you look carefully, the meaning becomes obvious. Pay attention to the word order. We don't want you to learn long lists of expressions but to get the feel of French construction so you will be able to understand any new expressions almost immediately.

3 Using the imperfect forms of *aller* and *devoir* is a literary device which allows the writer, while relating an event in the past, to cast an eye into his characters' futures.

Ce jour-là, qui aurait pu croire que ce petit garçon timide allait devenir Président?: Who could have believed, that day, that the shy little boy was to become President?

On l'a présenté à la femme qui allait devenir son épouse: He was introduced to the woman who was to become his wife.

****

The use of *devoir* suggests some form of constraint.
Leur mariage fut un grand événement au village mais ils devaient se quitter trois mois plus tard: Their wedding was a great event in the village but they were to separate three months later.
Je devais quitter ma ville natale à l'âge de deux ans: I was to leave my home town at the age of two.
The idea of constraint can only be rendered in English by changing the sentence.

4 *Autant* (as much, as many). Another familiar word, but let's look at some more of it's uses.
Tu as autant de talent que lui: You have as much talent as him,

and with **que**

Tu devrais l'aider d'autant qu'il est ton frère: You should help him all the more so since he's your brother. We may also say *d'autant plus que* without changing the meaning.

Idiomatic:
— *Je ne l'achèterai pas.* — *Cela vaut autant.* — I won't buy it. — Just as well.
— *J'aimerais autant aller au cinéma:* I'd just as soon go to the cinema.
And the example in our text with *Autant... autant,* balancing out two sides; on the one hand... on the other.
Autant vous l'aimez, autant il vous déteste: He hates you as much as you love him.
Autant j'approuve le premier projet, autant je suis réticent en ce qui concerne le second: I am as reticent about the second project as I am in favour of the first one.

Remember, sometimes it is impossible to find a corresponding idiom: this is why you must assimilate the French and use the English as a guide.

* *

CINQUANTE-SEPTIEME (57e) LEÇON

Honoré de Balzac

1 On dit que les fous construisent des châteaux en Espagne, que les névrosés les habitent - et que les psychiatres encaissent les loyers. **(1)**

2 Honoré de Balzac - sans doute l'un des plus grands romanciers de tous les temps - a créé un univers imaginaire tellement complet

3 qu'il devait l'habiter de plus en plus - laissant au monde réel les soucis d'argent qui le hantaient continuellement -, **(2)**

4 jusqu'au moment où cet univers « balzacien » devint sa réalité quotidienne et qu'il y mourut, nous laissant une peinture des mœurs hors pair. **(N.1) (3) (4)**

5 Honoré de Balzac naquit à Tours dans la dernière année du XVIIIe siècle et monta à Paris en 1814 pour y faire ses études.

UN TOURNANT EST INTERVENU DANS SA VIE QUAND IL S'EST ASSOCIÉ À UN HOMME D'AFFAIRES

NOTES

(1) This charming expression - equivalent to our 'build castles in the air' or 'to have pipe dreams' - comes from the time when French knights received fiefdom over castles in Spain which they had

57th LESSON

Honoré de Balzac

1 They say that madmen build castles in the air, that neurotics live in them and that psychiatrists collect the rent.

2 Honoré de Balzac - without doubt one of the greatest novelists of all time - created an imaginary universe so complete

3 that he came to live in it more and more - leaving to the real world his financial worries that continually haunted him

4 until the moment when this Balzacian universe became his daily reality and he died there, leaving us an unequalled painting of social morals.

5 Honoré de Balzac was born in Tours in the last year of the eighteenth century and came up to Paris in 1814 to study there.

NOTES (suite)

attacked and conquered. The expression can be made with the verbs *faire* and *bâtir* as well.
Faire le tour du monde en voilier ? Tu fais des châteaux en Espagne: Do the tour of the world in a sailing boat? You're dreaming.

(2) *Se soucier :* to worry about. *Elle se soucie trop des autres :* She worries too much about other people.
Un souci : a worry, a concern. *Votre réussite est mon seul souci :* Your success is my only concern.
We find the verb and noun form *(se) faire des soucis.*
Ne vous faites pas de soucis, tout s'arrangera : Don't worry about anything, everything will work out.
Insouciant also exists in English meaning heedless, uncaring.

(3) *Les mœurs* [mers] m. (always plural) means morals but, more broadly, the social customs and values of a society, a people or a country.
Cette pratique est passée dans les mœurs : That practice has become a custom.

(4) *Une jeune fille au pair* is a young foreign girl who lives in a family on an equal basis with the other members - or, at least, that's the literal meaning! As well as meaning: even (as opposed to 'odd') *pair* means equal (we saw that Hugo's father was *un pair de France :* this is where we get our word peer). *Hors pair :* peerless, without equal.

6 Il travailla chez un avocat et étudia le Droit mais, en même temps, il suivit les cours à la Sorbonne et obtint l'autorisation de ses parents **(5)**

7 de tenter sa chance comme écrivain. Installé dans sa mansarde parisienne, Balzac s'acharna à écrire une tragédie - qui ne connut aucun succès. **(6) (7)**

8 Ce fut alors que, pour gagner sa vie, il entra en collaboration avec un autre écrivain pour écrire des romans d'aventures « à succès ».

9 Un tournant dans sa vie, qui devait marquer son avenir et sa façon de percevoir le monde, intervint en 1825 lorsqu'il se lança dans les affaires.

10 Après s'être associé avec un libraire, il acheta une imprimerie ; il fréquenta alors le milieu des éditeurs, des journalistes et des écrivains, **(8)**

11 fréquentation dont il allait tirer profit dans ses futurs romans ; mais entre-temps, son imprimerie fit faillite et Balzac contracta de lourdes dettes. **(9)**

NOTES (suite)

(5) It becomes extremely difficult to translate between two countries' administrative or judicial systems, since the ideas, the practices and the names themselves are often different. We have already seen (Lesson 56) *un notaire* who is a notary but whose functions include those of a solicitor in Britain. *L'avocat :* corresponds in many ways to our barrister and *un avoué* to our solicitor, but remember that these terms are approximate in so far as their functions are not always the same.
Une loi : a law; *le Droit :* Law - in the abstract sense of the corpus of a country's ordinances. *Un étudiant en Droit :* a law student.

(6) Another eponym, François Mansart was a great French architect of the seventeenth century (traces of his work may still be seen in Paris today). He popularised (though did not invent) the curved roofs so typical of seventeenth and eighteenth century French architecture: *un toit mansardé. Une mansarde :* is a room built into such a roof; they used to be synonymous with the garret or attic of the struggling artist. They now tend to sell for a fortune!

6 He worked for a lawyer and studied Law but, at the same time, he followed classes at the Sorbonne and obtained his parents' permission

7 to try his luck as a writer. Installed in his Parisian attic, he worked unceasingly to write a tragedy - which had no success at all.

8 It was then that, to earn his living, he went into collaboration with another writer to write best-selling adventure novels.

9 A turning-point in his life, which was to mark his future and his way of perceiving the world, came about in 1825 when he went into business.

10 After going into partnership with a book-seller, he bought a printing business; he then began to frequent the circle of publishers, journalists and writers,

11 company from whom he was to draw a profit in his future novels; but, in the meantime, his printing business went bankrupt and Balzac contracted heavy debts.

NOTES (suite)

(7) *Il a un acharnement pour le travail :* he has an energetic passion for work.
Faire quelque chose avec acharnement : to do something with great energy.
So *s'acharner à quelque chose:* is to throw oneself totally into something.
Elle s'acharne à son travail comme s'il n'y avait rien d'autre : She goes at her work like there was nothing else.
The root of the word you may have recognised *la chair* (flesh) which we find in *la charcuterie.* The verb is an expression from venery when dogs were given the scent of meat before the hunt. With this in mind you can imagine the energy described by the verb *s'acharner!*

(8) *Un associé :* a partner; *s'associer à quelqu'un :* to go into partnership with. By extension, to associate with.
Je ne m'associe pas du tout à ses opinions : I don't associate myself at all with his/her opinions.
Une association is an association of people working together under a special statute in a non-profit-making enterprise.

(9) From *une faille:* a flaw, a fault, *la faillite* is the ultimate fault in business: bankruptcy (although less widely used, *la banqueroute* also exists); *faire faillite:* to go bankrupt.

12 Pour rembourser les cent mille francs qu'il devait, il se plongea dans la rédaction de romans et en « sortit » une dizaine en cinq ans.

13 Il essaya tous les styles et ses efforts prodigieux aboutirent à deux chefs-d'œuvre : Eugénie Grandet et Le Père Goriot. **(10)**

14 De là, il se mit à créer tout un monde autour des personnages de ses romans et ainsi à peindre une toile morale et sociale

15 qu'il baptisa « La Comédie Humaine ». Sa production était extraordinaire - il écrivit, en plus d'une dizaine de romans, de nombreuses pièces de théâtre.

16 Il s'était épris d'une Polonaise, Madame Hanska, à qui il rendit visite plusieurs fois à l'étranger et qu'il épousa en 1850. **(11) (12)**

17 Mais Balzac s'était épuisé ; il buvait des quantités de café, et avait ruiné sa vue en travaillant à la chandelle. **(13)**

18 Il mourut en 1851 ; son monde imaginaire s'était tellement emparé de lui que, sur son lit de mort, **(14)**

19 il réclama le médecin Horace Bianchon pour le sauver - mais ce docteur n'était qu'un personnage d'un de ses romans.

NOTES (suite)

(10) Do you recognise the root word? *Le bout:* the end. So *aboutir:* to end in, to lead to, to culminate in.
Ce petit sentier aboutit à une grande route : This little track leads into a main road. *Les négociations n'ont abouti à aucun résultat :* The negotiations have led to no result. *L'accord est l'aboutissement de tous ses efforts :* The agreement is the end result of all his/her efforts.
You see how important it is to look for the root-word? And once you have found it, how relatively simple it is to deduce its meaning?

12   To pay back the hundred thousand francs he owed, he threw himself into writing novels and 'brought out' ten or so in five years.

13   He tried all styles and his prodigious efforts led to two masterpieces: Eugénie Grandet and Le Père Goriot.

14   From there, he set to creating a whole world around the characters of his novels and thus to painting a moral and social canvas

15   that he christened 'The Human Comedy'. His output was extraordinary - he wrote numerous plays as well as ten or more novels.

16   He had fallen in love with a Polish woman - Madame Hanska, whom he visited several times abroad and whom he married in 1850.

17   But Balzac had exhausted himself; he drank huge amounts of coffee and had ruined his eyesight working by candlelight.

18   He died in 1851; his imaginary world had so taken possession of him that, on his death-bed,

20   he called for the doctor Horace Bianchon to save him - but this doctor was only a character in one of his novels.

NOTES (suite)

(11) Be careful: no elision *(qu'il)* because the preposition is dative - *à qui :* we only elide with the nominative.

(12) A mistake among some French people is to confuse *visiter* with *rendre visite à. On visite un château, on rend visite à une personne. Visiter* is used when one visits places; *rendre visite* when one visits a person (*visiter* a person may have pejorative overtones connected with the object of the visit...).

(13) The modern word for a candle is *une bougie* but we find *une chandelle* in familiar expressions like *faire des économies de bouts de chandelles :* to make useless savings (i.e. just saving the end of the candle instead of putting it out sooner).
Brûler la chandelle par les deux bouts : to burn the candle at both ends, and *travailler à la chandelle:* to work by candle-light.

(14) *S'emparer de quelque chose:* to take possession of something, to take over. *Il s'empare toujours de la conversation :* He always monopolises the conversation. *Les terroristes se sont emparés de l'ambassade :* The terrorists took over the embassy.

EXERCICES

1. Elle va tenter sa chance comme peintre - elle va monter à Paris. **2.** Un tournant est intervenu dans sa vie quand il s'est associé à un homme d'affaires. **3.** Il avait toujours des soucis d'argent ; pour rembourser ses dettes, il s'est plongé dans l'écriture. **4.** Il m'a rendu visite plusieurs fois quand j'étais malade. **5.** Balzac a travaillé avec acharnement, ce qui lui a coûté la santé. **6.** Tout ce qu'il a écrit a abouti à un monde imaginaire qui, à la fin, s'est emparé de lui.

Mettez les mots qui manquent.
Fill in the blanks.

1 *Restez à la maison* . . . . . ´ . . . . . *je* . . . .

Stay at home until I come back.

2 . . . . *qu'il* . ´ . . . . *à un libraire.*

It was then that he went into partnership with a bookseller.

3 . . . . . ´ . . . . *de Balzac, Madame Hanska*

accepta de l'épouser.

After falling in love with Balzac, Madame Hanska accepted to marry

him.

****

CINQUANTE-HUITIEME (58e) LEÇON

Le père Goriot

1 Le père Goriot, riche bourgeois, a marié ses filles et reste maintenant seul dans la pension de famille de Madame Vauquer ; **(1)**
2 ses enfants l'ont délaissé, ne lui rendant visite que pour demander de l'argent - et il se sacrifie toujours pour elles.

EXERCISES: **1**. She's going to try her luck as a painter - she's going up to Paris. **2**. A turning-point in his life came about when he went into partnership with a business-man. **3**. He always had financial worries; to pay back his debts he threw himself into writing. **4**. He visited me several times when I was ill. **5**. Balzac worked with unceasing energy, which cost him his health. **6**. Everything he wrote resulted in an imaginary world which finally took possession of him.

4 *Quand tu as des dettes comme ça, inutile de faire des*

. . . . *de* . . . .

When you have debts like that, it's useless making pinch-penny

savings.

5 *Il* . . . . *des écrivains* . . . . *il* . . . . . .

. . . . . *profit plus tard.*

He kept company with writers from whom he was to draw profit

later on.

Mots qui manquaient :

1. - jusqu'à ce que - revienne **2**. Ce fut alors - s'associa - **3**. Après s'être éprise - **4**. - économies - bouts de chandelles **5**. - fréquenta - dont - allait tirer -.

****

58th LESSON

Le père Goriot

1 Old man Goriot, a rich bourgeois, has married off his daughters and now remains alone in the family boarding-house of Madame Vauquer ;

2 his children have forsaken him, only visiting him to ask for money - and he always makes sacrifices for them.

NOTES **(1)** See Lesson 32, Note 3.

3 Vers la fin de la troisième année, le père Goriot réduisit encore ses dépenses, en montant au troisième étage et en se mettant à quarante-cinq francs de pension par mois.

4 Il se passa de tabac, congédia son perruquier et ne mit plus de poudre. [...] **(2) (3)**

5 Sa physionomie, que des chagrins secrets avaient insensiblement rendue plus triste de jour en jour, semblait la plus désolée

6 de toutes celles qui garnissaient la table [de la pension]. **(4)**

7 Quand son trousseau fut usé, il s'acheta du calicot pour remplacer son beau linge.

8 Ses diamants, sa tabatière d'or, sa chaîne, ses bijoux disparurent un à un.

9 Il devint progressivement maigre ; ses mollets tombèrent ; sa figure, bouffie par le contentement d'un bonheur bourgeois se vida démesurément. **(5)**

10 Durant la quatrième année de son établissement rue Neuve-Sainte-Geneviève, il ne se ressemblait plus. Le bon vermicelier de soixante-deux ans, **(6)**

11 qui ne paraissait pas en avoir quarante [...], qui avait quelque chose de jeune dans le sourire, semblait être un septuagénaire hébété, vacillant, blafard. **(7) (8)**

NOTES (suite)

(2) *Il s'est passé de tabac pendant la guerre :* He went without tobacco during the war. *S'il n'y a pas de sucre, je peux m'en passer :* If there is no sugar, I can do without it.

(3) *Une perruque :* a wig. *Un perruquier* is a wig-maker, but in the nineteenth century he was also the person who tended one's wig and hair. The following phrase means that Old Goriot no longer powdered his hair - a sign that he had let himself go.

(4) *Garnir:* to garnish, decorate, furnish, etc.
Un chapeau garni de plumes : a hat decorated with feathers. On many restaurant menus you will see *Tous nos plats sont garnis :* All our main dishes are served with vegetables.
The sense here is that the communal dining table is lined with people. (We find the sense of 'lined' in technical expressions like *les garnitures de freins:* brake linings.)

3 Towards the end of the third year, old man Goriot again reduced his expenditure by moving up to the third floor and limiting himself to 45 francs a month for board.

4 He did without tobacco, dismissed his hairdresser and no longer wore powder.

5 His face, which secret sorrow had imperceptibly made sad from day to day, seemed to be the saddest

6 of all those who lined the table [of the boarding-house].

7 When his wardrobe was worn out he bought calico to replace his beautiful linen.

8 His diamonds, his gold snuff-box, his chain and his jewels disappeared one by one.

9 He became gradually thin; his calves fell; his face, bloated with the contentment of bourgeois happiness, emptied inordinately.

10 During the fourth year of his life in the rue Neuve Sainte Geneviève he no longer looked himself. The fine sixty-two-year-old macaroni-maker,

11 who used to look only forty, whose smile held something young, seemed to be a seventy-year-old, vacant, shaking and pallid.

NOTES (suite)

(5) Notice that we have to use a reflexive verb (emptied itself) since the subject and the object of the verb are the same.

(6) One word in French - *les pâtes* - covers all that is made of pasta: spaghetti, noodles, macaroni, etc. Old Goriot had made his money from his pasta business, notably from the sale of vermicelli.

(7) Latin will help you here. *Un sexagénaire:* a man between sixty and seventy, *un septuagénaire* beween seventy and eighty, *un octogénaire* an eighty-year-old, *un nonagénaire* a ninety-year-old, *un centenaire* a man who has reached one hundred. Anything after, I suppose, could be called *un miracle.*

(8) Time to start building up your stock of adjectives. Remember that the first stage is to make them part of your reading vocabulary before you try and use them in speaking.
Hébété: dazed or vacant. *Hébété de tristesse:* bewildered with sadness. *Vacillant:* we know the English word vacillating, but applied to a person it means shaky, unsteady, uncertain. *Blafard:* pallid, wan; *une lumière blafarde:* a wan light.

12 Ses yeux bleus, si vivaces, prirent des teintes ternes et gris-de-fer, ils avaient pâli, ne larmoyaient plus, et leur bordure rouge semblait pleurer du sang.

13 Aux uns il faisait horreur ; aux autres il faisait pitié. [...] **(9)**

14 Un soir, après le dîner, Madame Vauquer lui ayant dit en manière de raillerie : « Eh bien, elles ne viennent donc plus vous voir, vos filles ? »

15 en mettant en doute sa paternité, le père Goriot tressaillit comme si son hôtesse l'eût piqué avec un fer. **(10) (11) (12)**

16 — Elles viennent quelquefois, répondit-il d'une voix émue. — Ah ! ah ! vous les voyez encore quelquefois ? s'écrièrent les étudiants. Bravo, père Goriot ! **(13)**

À DÉFAUT DE VOITURE, IL Y EST ALLÉ À BICYCLETTE

17 Mais le vieillard n'entendit pas les plaisanteries que sa réponse lui attirait ; il était retombé dans un état méditatif

18 que ceux qui l'observaient superficiellement prenaient pour un engourdissement sénile, dû à son défaut d'intelligence. **(14)**

12 His blue eyes, once so vivacious, took on dull and iron-grey tints; they had paled, they were no longer moist and their red edges seemed to weep blood.

13 In some he inspired horror, in others he caused pity [...].

14 One evening, after dinner, Madame Vauquer having said to him jokingly — Well, your daughters don't come and see you any more?

15 and putting his paternity into doubt, old Goriot winced as if his hostess had stung him with a hot iron.

16 — They come sometimes, he replied in an emotional voice. — Ah! ah! You still see them sometimes? cried the students. Bravo, old Goriot!

17 But the old man did not hear the jokes that his reply drew on him; he had fallen back into a meditative state

18 which those who observed him superficially took for senile torpor due to his lack of intelligence.

NOTES (suite)

(9) *Il me fait pitié :* I feel sorry for him.

(10) The past subjunctive, see **(N.1)** Lesson 64, can be used as a conditional. The sentence thus could read *... comme si son hôtesse l'avait piqué.* The subjunctive indicates that the action is even more remote than a conditional.

(11) *Le fer:* iron - *un fer à repasser:* a (clothes) iron, *un fer à friser:* curling tongs, *un fer à cheval:* a horse-shoe.

(12) Notice the construction of this sentence, with the use of the participle *(ayant)* and the placing of the clauses leading us up to the terrible picture of Old Goriot wincing in pain. To obtain the same effect in English, the sentence would have to be broken up: 'One evening, after dinner, Madame Vauquer jokingly said: — So, they don't come and see you any more, those daughters of yours? thus casting doubt on his fatherhood. Old Goriot winced as if his hostess had branded him with a hot iron.' This breaking-up of sentences is a general rule in translating from French into English.

(13) This refers to medical students, fellow lodgers at the boarding-house, who have decided that the old man is suffering from cretinism and who mock him constantly.

(14) *Un défaut:* a fault, a lack of. *L'accident était dû à un défaut d'attention :* The accident was due to a lack of attention.
A défaut de: for lack of. *A défaut de vin, nous bûmes de l'eau :* For lack of wine we drank water. (An alternative expression is *faute de*).

EXERCICES

1. Il a marié sa fille l'année dernière ; elle a épousé un banquier. **2.** Nous nous sommes sacrifiés pour elle ; nous nous sommes passés de beaucoup de choses. **3.** Après cinquante kilomètres de marche, ses chaussures étaient complètement usées. **4.** Il sortit de l'accident blafard et vacillant. **5.** Chaque fois que je le vois, il me fait pitié, il a l'air si triste. **6.** A défaut de voiture, il y est allé à bicyclette.

Mettez les mots qui manquent.
Fill in the blanks.

1 *Le contraire m'* . . . *étonné.*

The opposite would have surprised me.

2 *Son succès* . . . *a* . . . . . . *beaucoup d'attention.*

His success drew him a lot of attention.

****

CINQUANTE-NEUVIEME (59ᵉ) LEÇON

La France - Côte d'Azur et Provence (1)

1 Voilà que notre tour de France se poursuit ;
   nous nous sentons un peu las de toute cette
   bousculade : où irons-nous ? **(2) (3)**

NOTES

(1) Be very careful not to confuse *la province* [provans] - the provinces, and *la Provence* [provans].

(2) *Elle poursuit ses études cette année :* She's continuing her studies this year.
Les préparatifs pour le congrès se poursuivent : Preparations for the congress are going ahead.
Nous poursuivons notre tour : We are continuing our tour.

EXERCISES: 1. He married his daughter last year; she married a banker. **2.** We made sacrifices for her; we went without a lot of things. **3.** After walking fifty kilometres his shoes were completely worn out. **4.** He came out of the accident white and shaking. **5.** Each time I see him I feel sorry for him; he looks so sad. **6.** Since there was no car, he went by bicycle.

3 *Aux* . . . *il* . . . . *horreur, aux* . . . . . . *il*

   . . . .

In some he inspired horror, others felt sorry for him.

4 *Qu'est-ce qui* . . . *arrive ? Il ne* . . . .´ .

   . . . .

What is happening to him? He no longer looks himself.

5 *Son visage* . . . . *de* . . . .

His face became lined day by day.

Mots qui manquaient :

1. - eût - **2.** - lui - attiré - **3.** - uns - faisait - autres - faisait pitié **4.** - lui - se ressemble plus **5.** - se ridait - jour en jour.

****

59th LESSON

France - The Côte d'Azur and Provence

1 And now our tour of France carries on; we feel a little tired of all this pushing and shoving: where shall we go?

NOTES (suite)

Notre tour se poursuit : Our tour goes ahead.
Poursuivre (en justice) : to prosecute, to sue. *Il était poursuivi pour fraude :* He was prosecuted for fraud.
You may see the sign *Toute infraction peut donner lieu à des poursuites :* Any infringement may incur legal proceedings.
(3) *Las* is equivalent to *fatigué,* but is more weary than tired, more general than physical. *Je suis las de ce monde !:* I'm sick and tired of this world! (The feminine is *lasse*).

2 Si on vous parle de Saint-Tropez, Cannes, Nice, Menton ou Monte-Carlo, vous direz : - Riviera !

3 En France, nous appelons cette région la «Côte d'Azur » - car la mer et le ciel y sont (presque) toujours bleus.

4 La Côte d'Azur, c'est une certaine idée des vacances : soleil, plages, palmiers, palaces, luxe, animation ! **(4) (5)**

5 En été, c'est une assez bonne approximation de la Tour de Babel - une tour très, très peuplée !

6 Des millions d'« estivants » font du coude à coude, se disputant deux mètres carrés de sable ou une table de restaurant. **(N.2) (6) (7)**

7 - Stop ! C'en est déjà trop ! D'accord, c'est très beau mais cette foule grouillante me fatigue !

8 - Oui, mais pendant ce temps, à une dizaine de kilomètres à l'intérieur des terres, des lacs sauvages, **(8)**

9 des auberges fraîches et accueillantes vous attendent : c'est la calme Provence. **(9)**

10 La vraie Provence, pour qui la connaît, c'est un repas dans une de ces auberges, **(10)**

11 à une table tranquille, à l'extérieur ; l'ombre d'un figuier, d'un platane ou d'un olivier vous abritera du soleil... **(11)**

NOTES (suite)

(4) *Un palais :* a palace; *un palace :* a luxury hotel.
(5) Another of these words, like *une prestation* (see Lesson 43, Note 6), which covers a multitude of sins. The basic idea is that of animation, but it can be used for any situation where someone is employed to 'make things happen'. *L'animation* in a supermarket is a special display with salespeople proposing their wares to customers. *Un animteur* in a holiday camp is someone who is responsible for the holiday-makers' entertainment. The television often proposes *un débat animé par :* a debate chaired by... Once again, context is all-important since there is no exact equivalent.
(6) *Le coude :* the elbow. *Faire du coude à coude :* to jostle, to elbow.

2 If someone talks to you of Saint Tropez, Cannes, Nice, Menton or Monte-Carlo you will say: Riviera!

3 In France, we call this region the Côte d'Azur (Azure Coast) - because the sea and the sky are (almost) always blue.

4 The Côte d'Azur is a certain idea of holidays: sun, beaches, palm trees, great hotels, luxury, animation!

5 In summer, it's a fairly good approximation of the Tower of Babel a very, very crowded tower!

6 Millions of summer holiday-makers elbow each other, arguing over two square metres of sand or a restaurant table.

7 - Stop ! That's too much already! Agreed, it's very beautiful but this swarming crowd tires me!

8 - Yes but, in the meantime, about ten kilometres inland, wild lakes,

9 cool and welcoming inns are waiting for you: this is calm Provence.

10 The real Provence; for those who know it, it's a meal in one of those inns,

11 at a quiet table, outside; the shadow of a fig-tree, a plane-tree or an olive-tree will shade you from the sun...

NOTES (suite)

(7) Remember our rule on agreement of the past participle.
Les deux chauffeurs se sont disputés : agreement with the preceding reflexive direct object.
Ils se sont disputé la première place : no agreement since the preceding object is indirect.

(8) Normally *les terres* in the plural would apply to lands, i.e., someone's estate. *Ils sont venus braconner sur mes terres :* they came and poached on my land.
In our example, the phrase *à l'intérieur des terres* means inland. (*Terres* in the plural with an adjective presents no problem: *les terres lointaines, les terres étrangères,* etc.)

(9) *Frais* means both fresh and cool; *un ananas frais :* a fresh pineapple. *Une boisson fraîche :* a cool drink.

(10) A more elegant way of saying *pour celui qui la connaît.*

(11) *Une ombre* makes no distinction between a shadow and a shade. *Abriter* means to shelter. *Un abri de bus :* a bus shelter. *Il est à l'abri du danger:* He's out of danger's way.

12 Vous commencerez, bien entendu, par un pastis et, après un long, frais et délicieux repas, **(12)**

13 vous ferez une petite partie de pétanque entre amis, non ? **(13)**

14 Ensuite, comme ce sacré soleil vous aura « ensuqué » vous irez faire une petite sieste **(14)**

15 que bercera le chant de quelques cigales amicales. Ça ira comme programme ? - Es un programme que fai veni l'aigo a la bouco ! **(15) (16)**

16 Aussi, là-bas, les gens prennent leur temps ; tellement il fait beau, à quoi bon se presser ?

17 Assis à une table de restaurant en Provence, un client interpelle le serveur — Garçon ! Voulez-vous venir goûter à ma bouillabaisse ? **(17)**

18 — Mais, Monsieur, je n'ai pas le temps : j'ai deux clients à servir. Mais l'autre ne se décourage pas et, pendant une demi-heure,

NOTES (suite)

(12) *Le pastis,* typically southern, is a drink made with aniseed and diluted with water, as an aperitif. In Paris it is served in large glasses and gulped; in Provence, it is served in small measures and sipped for hours at café terraces...
The expression *Oh, quel pastis !* is not a shout of admiration for the distiller's art but an exclamation meaning: Oh, what a terrible situation!

(13) A persuasive way of asking a question: *Vous prendrez un autre pastis, non ?:* You'll have another pastis, won't you? You would really have to want to refuse an offer put in this way.

(14) *Ensuquer* is a southern slang word meaning to send to sleep.

(15) Look at the construction of the sentence and how the relative *que* makes it more economical. Instead of: *une sieste qui sera bercée par le chant...* we make *la sieste* the object by using *que.*
Ce soir, une émission qui vous sera présentée par... becomes *Une émission que vous présentera...*
The first sentence in both pairs is, of course, perfect French, the second examples are more... *la pratique.*
(*Une cigale* is a balm-cricket - for those who have never had the luck to hear a cicada.)

12 Of course, you'll begin with a pastis and, after a long, cool, delicious meal

13 you'll play a game of pétanque with your friends, won't you?

14 Afterwards, because that damned old sun will have 'knocked you out' you'll go for a little siesta

15 which will be lulled with the song of a few friendly cicadas. Will that do for a programme? (in Provençal) It's a programme which brings water to my mouth!

16 Also, down there people take their time; in such good weather what's the point of hurrying?

17 Sitting at a restaurant table in Provence, a customer calls over to the waiter — Waiter! Will you come and taste my bouillabaisse?

18 — But, sir, I haven't got time: I have two customers to serve. But the other man doesn't get discouraged and, for half an hour,

NOTES (suite)

(16) *La Provence* has its own language, *le provençal,* still spoken by mainly older people and which is similar to the Langue d'Oc once spoken in Gaul (see Lesson 50). In some ways, it resembles Spanish. Our extract means: It's a programme which makes water come to the mouth, i.e., it makes my mouth water.

(17) *La bouillabaisse* is one of these regional dishes which inspire as much debate as delectation. It was originally a fisherman's soup but now has taken on all the allure of haute cuisine. The name comes from Provençal.

Leçon 59

19   par intervalles, il répète sa demande :
      — Garçon, venez goûter à ma bouillabaisse !
      — Mais il est fada ! dit le garçon. **(18)**

20   Bon, d'accord, j'arrive ! Il s'asseoit à la table,
      passe la serviette autour du cou. Il approche
      l'assiette et demande : **(19)**

21   — Alors, la cuiller, où est la cuiller ? A quoi le
      client répond : — Ah ! **(20)**

EXERCICES

1. Je n'aime pas St-Tropez ; il y a trop de gens qui se
bousculent. Je suis las des foules. **2.** On doit toujours
faire du coude à coude pour avoir une table de restaurant.
3. L'auberge se trouve à une vingtaine de kilomètres à
l'intérieur des terres. **4.** Vous reprendrez bien du fromage,
non ? - Si vous voulez. **5.** Veux-tu approcher la table, s'il
te plaît ? **6.** Mes études se poursuivent l'année prochaine ; je vais apprendre le provençal.

Mettez les mots qui manquent.
Fill in the blanks.

1 *Voici une belle chanson* . . . .

  Mireille.

  Here is a beautiful song which Mireille will sing for you.

2 *Les* . . . . *une place*

  sur la plage.

  The holiday-makers fought over a place on the beach.

3 . . . . *il fait beau,* . . . . *se presser ?*

  The weather is so beautiful, what's the point of hurrying?

19 at intervals, he repeats his request — Waiter, come and taste my bouillabaisse! — He's crazy! says the waiter.

20 Right. O.K. I'm coming! He sits down at the table, puts the napkin around his neck. He pulls the plate towards him and asks:

21 Well, the spoon. Where's the spoon? To which the customer replies: — Ah!

NOTES (suite)

(18) — *Té ! Il est fada :* An expression from the South, meaning He's crazy!

(19) *Il s'approche de la table :* He moves over to the table.
Il approche la table : He brings the table nearer.

(20) There are two spellings for this word: *une cuiller* or *une cuillère*.

EXERCISES: 1. I don't like St-Tropez; there are too many people jostling each other. I'm tired of crowds.   **2.** You always have to elbow people to get a restaurant table.   **3.** The inn is about 20 kilometres inland.   **4.** You'll have some more cheese, won't you? - Yes please.   **5.** Will you bring the table closer, please?   **6.** My studies are continuing next year.   I'm going to learn Provençal.

4 *Mettez les boissons* . . . . *à . . . .*

soleil.

Put the cool drinks out of the sun.

5 . . . . *la   Côte d'Azur:*

regardez déjà les foules.

We are approaching the Cote d'Azur; look at the crowds already.

Mots qui manquaient :

1. - que vous chantera - **2.** - estivants se sont disputé - **3.** Tellement - à quoi bon - **4.** - fraîches - l'abri du - **5.** Nous nous approchons de -.

We hope these little excursions of ours are giving you a taste of France!

Leçon 59

SOIXANTIEME (60e) LEÇON

Le journal de vingt heures

1 — Madame, Mademoiselle, Monsieur, bonsoir ; d'abord les titres de l'actualité bien
remplie de ce soir : **(1)**

2 Préavis de grève dans les transports en
commun ; les syndicats entendent réduire la
durée hebdomadaire du travail. **(2) (3)**

3 Arrestation à Montpellier d'un gros bonnet de
la pègre ; la police a réussi un joli coup de filet.
(4)

4 Hausse des prix, plus zéro neuf pour cent : un
score plutôt médiocre ;

5 et, enfin, sports, le football : le Paris-St-
Germain face aux Belges ce soir au Parc des
Princes. Le coup d'envoi était il y a une demi-
heure.

6 Regardons maintenant ces informations dans
le détail :

7 Remous demain dans la capitale : les trois
principaux syndicats ont déposé hier soir un
préavis de grève de vingt-quatre heures dans
les transports en commun.

8 Avec le dossier, Jean Caban : — Trente-cinq
heures de travail hebdomadaires, la révision du
système des primes :

NOTES

(1) *Un titre :* a title or a headline. In the latter sense it can be used as a
verb: *L'affaire faisait les gros titres des journaux :* The affair made
the headlines of the newspapers.

(2) *Un préavis :* notice; *un préavis de licenciement :* notice of
dismissal. *Il a démissionné sans préavis :* He resigned without prior
notice.
As we have often pointed out, systems differ between countries.
In France, unions are required to give notice to the government of

60th LESSON

The eight o'clock news

1 — Ladies and gentlemen, good evening; first of all the headlines of tonight's full news programme.

2 Strike warning in the public transport system; the trade unions want to reduce the weekly work time.

3 Arrest in Montpellier of a big shot in the Underworld; the police brought off a nice haul.

4 Price increases, 0.9% more: a rather mediocre score

5 and, finally, sports, football: Paris St. Germain against the Belgians tonight at the Parc des Princes. Kick-off was half an hour ago.

6 Let's look in more detail at the news:

7 Unrest tomorrow in the capital; the three major trade unions last night gave a warning of a twenty-four hour strike in the public transport system.

8 With the story, Jean Caban: - Thirty-five hours a week and the revision of the bonus system;

NOTES (suite)

their intention to strike. This is called *un préavis de grève.*
Se mettre en grève : to go on strike - *une grève sauvage :* a wildcat strike (one without *préavis*) - *un gréviste :* a striker.
The origin of the word comes from the Place de Grève (now the Place de l'Hôtel de Ville) in Paris, where unemployed people would mass waiting to be chosen to work.
(*Une grève* also means a sea-shore; the Place de Grève was situated on the banks of the Seine.)

(3) Remember that *entendre* followed by an infinitive means to intend to. *Le gouvernement entend ainsi réduire le chômage :* The Government thus intends to, wants to, reduce unemployment.

(4) Television news uses a special, rather picturesque, vocabulary - especially in crime stories - of which we give you a sample here. *Un gros bonnet :* a big shot, an important person - *la pègre :* the underworld (especially of thieves) - (we will also see *le Milieu* which has the same meaning).
Un coup de filet : is a fishing expression (*un filet :* a net) - *un beau (ou joli) coup de filet :* a fine catch, haul.
This type of language is correct French and very useful in understanding mass media.

9 voilà ce que revendiquent la C.F.D.T., la C.G.T. et F.O. depuis quatre mois. Les négociations se poursuivaient entre patrons et syndicats jusqu'à hier soir. Ne trouvant aucun accord, les agents de la R.A.T.P. menacent de se mettre en grève à partir de ce soir minuit. **(5) (6)**

10 Dans les derniers mois, il y a déjà eu quelques grèves sauvages mais cette fois-ci, disent les responsables syndicaux, c'est une action concertée.

11 Dans le métro, une rame sur deux circulera et, côté bus, il y en aura un sur quatre. De beaux embouteillages en perspective ! **(7) (8) (9)**

12 — On le surnommait « Le Parrain » ou simplement « Didi ». Didier Colfani, trente-six ans, a longtemps été mêlé à des affaires plus ou moins crapuleuses. **(10) (11)**

13 Il a été condamné une première fois à quatre ans de prison dont deux avec sursis pour trafic de stupéfiants. **(12)**

14 Il refait surface dans le Milieu niçois où l'on parle de fabrication de faux billets sur la Côte d'Azur, **(4)**

15 et voilà qu'hier soir, les agents de la Brigade spéciale ont opéré une descente dans une boîte de nuit à Montpellier.

16 Colfani et deux complices ont été pris en flagrant délit avec des faux billets dans leur portefeuille, ainsi que des documents compromettants.

NOTES (suite)

(5) *Revendiquer :* to claim or demand. *Nous revendiquons nos droits :* We demand our rights. The noun is *une revendication.*

(6) *Un patron :* a boss. Often used in the plural in contrast to *les travailleurs. Les patrons* can be understood as the management for whom the correct name is *la direction.*

(7) Another piece of 'officialese', *une rame de wagons* is a string of carriages making up a train, but the S.N.C.F. or the R.A.T.P. often use it instead of the word *un train. Une collision entre deux rames de métro :* a collision between two metro trains. (*Une rame* also means an oar, *ramer :* to row.)

9 this is what the C.F.D.T., the C.G.T. and F.O. have been demanding for four months. Negotiations were going ahead between the management and trade unions until last night. Finding no agreement, the R.A.T.P. workers are threatening to go on strike from midnight tonight.

10 Over the last months, there have already been several wild-cat strikes but this time, say trade union officials, it is a concerted action.

11 In the metro, one train in two will run and, as for the buses, there will be one out of four. Fine traffic jams to look forward to!

12 He was nicknamed 'The Godfather' or simply 'Didi'. Didier Colfani, thirty-six, had for a long time been mixed up in rather sordid affairs.

13 He was first sentenced to four years in prison (two of which were a suspended sentence) for drug trafficking.

14 He re-appeared in the Nice underworld, where there was talk of forged banknotes on the Cote d'Azur

15 and then, yesterday evening, members of the Special Brigade raided a Montpellier night-club.

16 Colfani and two accomplices were caught red-handed with forged banknotes in their wallets, as well as compromising documents.

NOTES (suite)

(8) *Circulez !* a policeman might yell at you, pointing at your car. Drive on! (We know the word *la circulation :* traffic.)
Un train sur deux circulera : One train in two will run.

(9) This is an elision of *du côté de :* on the side of. *Les syndicats menacent de faire grève ; côté patrons, on s'inquiète :* The trade unions are threatening to strike; the management is worried.
Le travail est très intéressant et côté argent, je gagne plus : The work is very interesting and, from a money point of view, I'm earning more.

(10) *Surnommer :* to nick-name; *un surnom :* a nick-name.

(11) *Un parrain :* a god-father; *une marraine :* a god-mother; *un filleul :* a god-son; *une filleule :* a god-daughter; *un parrain* is also used to mean a sponsor (the verb: *parrainer*).

(12) *Un sursis* is a delay of execution of a sentence.
Quatre ans, dont deux avec sursis would mean that the sentence was two years *fermes* and two years suspended, only to be served in case of bad conduct.

17 Ils ont été mis sous les verrous à la prison centrale de la ville. **(13)**

18 Le juge d'instruction a ouvert une information pour faux et usage de faux. **(14)**

(à suivre)

EXERCICES

1. Voici les titres de l'actualité ce soir. **2.** Après le discours, il y a eu un remous dans la foule. **3.** Ils se mettront en grève à partir de demain dix heures. **4.** Je l'avais perdue de vue mais voilà qu'elle a refait surface il y a deux jours. **5.** La porte était fermée à clef et verrouillée ; nous n'avons pu entrer. **6.** Le tournoi de tennis est parrainé par une marque de cigarettes très connue.

Mettez les mots qui manquent.
Fill in the blanks.

1 *Les* . . . . *une*

augmentation . . . . . . *deux mois.*

The trade unions have been demanding an increase for two

months.

17 They were imprisoned at the central prison of the town.

18 The examining magistrate has begun legal proceedings for forgery and use of forged notes.

(to be continued)

NOTES (suite)

(13) *Un verrou* : is a bolt - *être mis sous les verrous* : to be put under lock and key. The verb is *verrouiller* [verooyay]. *N'oublie pas de verrouiller la porte quand tu rentres* : Don't forget to bolt the door when you come back.

(14) As we have already mentioned in Lesson 57, since legal systems are different, it is difficult to give an exact translation. When someone is arrested on criminal charges, a magistrate is put in charge of the preliminaries of the case. We say that he or she *instruit le dossier* - conducts the initial investigations. That magistrate is called *un juge d'instruction*.
Ouvrir une information is to begin this preliminary investigation. The official charge of forgery is *accusation de faux* although the verb to forge is *contrefaire* (whence our counterfeit).

EXERCISES: **1.** Here are the news headlines for this evening. **2.** After the speech, there was a movement of unrest in the crowd. **3.** They will go on strike from tomorrow at 10.00. **4.** I had lost sight of her but then she turned up again two days ago. **5.** The door was locked and bolted; we weren't able to get in. **6.** The tennis tournament is sponsored by a well-known brand of cigarette.

2 *Le festival commence demain ; il y a* . . . .

concerts . . . .

The festival begins tomorrow; there are some fine concerts to look forward to.

3 . . *côté* . . . *patrons, les* . . . .

semblent être prises en compte.

On the side of the employers, the demands seem to be taken into account.

4 . *cause* . . *la grève, il* . *'* . *aura* . . . *deux trains*

. . . *quatre.*

Because of the strike, there will be only two out of four trains.

****

SOIXANTE ET UNIEME (61ᵉ) LEÇON

Le journal de vingt heures (suite)

1 Le Quai d'Orsay a fait savoir ce matin que l'archéologue français arrêté en Nimie avait été entendu par les autorités **(1) (2) (3)**

2 et sera remis en liberté à la fin du mois. Plusieurs associations de droits de l'homme avaient émis des protestations auprès du gouvernement nimien.

3 D'après les dernières statistiques publiées par l'INSEE ce matin, l'indice de la hausse des prix est de zéro virgule neuf pour cent pour ce mois-ci, **(4)**

4 alors que le chômage serait en baisse, avec deux virgule six pour cent de moins pour les quatre derniers mois en données corrigées. **(5)**

NOTES

(1) Another trait of the news media is that of identifying the offices of certain ministries with their functions; thus *le Quai d'Orsay* is where *le ministère des Relations Extérieures* (Foreign Office) is to be found.

(2) *Faire savoir. Ils me l'ont fait savoir hier :* They let me know yesterday. Notice that the direct object *(le)* is not usually translated in English. When there is no pronoun in the expression: *Le ministre a fait savoir que...* the expression means let something be known or, more simply, announced. Thus our first sentence would read: The Foreign Ministry announced that the... etc.

5   *Les négociations s' . . . .*

pendant un an.

The negotiations had been going on for a year.

Mots qui manquaient :

1. - syndicats revendiquent - depuis - **2.** - de beaux - en perspective **3.** Du - des - revendications - **4.** A - de - n'y - que - sur - **5.** - étaient poursuivies -.

****

61st LESSON

The eight o'clock news (continued)

1   The Quai d'Orsay made it known this morning that the French archeologist arrested in Nimia has had a hearing before the authorities

2   and will be released at the end of the month. Several human rights organisations had made protests to the Nimian government.

3   According to the latest statistics published by INSEE this morning, the retail price index has risen by 0.9 per cent for this month

4   whereas unemployment seems to be going down, with 2.6 per cent less for the last four months in adjusted figures.

NOTES (suite)

(3) *Entendre* has yet another meaning, this time a legal one similar to our English: a (judicial) hearing. Our sentence means that the French archeologist had a hearing in front of the authorities.

(4) *L'INSEE, l'Institut national des statistiques et des études économiques :* the French Central Statistics Office.

(5) This use of the conditional is especially common in news writing, when it is not wanted to affirm something which has been reported.
La police aurait arrêté le criminel : The police have allegedly arrested the criminal. *Les chiffres seraient en baisse :* The figures appear to be falling. English needs to use a paraphrase depending on each context.

5 Conseil des Ministres demain à l'Elysée, le Président de la République se prononcera sur un éventuel remaniement au sein du Cabinet **(6) (7) (8)**

6 et sur la question que tout le monde se pose : y aura-t-il un changement d'occupant à Matignon ? **(9)**

7 Le sport maintenant, au Parc des Princes, où se jouent depuis bientôt cinquante minutes les huitièmes de finale de la Coupe d'Europe **(10)**

8 entre le Paris St-Germain et l'équipe belge d'Anvers. **(11)**

9 A la mi-temps, la marque était d'un but partout. Vous vous souviendrez que, lors de leur dernière rencontre, les deux équipes ont fait match nul. **(12) (13)**

10 Un mot du temps pour demain, qui sera maussade un peu partout sur le pays, avec des averses et le mistral et la tramontane dans le Midi. **(14)**

NOTES (suite)

(6) *Le Palais de l'Elysée :* the official residence of the French President.

(7) A 'faux-ami': *éventuel* means possible, theoretical. *Toute augmentation éventuelle fera l'objet d'une enquête :* Any future increase will be the subject of an enquiry.
Eventuel gives us the idea of a future possibility. *On doit s'assurer contre les accidents éventuels :* We must insure ourselves against possible accidents.
The substantive is *une éventualité ; l'éventualité d'un changement de Premier ministre.*

(8) Remember: *au sein de :* within.

(9) *L'Hôtel de Matignon* is the official residence of the Prime Minister. The sentence means: will there be a new Prime Minister?

(10) Whereas in English, we have matches leading up to the quarter-finals, then the semi-finals, then the finals, French counting goes exponentially back to the sixty-fourth - and beyond. *Les soixante-quatrièmes de finale :* the sixth set of matches before the finals. *Les huitièmes de finale* precedes the *les quarts de finale,* which is followed the *les demi-finales* then, finally... *La finale.* Hope you're good at maths!

(11) Be careful if you are driving in Belgium. Being a bilingual country, many towns have a French name and a Flemish name, as many foreigners have found out to their cost. The best known are *Anvers - Antwerpen; Mons - Bergen; Liège - Luik.*

5 Council of Ministers meeting tomorrow at the Elysée; the President of the Republic will declare his decision on a possible re-shuffle within the Cabinet

6 and on the question which everyone is asking: will there be a new prime-minister?

7 Sport now, at the Parc des Princes where the match before the quarter finals of the European Cup has been playing for almost fifty minutes

8 between Paris St. Germain and the Belgian team from Antwerp.

9 At half time, the score was one all. You will remember that, at their last meeting, the teams drew.

10 A word about the weather for tomorrow, which will be dull almost everywhere over the country, with showers and the Mistral and the Tramontane in the South.

NOTES (suite)

(12) *La marque* is the attempt to eradicate *le score* from the language. As you can see, it works every other time! *Ouvrir la marque :* to open the score.

(13) *Faire match nul :* to draw - *un match nul :* a draw.

(14) *Le mistral* and *la tramontane* are violent winds that blow periodically in the Southern part of the country. The Mistral blows from the north, or north west, towards the sea and the Tramontane is another northern wind blowing across (trans) the mountains (montana). They have a disturbing effect, and the expression *perdre la tramontane* means to become disorientated, to lose one's head.

11 Attention aux risques de brouillard sur les côtes et dans le bassin parisien.

12 Ce journal est maintenant terminé. Nous vous donnons rendez-vous pour une dernière page d'actualités à vingt-trois heures.

13 Bonsoir à toutes et à tous.

14 Un journaliste de la télévision effectuait un reportage "sur le vif" sur des familles nombreuses.

15 Il arrêtait des gens dans la rue en leur demandant combien d'enfants ils avaient.

16 Il fut étonné quand une jolie dame lui répondit :
— Dix.

17 — Dix, mais c'est extraordinaire ; et depuis combien de temps êtes-vous mariée ?
— Depuis douze ans.

18 — Mais pourquoi avez-vous arrêté ?
— C'est très simple : nous nous sommes acheté une télévision !

EXERCICES

1. On vous le fera savoir à la fin de la semaine. 2. D'après ce qu'ils ont dit, cet homme serait un escroc. 3. Je ne peux pas me prononcer sur ce sujet si je n'ai pas assez d'informations. 4. Y aura-t-il un nouveau Premier ministre, c'est la question que tout le monde se pose. 5. La demi-finale se rejouera la semaine prochaine, la dernière fois les deux équipes ont fait match nul. 6. Il a enquêté "sur le vif".

Mettez les mots qui manquent.
Fill in the blanks.

1 *Les gangsters* . . . . *utilisé une voiture volée,*

. . . . *nos informations.*

According to our information the gangsters appeared to have used a

stolen car.

11 Be careful of the risks of fog along the coasts and in the Parisian basin.

12 This bulletin is now finished. We'll be back with a last look at the news at 11.00 p.m.

13 Goodnight.

14 A television journalist was doing an 'on the spot' report on large families.

15 He was stopping people in the street, asking them how many children they had.

16 He was astonished when an attractive lady answered: — Ten.

17 — Ten! But that's extraordinary. How long have you been married? — For twelve years.

18 — But why have you stopped? — It's very simple: we bought a television!

EXERCISES: 1. We will let you know at the end of the week. **2.** From what they said, this man appears to be a crook. **3.** I can't announce a decision on this subject if I don't have enough information. **4.** Will there be a new Prime Minister? That's the question everyone is asking. **5.** The semi-final will be replayed next week; the last time, both teams drew. **6.** He enquired 'on the spot'.

2 *Une victoire* . . . . *leur* . . . .

de gagner la Coupe d'Europe.

A possible victory would allow them to win the European cup.

3 *Le* . . . . *a* . . . . *que le*

prisonnier avait été . . . . *par les autorités.*

The Ministry announced that the prisoner had had a hearing before

the authorities.

4 *L'* . . . . . . *de la* . . . . . . *des* . . . . *a pris deux*

. . . .

The retail price index rose by two per cent.

283

5 . . . . *de* . . . . -*vous mariée ?*

How long have you been married?

****

SOIXANTE-DEUXIEME (62ᵉ) LEÇON

La poésie n'est pas si difficile

1 Quel plaisir que de découvrir la langue d'un pays à travers sa littérature ! **(1)**

2 Jusqu'ici nous n'avons lu que des extraits de romans ; il est maintenant temps de regarder un peu **(2)**

3 dans ce ''miroir brouillé'' (comme disait Aragon) qu'est la poésie. **(3) (4)**

4 On a tort de dire que d'essayer de lire des poèmes dans une langue étrangère est difficile -

5 certes il est des poètes qui sont plus ''difficiles'' que d'autres, mais la littérature française en offre un tel choix - **(5)**

NOTES

(1) We are familiar with the exclamatory use of *Quel(le). Quel bruit !:* What a noise! If we wish to continue adding a verb: What a noise they make!: *Quel bruit ils font !*
But if we wish to qualify, further, our exclamation: What a pleasure it is to visit the countryside, we insert the relative *que* and the *de,* which introduces the infinitive, the logical subject: *Quel plaisir que de visiter la campagne !*
In spoken language, one tends to drop the *que.*

(2) *Jusqu'ici* also has a temporal meaning. *Ils ont marché jusqu'ici :* They walked here. *Jusqu'ici nous avons vu trois monuments :* Up till now, we have seen three monuments.

(3) We know *débrouiller* - now the 'opposite': *brouiller,* which means to mix up, to confuse. Coming from the same root word as *le brouillard* (fog), it covers any idea of obscuring, blurring. *Le voleur a brouillé les pistes :* The thief mixed up the trails leading to him. *Brouiller une transmission :* To jam a broadcast. *Les œufs brouillés :* Scrambled eggs (well, they **are** mixed up!). *Il est brouillé avec son frère :* He has fallen out with his brother.

(4) Louis Aragon, a contemporary twentieth century poet, is above all known for his political *engagement* in the Communist Party.

Mots qui manquaient :

1. - auraient - d'après - **2.** - éventuelle - permettrait - **3.** - ministère - fait savoir - entendu - **4.** - indice - hausse - prix - pour cent **5.** Depuis combien - temps êtes -.

****

62nd LESSON

Poetry isn't that difficult

1 What a pleasure to discover the language of a country through its literature!
2 Up until now we have only read extracts from novels; it's now time to look a little
3 into that 'blurred mirror' (as Aragon said) which is poetry.
4 It is wrong to say that to try and read poems in a foreign language is difficult -
5 of course there are poets who are more 'difficult' than others, but French literature offers such a choice -

NE VERSEZ PLUS DE VIN, LE VERRE DÉBORDE DÉJÀ

NOTES (suite)

(5) A literary device - rather declamatory in tone - which replaces *il y a. Il est des hommes qui ont un grand destin :* There are men who have a certain destiny. Again, rarely used in spoken language. which prefers *il y a.*

6 de Ronsard à Lamartine en passant par Baudelaire - que tout le monde peut y trouver son content. **(6) (7)**

7 Nous avons choisi un poème de celui qui a peut-être inventé la ''nouvelle poésie'', Arthur Rimbaud. **(8)**

8 Quoi qu'il en soit, il a donné à la poésie un nouveau souffle avec le vers libre

9 et une imagination débordante, éclatante, qui explique en quelque sorte pourquoi ce génie s'est arrêté d'écrire à l'âge de... vingt et un ans !

10 Voici un sonnet qui s'intitule : Le Buffet.

11 C'est un large buffet sculpté, le chêne sombre, **(9)**
    Très vieux, a pris cet air si bon des vieilles gens ;

12 Le buffet est ouvert, et verse dans son ombre
    Comme un flot de vin vieux, des parfums engageants. **(10)**

13 Tout plein, c'est un fouillis de vieilles vieilleries, **(11)**
    De linges odorants et jaunes, de chiffons

14 De femmes ou d'enfants, de dentelles flétries, **(12)**
    De fichus de grand-mère où sont peints des griffons.

NOTES (suite)

(6) Pierre de Ronsard was a sixteenth century humanist and poet, he became leader of *La Pléiade,* a group of poets including the great Joachim du Bellay. *La Pléiade* is now the name given to the series of books which publishes the greats of French literature.
Alphonse de Lamartine (1790-1869) is an example of the constant link between politics and art in France. Many ministers and presidents have been fine writers, as was Lamartine. His poetry celebrates nature and the link with the sentiments of love and devotion.
Charles Baudelaire (1821-1867), the tortured 'poet of the Devil', explored the heights and depths of the soul. He is best known for his collection of poems *Les Fleurs du Mal* (The Flowers of Evil).

6   from Ronsard to Lamartine by way of Baudelaire -
    that everyone can find satisfaction.
7   We have chosen a poem by the person who perhaps
    invented 'new poetry', Arthur Rimbaud.
8   Be that as it may, he gave new life to poetry with
    free verse
9   and an overflowing, dazzling imagination which
    explains in some way why this genius stopped
    writing at the age of... twenty-one.
10 Here is a sonnet entitled 'The Sideboard'.

11 It is a large, carved sideboard; the dark oak
    So old, has adopted the fine air of old people;
12 The sideboard is open, and pours out into its
    shadow
    Like a flow of old wine, the smell of inviting
    perfumes.
13 Full-up it is a jumble of old, out-of-date objects
    Yellow and fragrant linen, scarves
14 Of women and children, soiled lace
    Grandmother's shawls painted with griffons.

NOTES (suite)

(7) The expression *y trouver son content* means to find one's
satisfaction, one's contentment. *J'en ai mon content* : I have had
my fill.

(8) Arthur Rimbaud (1854-1891) showed a rebellious nature from the
very beginning of his life, mixing poetry with social and moral
revolution. He abandoned writing at the age of twenty-one, when
he declared that poetry was powerless to change life. He became
a traveller and ran arms to Abyssinia before his death at the age of
thirty-seven. We do not have the space here to present any of his
major works, but the sonnet *Le Buffet* shows his fascination with
the exploration of colours, sounds and symbols. His work was a
major force in changing the nature of French poetry.

(9) *Sculpter* (the p is silent) means both to sculpt stone and to carve
wood. *Un sculpteur* : a sculptor; *un sculpteur sur bois* : a wood
carver (the verb to carve meat is *découper*).

(10) *Engageant* : attractive, engaging, charming.
We mentioned, earlier, that Aragon was very *engagé*. Used
especially in the sense of a political movement, it applies to
someone who is deeply committed.

(11) *Les vieilleries* : old-fashioned things, out-of-date objects. It is a
poetic word heightened here by the adjective *les vieilles vieilleries*
(the opposite is *les nouveautés*).

(12) *Flétrir* : (transitive) to fade, to make withered.
The adjective means faded, wilted - or applied to clothes, etc.,
dirtied, stained.

15 C'est là qu'on trouverait les médaillons, les mèches

De cheveux blancs ou blonds, les portraits, les fleurs sèches

16 Dont le parfum se mêle à des parfums de fruits.

Ô buffet du vieux temps, tu sais bien des histoires

17 Et tu voudrais conter tes contes, et tu bruis **(13) (14)**

Quand s'ouvrent lentement tes grandes portes noires.

(Our translation of the sonnet is merely a rendition; it does not attempt to be poetry, but to help you appreciate the original. Perhaps you would now like to attempt a proper translation...?)

EXERCICES

1. La pluie brouillait les carreaux ; dehors nous ne vîmes rien. **2.** Ne versez plus de vin, le verre déborde déjà. **3.** Cet écrivain a un talent éclatant ; c'est un vrai génie. **4.** Les verres tombèrent à terre avec un bruit éclatant. **5.** Je ne peux plus prendre de travail ; je suis débordé ! **6.** Nous sommes allés de Paris à Marseille en passant par Lyon.

Mettez les mots qui manquent.
Fill in the blanks.

1 . . . . *lire de la poésie !*

What a pleasure it is to read poetry!

2 . . . . *de dire que c'est difficile.*

It is wrong to say that it is difficult.

3 . . . . , *il* . . . *des poètes compliqués,*

Certainly, there are complicated poets,

15 There's where we would find the medallions, the locks
Of grey or blond hair, the portraits, the dry flowers
16 Whose perfumes mingle with the smell of fruit.
Yesteryear's sideboard, you know many stories
17 And would tell your tales; and you murmur
When your great black doors slowly open.

NOTES (suite)

(13) *Un conte :* a short story; *conter :* to tell a tale. *Un conte de fées :* a fairy-tale ; *un conteur :* a story-teller. As in English, these 'tales' can also be understood as tall stories, exaggerations.
(14) From the verb *bruire.* Not in common use (except for the present participle *bruyant :* noisy), it means 'to make a continuous noise'. It is up to your poetic imagination to choose an English verb that fits the context. We have chosen: to murmur; it could also be to hum, to rustle, to rumble... etc.

EXERCISES: 1. The rain was blurring the window panes; outside we could see nothing. **2.** Don't pour any more wine, the glass is already overflowing. **3.** That writer has a dazzling talent; he's a real genius. **4.** The glasses fell to the ground with a crash. **5.** I can't take on any more work; I'm overworked! **6.** We went from Paris to Marseilles by way of Lyons.

4 *mais* . . . . . ' . . . *nous* . 'avons rencontré . . . . . .

difficulté.

but up till now, we have not come across any difficulties.

5 . ' . . . . 'on . . . . *la tombe de Rimbaud.*

That's where we will find Rimbaud's tomb.

Mots qui manquaient :

1. Quel plaisir que de - **2.** On a tort - **3.** Certes - est - **4.** - jusqu'ici - n - aucune - **5.** C'est là qu - trouvera -.

SOIXANTE-TROISIEME (63ᵉ) LEÇON

REVISION ET NOTES

1   We have already touched briefly on the imperfect, the past and the pluperfect subjunctive. In this final section on grammar, we will look at the rules for the formation and use of these three tenses. First of all, it is important to point out that, in spoken French, the present subjunctive is used **almost exclusively**. We want you to know a little about the others so that you will recognise them when you come across them, and this is really only likely in literature (and even modern writers tend to avoid the imperfect and the pluperfect subjunctives because they 'sound' awkward).

So, first the imperfect subjunctive:

Formed by dropping the last letter of the first person singular of the *passé simple* (e.g. *donnai - donna*) and adding the following endings: *-sse; -sses;* *ˆt; -ssions; -ssiez; -assent.*

The vowel in the 3rd person singular is either an *a* or a *u* depending on the verb.

It follows a main verb in the imperfect or pluperfect indicative or the conditional. So, 'perfect' French would give us:

Je voudrais que vous me le donnassiez demain, but we would always use the present subjunctive in speech or letter-writing: *Je voudrais que vous me le donniez demain.*

Here are some more examples in their literary and spoken forms:

Je serais content que vous vinssiez me voir... que vous veniez me voir. Il avait demandé qu'on le réveillât... qu'on le réveille. Nous ne nous attendions pas qu'elle commençât... qu'elle commence. Notice the different tenses of the main verb; notice also the circumflex over the 3rd person singular. This is important because the third person singular of the imperfect subjunctive of *être* and *avoir* (*eût* and *fût*) are sometimes used elegantly to express the conditional *aurait* and *serait* (we saw this in the extract from Le Père Goriot, lesson 58; *... comme si son hôtesse l'eût piqué*). We must not confuse these forms with the same persons in the *passé simple*. *Il fut un temps :* One upon a time; *il eut une grande suprise :* he had a great surprise. Notice there is no circumflex.

The past subjunctive is still used in spoken language. Formed by the past participle of the verb to the present subjunctive of *avoir* (or for reflexive or motion verbs: *être*):

que
┌ *j'aie donné*
│ *tu aies donné*
└ *il/elle ait donné*

que
┌ *nous soyons partis*
│ *vous soyez partis*
└ *ils soient partis*

(Notice the agreement of the past participle with the plural pronouns when conjugated with *être*.)

This tense corresponds to the use of the *passé composé* in the indicative. For example:

Je crois qu'il est parti hier but, subjunctive,
Je doute qu'il soit parti hier.
Je crains qu'il n'ait oublié : I'm afraid he has forgotten.
J'ai peur qu'ils se soient trompés : I'm worried they've made a mistake.

This form replaces, in spoken language, the Pluperfect Subjunctive. Formed by adding the past participle of the verb to the imperfect subjunctive of *avoir* (or *être* where relevant):

que
┌ *j'eusse donné*
│ *tu eusses donné*
└ *il eût donné*

que
┌ *nous fussions partis*
│ *vous fussiez partis*
└ *ils fussent partis*

This tense corresponds to the pluperfect in the indicative, so:

Je croyais qu'il était parti
Je doutais qu'il fût parti

The spoken language should use the past subjunctive *(Je*

doutais qu'il soit parti) but, even more commonly, would use the present subjunctive.

So, the sequence of tenses, in written French, is the following:

After the present
      future   ] indicative
      passé composé]

use the **present**
subjunctive or past
subjunctive if there
is a verb and a
past participle

After the imperfect
      passé simple   ] indicative
      pluperfect   ]
      conditional   ]

use the **imperfect**
subjunctive or the
pluperfect if there
is a verb and a
past participle

We hope that this information does not frighten you off! We can only repeat that the pluperfect and imperfect subjunctives are used uniquely in **literary** French.

Look once again at the constructions and the sequence of tenses and make sure that you can use the present subjunctive correctly!

2   Etymology - the origin of words - is more than just an entertaining pastime, which is why we have often spent time explaining the origin and development of words. It can help you locate, understand and construct words

****

without the help of a dictionary. Look for the root of any new word and try and fit it into the context.

A knowledge of prefixes is very useful: here are some of the more common ones:

a-	= without	*amoral; aphone*
com-	= with	*compagnon; compatriote*
dé-	= un-	*déshérité; défaire*
im-	= in	*immersion; impliquer*
in-	= in	*inscrire; interner*
inter-	= between	*interview; interrompre*
mé-	= un- mis-	*mécontent; mésaventure*
re-	= again	*relire; refaire*

Another way to find English words is to go back to the old French spellings. For example, a circumflex indicates that an 's' used to exist in the old word. Look at these examples:

une forêt - forest
un intérêt - an interest
un mât - a mast
une requête - a request

Or when we see words beginning in *ét-*, *ép-* or even *éc-* it usually indicates that the initial letter in Latin was an 's'. Once again:

écarlate - scarlet
une étable - a stable
épars - sparse
épeler - to spell
établir - to establish
une épice - a spice

It can be quite an adventure, tracing words back to their origins and, more often than not, it is a great help in building up our vocabulary.

* *

SOIXANTE-QUATRIEME (64e) LEÇON

Langues et langages I (1)

1 Comme vous avez pu le constater jusqu'à présent, la langue française est pleine de richesses.

2 Vous avez étudié - agréablement, nous l'espérons - le langage de tous les jours,

3 la langue littéraire et celle des médias, entre autres.

4 En France (ou dans l'Hexagone, comme on l'appelle parfois), on trouve aussi d'autres langues régionales, qui sont plus que des dialectes, (2)

5 en ce qu'elles possèdent non seulement une grammaire et un vocabulaire particuliers, (3)

6 mais aussi une vraie littérature : on dénombre le breton, l'occitan, le provençal (dont vous avez eu un petit échantillon),

7 sans oublier la langue de l'Ile de Beauté, le corse. (4)

8 Depuis quelques années, il y a une forte renaissance d'intérêt pour ces langues - et les écoliers peuvent même passer une partie de leur baccalauréat en une langue régionale, s'ils le désirent. (5)

NOTES

(1) We may say that *une langue* is the system of expression shared by a people, whereas *le langage* is the abstract idea of language. We talk of *les langues latines* or *les langues orientales* but we would speak of *un langage visuel* or *un langage conventionnel*. Unfortunately English makes no distinction between the two ideas at this level. The second meaning of *un langage* - as we use it in this lesson - is that of particular form of speech, a way of expression which is part of the national language. Here we would talk of *le langage courant, le langage académique,* etc. This lesson - and the next - highlight the different forms of expression within the French language.
Another word having the same meaning as *le langage* in this context, we come across in line 12 - *le parler.*

64th LESSON

Languages and types of speech I

1 As you have noticed until now, the French language is full of riches.

2 You have studied - agreeably, we hope - everyday forms of expression

3 the literary language and that of the media, among others.

4 In France (or in The Hexagon, as it is sometimes called) we also find other regional languages, which are more than dialects

5 in that they have not only a grammar and a vocabulary peculiar to them

6 but also a real literature : we can count Breton, Occitan, Provençal (of which you have had a small sample)

7 not forgetting the language of the Isle of Beauty - Corsican.

8 For several years, there has been a strong renaissance of interest for these languages - and schoolchildren may now take a part of their baccalauréat in a regional language if they so wish.

NOTES (suite)

(2) Mainland France, if looked at quickly, presents the form of a hexagon. *L'Hexagone,* which is *à la mode* in certain forms of discourse, discounts the French overseas departments and territories *(les D.O.M.-T.O.M.).*

(3) *En ce que :* in so far as. *Cette machine est nouvelle en ce qu'elle est entièrement automatique :* This machine is new in that/in so far as it is entirely automatic.
Not to be confused with *en ce* **qui** : As far as...
En ce qui me concerne, j'accepte votre proposition : As far as I'm concerned, I accept your proposition. *En ce qui concerne ma société, j'en suis moins sûr :* As far as my company is concerned, I'm less sure.

(4) *La Corse :* Corsica (also called *l'Ile de Beauté*); *le corse :* the Corsican language. *Un Corse :* a Corsican.

(5) *Le baccalauréat* (abbreviated to *le bac* or *le bachot*) is the secondary-school leaving certificate, taken between the ages of sixteen and eighteen. Children may take a modern-language option in a regional language.

9 Si elles vous intéressent, vous pouvez en apprendre plus long avec les excellentes méthodes ASSIMIL. **(6)**

10 A l'intérieur du français même, on trouve aussi d'autres modes d'expression comme, par exemple, l'argot.

11 Cette "langue verte" était à l'origine, au XVe siècle, le langage des Coquillards - ces voleurs qui portaient la coquille des pèlerins de Saint-Jacques de Compostelle -, **(7) (8)**

12 inventé pour se protéger des intrus. Là-dessus, au fil des siècles, se sont greffés d'autres parlers - ceux des métiers par exemple - **(9)**

13 pour former une façon originale - et crue - de s'exprimer. **(10)**

14 Pour peu que vous flâniez dans certains quartiers de Paname, pardon, de Paris, vous entendrez "jacter" les "titis parisiens" **(11) (12)**

15 et vous n'''entraverez'' (ou comprendrez) pas grand-chose. **(13)**

NOTES (suite)

(6) *Je voudrais en savoir plus long :* I would like to know more about it.
Son visage m'en dit plus long que ses explications : His face tells me more than his explanations.
This is another way of saying *davantage*.

(7) *'La langue verte'* is a synonym for *l'argot*. The idea is that of unripe fruit which has an acid, biting quality.
Une histoire verte : a racy story.

(8) Pilgrims leaving for the shrine of St. John of Compostella (their meeting-place in Paris - la Tour St-Jacques - still stands off the rue de Rivoli) wore cockle-shells in their caps and shawls, which is why scallops are called *des coquilles St-Jacques* (f.). The Coquillards disguised themselves as pilgrims to lure the unwary.

(9) *Voyez-vous cette table ? Posez le colis là-dessus :* Do you see that table? Put the parcel on it.
Là-dessus se sont greffées d'autres langues : i.e. the other languages grafted themselves on to *l'argot*.
Là-dessus also has a temporal meaning of : Thereupon...
Ils ont commencé à parler politique ; là-dessus je me suis énervé : They began talking politics; thereupon I got angry.

9   If the languages interest you, you can learn more with the excellent ASSIMIL methods.

10 Within French itself, we also find other modes of expression like, for example, slang.

11 This 'sharp language' was originally, in the fifteenth century, the speech of the Coquillards - those thieves who wore the shell of the pilgrims of St. John of Compostella,

12 invented to protect themselves from intruders. Down through the centuries other forms of expression grafted themselves therupon - the language of trades for example -

13 to form an original - and unrefined - way of expressing oneself.

14 All you have to do is stroll through certain quarters of Paris and you will hear the native Parisians speaking -

15 and you won't get (or understand) much.

NOTES (suite)

(10) *Cru* means raw or unrefined. *La viande crue :* raw meat; *la vérité toute crue :* the naked truth; *une lumière crue :* a glaring light.
Un cru : a growth, for wines; where the quality of a particular wine depends on which growth the grapes come from. The finest is *le premier grand cru classé.* Since *cru* is also the past participle of the verb to believe, certain wits began declaring that, after certain Bordeaux wines were found to be mixed with wines of different origins and inferior quality, *le premier cru* should mean: at first believed to be...

(11) *Pour peu qu'on l'encourage, il le fera à fond :* All you have to do is to encourage him, and he will do it thoroughly. *Pour peu que* (with the subjunctive): all it needs, all you have to do is... We could also translate our sentence: Should you stroll... etc. We also see *peu* used as the opposite of *très* in line 20.

(12) *Paname* is one of the several slang words for Paris.

(13) In this and the preceding line we see some real Parisian argot. We do not suggest you use it because it would sound comical coming from someone who is not from a certain part of Parisian life (imagine a Frenchman speaking in Cockney rhyming slang: clever, funny, maybe - but out of place). You can still hear *l'argot parisien* in some quarters of Paris, or in the songs of Edith Piaf or Yves Montand.
Jacter : to talk; *entraver :* to understand.
Le "titi parisien", coming from the elliptical Parisian pronunciation of *petit,* is the Parisian-born-and-bred of working class origins, similar to a London cockney.

16 Mais où s'arrête l'argot et où commence le langage populaire ? Beaucoup de mots argotiques sont devenus monnaie courante.

17 Vous entendrez les gens de tous bords parler de leur ''fric'', leur ''boulot'' ou leur ''bagnole'',

18 au lieu de leur argent, leur travail ou leur voiture - ces mots, parmi d'autres, sont passés dans les mœurs.

19 Un grand explicateur de l'argot pense que la langue verte est la première défense des deshérités.

20 Somme toute, c'est une façon peu élégante mais croquante de dépeindre certains côtés d'une société qui se reflète dans une langue parfois trop pure. **(14) (15)**

EN CE QUI CONCERNE L'ARGOT, NOUS VOUS CONSEILLONS DE NE PAS L'UTILISER

EXERCICES

1. Dans cette étude de la langue française vous avez appris, entre autres, le langage familier, le langage de tous les jours. 2. En ce qui concerne l'argot, nous vous conseillons de ne pas l'utiliser. 3. Si vous le désirez, vous pouvez apprendre les langues régionales françaises. 4. Ils ont commencé à parler l'argot ; là-dessus je n'ai rien compris. 5. Expliquez-m'en plus long ; votre projet m'intéresse. 6. Ce quartier est fréquenté par des gens de tous bords. 7. Cette expression est devenue monnaie courante.

16 But where does slang stop and where does popular expression begin? Many slang words have become everyday currency.

17 You will hear people from all walks of life talking of their 'fric', their 'boulot' or their 'bagnole'

18 instead of their money, their work or their car - these words, among others, have passed into common use.

19 A great exponent of slang thinks that the 'sharp language' is the first defence of those with nothing.

20 When all is said and done, it's a not very elegant but crisp way of depicting certain sides of a society which is reflected in a language which is sometimes too pure.

NOTES (suite)

(14) *Somme toute :* when all is said and done (literally the sum of everything). *On a beau se plaindre, somme toute, ce n'était pas si mal :* Although we complained, after all, it wasn't so bad.
It can be placed at the beginning or in the middle of a phrase.

(15) Although we agree that *l'argot* gives a certain spice to French, we do not advise you to use even the popular words we saw here *(fric, bagnole, boulot).* Slang is a question of background, of feeling. After speaking French with a variety of people you may begin to feel when such words are appropriate but, even then, we advise caution. Unless one has a sufficient mastery of the language, one will sound quaint - or worse, vulgar. However, such pious words don't touch the Frenchman in the street and it is worthwhile building up your passive knowledge of these words and expressions if you envisage visiting France, reading certain modern authors (Céline, or Boris Vian, for example) or watching modern films.

EXERCISES: 1. In this study of the French language, you have learned among other things, familiar language, the everyday form of expression. **2.** As far as slang is concerned, we advise you not to use it. **3.** If you so wish, you may learn the French regional languages. **4.** They began speaking slang, thereupon I understood nothing. **5.** Tell me more; your project interests me. **6.** This quarter is frequented by people from all walks of life. **7.** This expression has become common.

Leçon 64

Mettez les mots qui manquent.
Fill in the blanks.

1 . . . . *que* . . . . *à Ménilmontant*,* .

Should you stroll through Ménilmontant,

2 *vous entendrez l'argot. - Qu'est-ce ? - Le* . . . .

de tous les jours.

you will hear slang. - What's that? - Everyday speech.

3 *C'est vulgaire* . . . . ' . . . . *le*

. . . . . . *des voleurs.*

It is vulgar in so far as it was the speech of thieves.

****

SOIXANTE-CINQUIEME (65e) LEÇON

Langues et langages II

1 Hier, nous nous sommes intéressés à l'argot - véritable langage parallèle ; aujourd'hui, nous allons parler d'un autre phénomène

2 - n'en déplaise aux puristes -, celui que l'on appelle le ''franglais'', qui est à la fois événement linguistique et manifestation sociale. **(1) (2)**

NOTES

(1) This expression comes from the verb *déplaire* (to displease) - we see the present subjunctive used as an imperative. *N'en déplaise à...* is used apostrophically to mean: with all due respect to... and is usually spoken when one is about to say something which will shock the person or group in question! *N'en déplaise à Monsieur le député, son projet de loi est futile !:* With all due respect to Mr Député, his Bill is futile! *Je le ferai moi-même, ne vous en déplaise :* I will do it myself if you have no objection.

4 *Ils m'ont dit que le film était mauvais ;* . . . . .

. . . . . , *je l'ai aimé.*

They told me the film was bad, but I enjoyed it after all.

5 *Ces mots* . . . . *dans* . . . .

au quinzième siècle.

Those words had passed into use in the fifteenth century.

**** Ménilmontant : a working-class district in the north-east
of Paris which is considered the home of the* 'titi parisien'.**

Mots qui manquaient :

1. Pour peu - vous flâniez - **2.** - langage **3.** - en ce que c'était - parler -
4. - somme toute - **5.** - étaient passés - les mœurs -.

****

65th LESSON

Languages and types of speech II

1 Yesterday, we took an interest in slang - a real
parallel language; today we are going to speak
about another phenomenon
2 - with due respect to the purists - that which is
called 'franglais', which is both a linguistic event and
a social occurence.

NOTES (suite)

(2) *Une manifestation* is another one of these wonderfully vague
words like *une prestation* or *une intervention* whose comprehen-
sion depends so much on the context. It comes from the verb
manifester (to show, as in a sign). *Les premières manifestations de
cette maladie... :* The first signs of this illness... *Dans le cadre du
Festival de Musique, plusieurs manifestations sont prévues :* Under
the auspices of the Music Festival, several activities are planned
(they may be concerts, workshops, lectures, etc.). So *une
manifestation* is a showing of... whatever the context leads you to
understand.
One immutable meaning, however, is that of a demonstration,
usually of protest. *Les manifestations de rue en mai 1968 :* The
street demonstrations in May 1968.

3 En fait, le "franglais" n'est ni langue ni vraiment langage mais est constitué par un certain nombre d'expressions et mots anglais et américains

4 (qui ne sont pas toujours utilisés à bon escient), qui figurent de plus en plus dans le langage de tous les jours et dans les médias. **(3)**

5 Certains sont des mots dits d'emprunt, c'est-à-dire qu'ils signifient des choses pour lesquelles il n'y a pas de mot français ;

6 c'est ainsi que nous trouverons un smoking, un self, un footing ou un parking usités couramment. **(4) (5)**

7 Dans certains domaines aussi - des sports ou des techniques -, lorsque la France adopte la chose, le Français adopte le mot qui l'accompagne.

8 Si cela fait longtemps que ces mots sont arrivés, ils sont pour ainsi dire "francisés", ainsi les mots *un boulingrin* **(6)**

9 ou *une redingote* ne choqueraient personne ; après tout, la langue française a assez prêté de mots à son tour. **(7)**

NOTES (suite)

(3) Recognise the root-word? Science, i.e., knowledge. Used mainly in the expression *à bon escient* which means with full knowledge, or correctly.
Il dépense son argent à bon escient : He spends his money wisely, knowing what he is doing.
Il ne faut agir qu'à bon escient : You must only act wittingly.

(4) We said that many franglais words were not always used *à bon escient*. Well...
Un smoking : a dinner jacket (tuxedo) or evening suit; *un self :* a self-service restaurant; *un footing :* a run; *un parking :* a car park. As you can see, the original word has some connection with its English counterpart but, somewhere along the way, something happened!

(5) *Usité* has a much narrower meaning than *utilisé*. First of all, it only exists in this participial form, and it applies mainly to use of language. *Cette expression n'est plus usitée :* This expression is no longer in use.

3 In fact 'franglais' is neither a language nor really a form of speech, but is made up of a certain number of English and American words and expressions

4 (which are not always used in the correct way) which appear more and more in everyday speech and in the media.

5 Some are called 'loan words' i.e., they signify things for which there is no French word

6 thus we will find *un smoking, un self, un footing* or *un parking* used commonly.

7 In certain fields also - sports or technologies - when France adopts the thing, French adopts the word that accompanies it.

8 If the words arrived a long time ago, they have been 'Gallicised' so to speak; thus the words *un boulin-grin*

9 or *une redingote* would shock nobody; after all, the French language has lent out enough words in its turn.

NOTES (suite)

(6) *Un boulingrin,* meaning a plot of grass or small lawn, entered French in the seventeenth century as... a bowling green. It is interesting to note, however, that bowl came originally from French!

(7) *Une redingote :* a frock coat was a later, eighteenth century, deformation of a riding coat. There are many such words and following their passage back and forth across the Channel is a fascinating study once one has a knowledge of French.

10 Mais il est des mots de franglais qui sont utilisés par snobisme (tiens...). Quand le mari est dans le marketing, sa femme fait plutôt son shopping que son marché. **(8) (9)**

11 On doit éviter de tels abus et, périodiquement, l'Académie française, voire le gouvernement même, à coups de lois, **(10) (11)**

12 mènent la bataille contre cette prétendue ''invasion'' - qui n'en est pas une en vérité **(12)**

13 car, si certains de ces mots ont fait souche de ce côté de la Manche ou de l'Atlantique, **(13)**

14 il existe bel et bien des équivalents ''bien de chez nous'' pour la plupart de ces intrus. **(14) (15)**

15 Et ne soyons pas xénophobes : une langue s'enrichit au contact de ses voisines. Déjà, au XVIIIᵉ siècle, un auteur français avait écrit **(16)**

NOTES (suite)

(8) Yet another loan word that has taken root. Legend has it that snob comes from English public schools where those pupils who had money but no noble breeding were branded as *S.Nob.* (sine nobilitas, Latin for without nobility). French has adopted the word and, like all foreign adjectives, it is invariable. *Ils sont très snob.* *Le snobisme :* snobbery. When loan words are adopted as verbs, they become part of the first conjugation, e.g., to kidnap: *kidnapper.*

(9) There really seems to be no equivalent for *le marketing.* Perhaps future edicts will impose a proper French word. *Faire du shopping* is a snobbish abomination which should be replaced by *faire son marché* if one is buying food, and *faire des courses* or *des achats* if one is shopping for other things.

(10) Nothing to do with the verb to see, its root is the Latin word *verus* - true. In old-fashioned usage, it was an exclamation similar to: Indeed! Nowadays - sometimes followed by *même* - it means... and even. *Ce texte est difficile, voire impossible à comprendre :* This text is difficult, even impossible, to understand. It can be replaced by *et même.*

(11) Again, our famous *coup.* The expression *à coup de* means, literally, by blows of. *Ils l'ont tuée à coups de couteau :* They stabbed her to death. *Je l'ai cassé à coups de marteau :* I broke it with a hammer The idea of *à coups de* translating the repetition of the action. *On l'a guéri à coups de médicaments :* He was cured by doses of medicine. Our sentence here means the government made several laws to wipe out Franglais.

10 But there are 'franglais' words which are used snobishly (well, well...). When the husband is in marketing, his wife does her 'shopping' rather than her market.

11 Such abuses should be avoided and, periodically, the French Academy, even the government itself, with bursts of laws,

12 leads the battle against this so-called 'invasion' - which is not really one, in fact,

13 for if certain words have settled on this side of the Channel or the Atlantic,

14 there really do exist 'good French' equivalents for most of these interlopers.

15 And let's not be too xenophobic: a language enriches itself by contact with its neighbours. Already, in the eighteenth century, a French author had written

NOTES (suite)

(12) We have already seen the expression *soi-disant. Ce soi-disant intellectuel :* This so-called intellectual. Correctly speaking, only a person can be qualified as *soi-disant* since only a person can 'say of himself'. The correct adjective for a so-called object is *prétendu(e)*. (Remember , the verb *prétendre* is a faux-ami meaning to claim, to insist.) However, in everyday French, *soi-disant* is admitted for objects. We wish to give you the choice.

(13) *Une souche* is a tree stump, complete with roots, which gives us the expression *Dormir comme une souche :* To sleep like a log. *Faire souche :* means to take root and proliferate. *Une famille de vieille souche :* an old-established family. Used with languages, it means that a word settles in a language and gives rise to derivatives. *Ce mot est de souche latine :* This word is of Latin origin, of Latin stock.

(14) *Bel et bien :* well and truly. *Vous le croyiez mort, mais il est bel et bien vivant :* You thought he was dead, but he's well and truly alive. *Je vous ai bel et bien dit de ne plus revenir :* I told you clearly not to come back.

(15) A wonderful Gallicism: *bien de chez nous :* typically French, but it has an affectionate quality. *C'est un petit vin bien de chez nous.* (No translation necessary.)

(16) *Xénophobe* [gzenofob] someone who has a fear of foreigners, who is xenophobic. However, over the past few years, the word has too often been used to express hatred of foreigners - or plain racism. The word is less learned-sounding in French than in English

16 que, entre l'anglais et le français, ''nous établirons, pour chercher l'abondance, un commerce de mots, sans change ni tarif''.

17 Ainsi voit-on que le français est riche de tous ces parlers ''marginaux'' et nous espérons que vous profiterez de cette abondance.

18 Un auteur, candidat à l'un des quarante sièges à l'Académie française, a fait cette confidence a un ami : **(17)**

19 — Si je suis élu, je serai Immortel ; mais si je ne suis pas élu, je n'en mourrai pas !

EXERCICES

1. Cette expression est prétentieuse, voire snob ; il faut l'éviter. **2.** J'étais tellement fatigué que j'ai dormi comme une souche ! **3.** Il ne faut rien prédire qu'à bon escient. **4.** La police a enfoncé la porte à coups de bâtons. **5.** C'est bel et bien mon père qui a conçu ce bâtiment. **6.** S'il ne gagne pas le premier prix, il n'en mourra pas. **7.** Ce soi-disant artiste et ses prétendues œuvres me déplaisent profondément.

Mettez les mots qui manquent.
Fill in the blanks.

1 *Il faut utiliser ces mots* . . . .

These words must be used correctly/in the right place.

2 *Certains sont des* . . . . *d'''* . . . . ''

Some of them are called 'loan words'.

3 . . . . *qu'il* . . . *arrivé.*

He arrived a long time ago/He has been here for a long time.

16 that, between English and French 'we will set up - to seek wealth - a trade of words without exchange transactions or tariffs'.

17 Thus we can see that French is rich from all these 'marginal' forms of expression and we hope that you will take advantage of this wealth.

18 An author who was a candidate for one of the forty seats in the Académie Française, confided this to a friend:

19 — If I am elected, I will be an Immortal, but if I'm not elected, I won't die of it!

NOTES (suite)

(17) *L'Académie française* has forty members who are called *Les Immortels,* so it seems strange that the only way one can enter the Academy is to be elected to a seat left vacant by *un académicien* who dies...

EXERCISES: **1.** This expression is pretentious, even snobbish; it must be avoided. **2.** I was so tired that I slept like a log! **3.** You must predict nothing unless you know. **4.** The police broke down the door with batons. **5.** It really is my father who designed that building. **6.** He won't die if he doesn't win the first prize. **7.** That so-called artist and his so-called works thoroughly displease me.

4 *Ainsi . . . . . - . . qu'on est . . . . ses*

connaissances.

Thus we see that one is rich in one's knowledge.

5 *C'est un mot . . . . !*

[See note 15]

Mots qui manquaient :

1. - à bon escient 2. - mots dits - emprunt 3. Cela fait longtemps - est - 4. - voit-on - riche de - 5. - bien de chez nous.

SOIXANTE-SIXIEME (66e) LEÇON

L'Alsace et La Lorraine

1 Notre tour des régions de France tire à sa fin ; nous allons aujourd'hui vers l'est pour visiter l'Alsace et La Lorraine.

2 Ces deux régions ont été longtemps un symbole patriotique pour le Français moyen :

3 Pendant près d'un siècle, elles ont été l'un des enjeux des terribles guerres franco-allemandes, puis mondiales. **(1)**

4 Annexées à l'Empire allemand en 1871, elles furent à nouveau rattachées à la France en novembre 1918. **(2)**

5 Réoccupées pendant la deuxième guerre, elles durent attendre la Libération de 1944 pour, enfin, être rendues françaises. **(3)**

6 Temps révolus, heureusement ! De nos jours ces deux provinces sont régulièrement envahies par des Allemands, certes, **(4)**

NOTES

(1) We recognize the root word *le jeu* (game, gambling); what is *en jeu* is the stake, *l'enjeu. La survie de la région est en jeu :* The survival of the region is at stake.
Retirer son enjeu : means to withdraw one's stake in a game - or one's involvement in an undertaking.
Il nous a promis de nous aider à créer la société, puis il a retiré son enjeu : He promised to help us set up the company, then he backed down.

(2) The prefix *re-* or *r-* usually means: again (*rappeler, rattraper,* etc.). However, in some verbs the *re-* serves a double function: that of repetition OR that of bringing closer. thus if we say *Le chien s'est enfui, il faut le rattacher,* we mean that the dog must be tied up again; but if we say, for example, that *L'Alsace fut rattachée à la France,* it means, simply, that Alsace was attached - brought closer to, France. *C'était le seul lien qui le rattachait à son passé :* It was the only link that attached him to his past. This is why we must add *à nouveau* to indicate that the incorporation of the province happened again.
Another verb in the same category is *rapprocher* which means to bring closer to. It takes a little practice to distinguish when *re-* really means: again. It helps to memorize our examples.

66th LESSON

Alsace and Lorraine

1   Our tour of the regions of France draws to an end; today we are going east to visit Alsace and Lorraine.
2   These two regions were, for a long time, a patriotic symbol for the average Frenchman:
3   For more than a century, they were one of the stakes of the terrible wars - Franco-German, then world wars.
4   Annexed by the German Empire in 1871, they were re-attached to France in November 1918.
5   Re-occupied during the second World War, they had to wait for the Liberation in 1944 to, at last, be French.
6   Those times are over, fortunately ! Nowadays, these two provinces are regularly invaded by Germans, it is a fact,

NOTES (suite)

(3) The past tense of *devoir*. Be careful with the third person singular of the passé composé: it has two possible meanings. *Il a dû partir, je ne vois pas sa voiture :* He must have left, I can't see his car (i.e. supposition).
Il a dû partir pour un rendez-vous urgent : He had to leave for an important appointment (certainty).

(4) *Pour s'engager dans l'armée, il faut avoir dix-huit ans révolus :* To join the army, you must be eighteen, i.e., have turned eighteen.
Révolu means a period of time completed.
Le temps des guerres est révolu : The days of wars are over.
Ces temps sont révolus : Those days are over.

7   mais des Allemands touristes, souriants et amicaux ; et si l'on garde un mauvais souvenir,

8   cela se traduit plutôt par des boutades, tel ce touriste d'Outre-Rhin qui demanda, à un autochtone, en regardant un ciel gris et nuageux au-dessus de Strasbourg, **(5)**

9   s'il faisait toujours un temps aussi maussade en Alsace ; à quoi la réponse fut : — Pas du tout !

10 Ces nuages sont des emballages vides qui reviennent de chez vous !

11 On y parle français, mais aussi des langues régionales comme l'Elsasser, très influencées par la langue allemande.

12 Strasbourg - capitale de l'Alsace - a une vocation européenne (le Conseil de l'Europe y siège). **(6)**

13 L'Alsace est un pays typique de vignobles et de chasses, d'industries et - vous vous en serez doutés - de gastronomie ! **(7)**

14 La Lorraine, elle, est plus tournée vers l'industrie : mines de fer, de charbon, aciéries.

15 Sans oublier l'art : cristalleries d'une renommée mondiale (Baccarat et St-Louis) et la merveilleuse place Stanislas à Nancy, **(8)**

NOTES (suite)

(5) *Un autochtone :* a native of a particular place, region or country, one born there. *L'afflux des touristes a beaucoup dérangé les autochtones :* The influx of tourists upset the locals very much. One would also say *Il est originaire d'ici.*

(6) *Le siège :* the seat. As in English we say a seat of learning, meaning the centre, so *le siège social* of a company would be its head office. Although we can say *Le Conseil a son siège à Strasbourg;* it is simpler to use the verb *siéger : Le Conseil siège à Strasbourg.* It is also used for a court or tribunal which 'sits'. *La Cour d'Appel siège six fois par an :* The Court of Appeal sits six times a year.

(7) The verb *douter* and its reflexive form sometimes pose problems for learners of French.
Je doute de sa sincérité : I doubt his/her sincerity. The negative is simple: *Je ne doute pas...*
The reflexive form gives us *Il se doutait de quelque chose :* He

7   but by smiling and friendly German tourists; and if there are any bad memories

8   they are translated into jokes, such as the German tourist who, looking at a grey and cloudy sky over Strasbourg, asked a native

9   if the weather was always so dull in Alsace; to which the answer was: — Not at all!

10   Those clouds are just the empty wrappings coming back from your country!

11   French is spoken there, but also regional languages like Elsasser, much influenced by the German language.

12   Strasbourg - capital of Alsace - has a European vocation (The Council of Europe has its headquarters there).

13   Alsace is a typical region of vineyards, hunting, industries and - you won't be surprised - gastronomy!

14   Lorraine is more oriented toward industry: iron and coal mines, steel-works.

15   Without forgetting art: crystal-ware of world renown (Baccarat and St. Louis) and the marvellous Stanislas Square in Nancy,

NOTES (suite)

suspected something was wrong. The negative, too, is regular. Now look as these expressions.
Il est très honnête - Je n'en doute pas : He's very honest - I don't doubt it.
Il est très mécontent - Je m'en doute : He's not very pleased - I suppose he is.
The idiomatic sense of *je m'en doute* is: I suppose, I'm sure.
Be very careful of the letter before *en!*
Notice also these idiomatic uses:
Elle a oublié de le rapporter - Je m'en doutais !: She forgot to bring it back - I thought as much!
La partie la plus intéressante - vous vous en serez doutés - est la fin : The most interesting part - you won't be surprised to hear - is the end.
Pay special attention to the context!

(8) *Une cristallerie :* a crystal works; *de la cristallerie :* crystal-ware. This confusion often occurs with craft-ware. *Une dentellerie :* a lace factory; *de la dentellerie :* lace-ware; *une bijouterie :* a jeweller's shop, or trade; *de la bijouterie :* jewellery.
Make sure whether the noun is singular or collective.

16 qui, à elle seule, ''vaut le voyage'' comme dirait un guide touristique célèbre !

17 Régions au particularisme développé, attachantes et souriantes, l'Alsace et La Lorraine vous attendent !

EXERCICES

1. Je pense qu'elle a dû partir ; il n'y a personne dans son bureau. **2.** Après la guerre, les deux pays se sont rapprochés à nouveau. **3.** Nos vacances tirent à leur fin : pourquoi fait-il un temps si maussade ? **4.** — Je me souviens, qu'en 1914... — Hé, grand-père, ces temps sont révolus ! **5.** Dans toutes les régions de France, la spécialité - vous vous en serez doutés - est la gastronomie. **6.** Cette ville vaut vraiment le voyage ; il y a une splendide cathédrale du XIVᵉ siècle.

Mettez les mots qui manquent.
Fill in the blanks.

1 *Il y a eu un appel urgent ; ils* . . . .

  tout de suite.

  There was an urgent call; they had to leave straight away.

2 *Elle* . . . . *leur bonne volonté.*

  She doesn't doubt their good will.

3 *Notre cheval a perdu ! — Je* . . ' . . . .

  Our horse lost! — I was sure of it.

****

16 which alone 'is worth the journey' as a famous tourist-guide would say!

17 Regions with a highly developed regional identity, engaging and cheerful, Alsace and Lorraine await you!

NOTES (suite)

(9) *Le particularisme :* particularism - the desire of a community or a population to conserve its own identity within a state. We translate it here by: regional identity.

EXERCISES: 1. I think she must have left; there is no-one in her office. **2.** After the war, the two countries moved closer together once more. **3.** Our holidays are drawing to an end: why is the weather so dull? **4.** — I remember, in 1914... — Heh, grandad, times have changed! **5.** In all the regions of France, the speciality - you won't be surprised to hear - is gastronomy. **6.** That town is really worth a journey; there's a splendid fourteenth century cathedral.

4 *Le* . . . . *de l'Europe* . . . . . *à Strasbourg.*

The Council of Europe has its headquarters in Strasbourg.

5 *C'est une région* . . . . *touristique.*

Je . ' . . . . . . *pas, mais c'est trop loin.*

It's a region which is devoted to tourism.

I don't doubt it, but it's too far away.

Mots qui manquaient :

1. - ont dû partir - **2.** - ne doute pas de - **3.** - m'en doutais **4.** - Conseil - siège - **5.** - à vocation - n'en doute -.

****

SOIXANTE-SEPTIEME (67e) LEÇON

La littérature du XXe siècle

1 Dans nos extraits littéraires jusqu'à présent, nous nous sommes cantonnés au XIXe siècle ; le problème, quand on parle des auteurs de notre temps, **(1)**

2 n'est pas qui citer, mais qui omettre ! Va-t-on passer sous silence Anatole France, Paul Claudel, André Gide, Paul Valéry ? **(2)**

3 Qui oserait passer à côté d'un André Malraux ou d'un Jean-Paul Sartre ? **(3)**

4 Non, nous avons tranché ; nous allons vous présenter un auteur qui eut peut-être la plus grande influence sur le roman contemporain. **(4)**

5 C'était un homme maladif, qui passa beaucoup de sa vie sur un lit de malade et qui écrivait l'histoire de sa vie intérieure

6 en essayant d'échapper au temps : Marcel Proust.

7 Sa vaste œuvre ''A la Recherche du Temps Perdu'' fut inspirée par un petit incident, désormais célèbre...

8 — [...] Un jour d'hiver, comme je rentrais à la maison, ma mère, voyant que j'avais froid, me proposa de me faire prendre, contre mon habitude, un peu de thé.

NOTES

By now you will have realised that we have left more and more vocabulary-checking to your own initiative. We hope you have bought a dictionary. We only pick out words that pose special difficulties or those whose etymology may help you to build related words. When reading through this passage of Proust, don't let the words you don't know prevent you from enjoying the passage as a whole.

67th LESSON

The literature of the twentieth century

1 In our literary extracts up to now, we have confined ourselves to the nineteenth century; the problem when speaking of the authors of our time

2 is not who to quote but who to omit! Can we ignore Anatole France, Paul Claudel, André Gide, Paul Valéry?

3 Who would dare bypass an André Malraux or a Jean-Paul Sartre?

4 No, we have decided; we are going to introduce an author who had, perhaps, the greatest influence on the contemporary novel.

5 He was a sickly man, who spent much of his life on a sick-bed and who wrote the story of his interior life,

6 trying to escape time: Marcel Proust.

7 His vast work 'In Search of Lost Time' was inspired by a little incident which is henceforth famous...

8 — One winter's day, as I was returning home, my mother, noticing that I was cold, offered to have me take a little tea, against my habit.

NOTES (suite)

(1) Found especially in Swiss - but also in French - demographic vocabulary, *un canton* is a part of a *département* (or one of the states of the Confederation in Switzerland).
Se cantonner means to limit oneself to this part, especially used in academic language.
Nous allons nous cantonner à cette partie de l'œuvre : We are going to confine ourselves to this part of the work.

(2) The verb *ignorer*, if you remember, means to be unaware of. Our verb to ignore has many possibilities. When we ignore something or someone by not talking about them, the French equivalent is *passer sous silence.*
Vous avez encore eu une contravention ! Passons sous silence l'amende que vous avez eue la semaine dernière !: You've got another parking ticket! Let's not talk about the fine you got last week!

(3) We will not give you any biographical notes about these authors. Why not try reading some of them for yourselves?

(4) *Une tranche :* a slice; *trancher :* to cut into slices.
It also means to make a final decision, to cut short a debate or an argument. *Assez parlé ; tranchons :* We've talked enough; let's decide. *Ils se disputaient depuis des semaines ; j'ai tranché le différend :* They had been arguing for weeks; I settled the quarrel.

Leçon 67

9   Je refusai d'abord et, je ne sais pourquoi, me ravisai. Elle envoya chercher un de ces gâteaux courts et dodus appelés Petites Madeleines, **(5)**

10   qui semblent avoir été moulés dans la valve rainurée d'une coquille St-Jacques.

11   Et bientôt, machinalement, accablé par la morne journée et la perspective d'un triste lendemain,

12   je portai à mes lèvres une cuillerée de thé où j'avais laissé s'amollir un morceau de madeleine. **(6) (7)**

13   Mais à l'instant même où la gorgée mêlée des miettes de gâteau toucha mon palais, je tressaillis, attentif à ce qui se passait d'extraordinaire en moi.

14   Un plaisir délicieux m'avait envahi, isolé, sans la notion de sa cause. Il m'avait aussitôt rendu les vicissitudes de la vie indifférentes,

15   ses désastres inoffensifs, sa brièveté illusoire, de la même façon qu'opère l'amour, en me remplissant d'une essence précieuse **(8)**

16   ou plutôt, cette essence n'était pas en moi, elle était moi.

17   J'avais cessé de me sentir médiocre, contingent, mortel. D'où avait pu venir cette puissante joie ? Je sentais qu'elle était liée au goût du thé et du gâteau,

9   I first of all refused and, I do not know why, changed
    my mind. She sent for one of those short, plump
    cakes called Little Madeleines

10 which seem to have been moulded in the fluted
    valve of a scallop-shell.

11 And soon, mechanically, overwhelmed by the dreary
    day and the prospect of a sad morrow

12 I brought to my lips a spoonful of tea in which I had
    allowed a piece of madeleine to soften.

13 But at the very instant that the mouthful mixed with
    cake-crumbs reached my palate, I quivered, atten-
    tive to the extraordinary thing which was taking
    place within me.

14 A delicious pleasure invaded me, isolated, without
    an idea of a cause. It immediately rendered
    indifferent the vicissitudes of life,

15 its disasters became inoffensive, its brevity was
    illusory, in the same way that love operates, filling
    me with a precious essence

16 or rather, this essence was not in me, it **was** me.

17 I had ceased to feel mediocre, contingent, mortal.
    Whence could have come this powerful joy? I felt
    that it was linked to the taste of the tea and the cake

NOTES (suite)

(5) The root is *l'avis* (m), the opinion. *Se raviser :* to change one's
    opinion, one's mind. In spoken language, we would tend to say
    changer d'avis.

(6) Look at the following constructions:
    un bras - une brassée : an arm - an armful;
    une cuillère - une cuillerée : a spoon - a spoonful;
    une bouche - une bouchée : a mouth - a mouthful of food.
    The word *une gorgée* also means a mouthful, but of liquid; it can
    be *une grande gorgée :* a gulp or *une petite gorgée :* a sip. A
    handful is *une poignée,* literally a fist-full.

(7) The root word is *mou* (feminine *molle*): soft. *S'amollir :* to go soft.
    There is also the verb *ramollir,* which belongs to those verbs
    discussed in Lesson 66 Note 2, and follows the same rules.

(8) Notice the construction: instead of... *de la même façon que
    l'amour opère* we find the more literary... *qu'opère l'amour.*(Cf.
    Lesson 59, Note 15.)

18 mais qu'elle les dépassait infiniment, ne devait pas être de même nature. **(9)**

19 D'où venait-elle ? Que signifait-elle ? Où l'appréhender ? **(10)**

EXERCICES

1. On ne peut pas étudier toute l'œuvre : il faut se cantonner au premier volume. **2.** Après de longs débats, le Tribunal a tranché en faveur de la femme. **3.** J'avais l'intention de partir ce week-end, mais j'ai changé d'avis. **4.** Il a fait de la prison, il vaut mieux passer ça sous silence. **5.** Les enfants avaient tellement soif : ils ont bu leur limonade à grandes gorgées. **6.** Cet argent m'avait rendu la vie plus facile.

Mettez les mots qui manquent.
Fill in the blanks.

1 *Vous avez l'air malade ; j' . . . .*

le médecin.

You look sick; I'll send for the doctor.

2 *Il le fait . . . .*

. . . . mon père.

He does it in the same way my father did.

3 *Je me suis fait mal ; il y avait un clou . . .*

. . . . du mur.

I have hurt myself; there was a nail sticking out of the wall.

4 *Vous êtes . . . . l'essentiel.*

You have gone past the most important point.

6 Let's out of delicacy, leave them while Laurent proposes and while Anne-Marie hesitates lengthily

7 - at least ten seconds - before accepting.

8 Afterwards, there was turmoil in both families. Laurent did not want a religious ceremony,

9 he preferred to get married at the Town Hall, surrounded by his mates, but after a brief interview with his father and his future father-in-law, he changed his mind...

10 Afterwards, they had to choose the date, publish the banns, choose the witnesses, reserve a hall for the party.

11 The choice of her wedding-dress put Anne-Marie into a state - and then they had to choose the wedding-rings...

12 But finally, everything came back into order and D-Day arrived at great pace.

13 Laurent had chosen two friends from university to be his witnesses - and they were much more nervous than him.

14 In the car before leaving for the church, they were asking one another : — Right, we haven't forgotten anything? — No, I've got the telegrams

NOTES (suite)

(9) Not a handsome father but a father-in-law. There is also *la belle-mère* : mother-in-law. Brothers, sisters-in-law follow the same principle.
But the same words are used for step-father and step-mother so we have to be careful. This gives us the following slight complication: *un beau-fils* can mean son-in-law **OR** step-son, so there is another word for the marital relation: *le gendre*. With *belle-fille* (step-daughter or daughter-in-law), the other word is *la bru*, but since this sounds so unpleasant, people tend to avoid it and take a risk of confusing others!

(10) *Une bague :* a ring worn on the finger (although recent times have shown that it can be worn elsewhere!). *Une alliance :* a wedding-ring. *Un anneau* is any other kind of ring.

(11) *Le jour J,* D-Day, the great day.
L'heure H, zero-hour.

(12) The marrying couple choose friends to be their witnesses, *les témoins* (m). There is no actual equivalent of the best man.

(13) *Inquiet :* worried, or nervous. *Nerveux :* means excitable, highly-strung (unless applied medically, where it has the same meaning as in English). The French often talk of *une voiture nerveuse*. The car is not neurotic, just responsive, sporty.

15 — Et moi, j'ai les fleurs et leurs billets d'avion.
Allons-y. Ils démarrèrent en trombe, sifflant la
Marche Nuptiale à tue-tête. **(14)**

16 Ils n'avaient guère fait qu'une centaine de
mètres lorsque Pierre pila. — Qu'est-ce que tu
as ? demanda Alain. — Tu as oublié quelque
chose ?

17 — Oui, répondit Pierre ! On est partis sans lui.

18 Malgré de petits désastres de ce genre, tout se
passa merveilleusement bien. Après les deux
cérémonies, les invités firent une fête qui dura
jusqu'à l'aube,

19 tandis que, discrètement, vers deux heures du
matin, les nouveaux mariés partaient pour leur
lune de miel.

20 Pierre et Alain regardèrent disparaître la voiture. Pierre dit : — Quand je pense à toutes les
femmes qu'il a rendues heureuses !

21 — Mais voyons, répondit Alain. Tu n'es pas
très discret, le jour de leur mariage.

22 — Non, je veux dire toutes les femmes qu'il a
rendues heureuses en épousant Anne-Marie.

EXERCICES

1. Quand il a eu fini ses études, il s'est marié, bien qu'il ne
s'entendît pas très bien avec la belle-famille. 2. Mais il
allait leur rendre visite souvent et, de fil en aiguille, ils ont
oublié leurs disputes. 3. Avant le jour J, la maison était en
branle-bas. 4. Comme vous pouvez le constater, nous
n'avons pas perdu notre temps. 5. Pour ma part, je ne
veux qu'une cérémonie civile. 6. — Tu as les yeux tout
rouges. — Oh là là, j'ai fait une de ces fêtes hier soir !

Mettez les mots qui manquent.
Fill in the blanks.

1 *Quand ils* . . . . . . *choisi la date, ils* . . . .

une salle pour la . . . .

When they had chosen the date, they reserved a hall for the party.

15 — And I've got the flowers and their plane tickets. Let's go. They pulled off like a whirlwind, whistling The Wedding March at full blast.

16 They had hardly gone about a hundred metres when Pierre slammed on the brakes. — What's the matter? asked Alain. — Have you forgotten something?

17 — Yes, answered Pierre, Laurent. We've left without him.

18 Despite some small disasters of this nature, everything went off wonderfully well. After the two ceremonies, the guests partied until dawn

19 whilst, discreetly, around 2.00 a.m., the newly-weds left on their honeymoon.

20 Pierre and Alain watched the car disappear. Pierre said : — When I think of all the women he has made happy!

21 — Oh, come on! replied Alain. You're not very discreet, on their wedding-day.

22 — No, I mean all the women he has made happy by marrying Anne-Marie.

NOTES (suite)

(14) Two expressions connected with *les voitures nerveuses - démarrer en trombe :* to drive off, pull away in a cloud of dust (*une trombe* is a waterspout, *une trombe d'eau :* a cloud-burst) - *piler :* to slam on the brakes (literally the verb means to pound or to grind - *la glace pilée :* crushed ice).

EXERCISES: 1. When he had finished his studies he got married, although he did not get on well with his family-in-law.   **2.** But he often visited them and, gradually, they forgot their arguments.   **3.** Before D-day, the house was in a commotion.   **4.** As you can see, we haven't wasted our time.   **5.** As far as I am concerned, I only want a civil ceremony.   **6.** — Your eyes are all red. — Oh lord, I had such a party last night!

2 *Les* . . . .

. . . . *la voiture.*

The witnesses watched the car disappear.

3 Il y a eu un . . . . - . . . *pendant deux jours puis tout*

   est . . . . *l'* . . . . .

   There was turmoil for two days then everything fell back into order.

4 Il . . ' avait . . . . *que cent mètres quand il*

   . . . . .

   He had scarcely gone a hundred metres when he slammed on the

   brakes.

****

SOIXANTE-NEUVIEME (69e) LEÇON

De la bonne chère (1)

1 Il a beaucoup été question dans ce livre de gastronomie - et ce n'est pas seulement dû à la gourmandise de l'auteur.
2 Dans un pays qui prend parti passionnément pour les idées, et d'habitude celles qui vont à l'encontre des idées du voisin, (2)
3 la cuisine est une façon de réunir femmes et hommes autour d'une table pour oublier, le temps d'un repas, leurs querelles,
4 parce qu'on n'y parle que de ce qu'on a mangé à d'autres repas !
5 Comme disait Brillat-Savarin : La table est le seul endroit où on ne s'ennuie jamais pendant la première heure. (3)

NOTES

(1) *Il aime la bonne chère :* He likes good food. The notion of *la bonne chère* covers all aspects of eating and drinking well. One of the wittiest cookery writers in French - Dr. Edouard de Pomiane - has left us his comprehensive and entertaining *Code de la bonne chère.*

5   *Nous les avons* . . . . . . *de* . . . .

quelque temps.

We lost sight of them some time ago.

Mots qui manquaient :

1. - eurent - retinrent - fête **2**. - témoins regardaient disparaître - **3**. - branle-bas - rentré dans - ordre **4**. - n - guère fait - a pilé **5**. - perdus - vue depuis -.

****

69th LESSON

Of good food

1   There has been a lot of talk in this book about gastronomy - and it is not only due to the greediness of the author.

2   In a country which passionately takes sides for ideas, and usually those which go against the neighbour's ideas,

3   cuisine is a way of gathering women and men around a table to forget, for the space of a meal, their quarrels

4   because one only talks about what one has eaten at other meals!

5   As Brillat-Savarin said: — Table is the only place where one is never bored for the first hour.

NOTES (suite)

(2) *Aller à l'encontre de quelqu'un ou de quelque chose :* to go against. *Ces idées vont à l'encontre de tout ce que nous connaissons déjà :* These ideas go against everything we already know. *Nous n'avons rien à dire à l'encontre de :* We have nothing to say against...

(3) Anthelme Brillat-Savarin (1755-1826). A magistrate who is best known for his witty treatise on gastronomy *La physiologie du Goût.*

6 Etrange coutume. Vous, l'étranger, l'invité d'honneur, vous vous pâmez sur un plat - disons un cassoulet - **(4)**

7 qu'a mijoté votre hôtesse pendant des heures. Vous lui exprimez votre délectation - et elle vous répond : **(6)**

8 — Mouais... mais c'était meilleur la dernière fois ! **(7)**

9 Alors vous sortez de table rassasié avec encore sur le palais ces parfums de rêve,

10 ayant la nette impression que vous êtes toujours passé à côté des meilleurs festins qui aient jamais été !

11 Même la langue est embaumée des odeurs de gourmandise, de cuisine et de gastronomie... **(8)**

NOTES (suite)

(4) Remember that un *étranger* means both foreigner and stranger. The accepted translation of Camus' novel *L'Etranger* is The Outsider.

(5) *Pâmer.* Literally means to faint but it is used in the reflexive to describe an excessive emotion. *Il se pâma de rire :* He swooned with laughter. *Se pâmer sur quelque chose :* to go into raptures over. The verb commonly used for to faint is *s'évanouir*.

(6) *Mijoter* is an idea essential to good cooking. It means to cook for hours, with care and attention. *Les plats mijotés* are much lauded in French cooking.
Used metaphorically, it is similar to the English idiom: to cook something up. *Ces deux-là, je suis certain qu'ils mijotent quelque chose :* I'm certain that those two are cooking something up, hatching a plot.

(7) A phonetic rendition of a hesitant, dubious *oui*.

(8) We beg your indulgence for a few lines. We have cobbled together some of the more common expressions using food as a metaphor. We will attempt to explain some of them below - our English translation opposite simply gives the meanings since, for most, there are no equivalents. (If we did the same thing in reverse, it would take the form of English expressions deriving from sports... or the weather.)
C'est la fin des haricots : That's the end of everything, the last straw; since beans were usually the last thing left in the store-cupboard, when they were gone, that was it!
Les carottes sont cuites : This has the same meaning as the above but the origin is unclear and the only hypotheses scatological!
Il n'est pas dans son assiette : He is uneasy, doesn't feel very well.
Il travaille le week-end pour mettre du beurre dans les épinards : Spinach was a dish for poor people because it grows abundantly

6 A strange custom. You, the foreigner/stranger, the guest of honour, you go into raptures over a dish - let's say a dish of cassoulet -

7 which your hostess has nursed gently on the fire for hours. You express your delight - and she replies:

8 — Ye-e-e-s, but it was better last time!

9 So you leave the table replete, and with the dream-like flavours still on the palate

10 having the clear impression that you have always missed the best feasts that ever were!

11 Even the language is embalmed with smells of 'gourmandise', cuisine and gastronomy...

NOTES (suite)

but, alone, has no gastronomic interest at all. However, put a little butter in it and... well, it's not so bad!

The expression means to supplement one's income, to give a little bit of luxury to something which otherwise would be hard... to swallow!

Je ne sais pas si c'est du lard ou du cochon. Le lard is pig-fat, cheap and filling; *le cochon* provides leaner, more delicate meat. If you don't know whether something is *du lard ou du cochon* you don't know whether it is a risky proposition or a sure-fire thing; whether it's full of promise or likely to fall flat.

Son affaire part en brioche : His business is going very badly - *la brioche,* unlike bread, is soft and flakes away easily.

Nous en parlerons entre la poire et le fromage : We'll talk about it at an opportune moment, when we're comfortable. In the olden days, vegetables were scarce. After the main dish of roast meats, it was usual to eat a pear to clear the palate and prepare oneself for the cheese course, a little like we eat salad today. What better moment to talk about a delicate matter, or to share a secret?

Couper la poire en deux : to compromise, to go fifty-fifty. As we have seen, pears were a great delicacy and, if there was only one left, what else could one do than compromise by cutting it in two?

Une auberge espagnole was considered poor: in order to eat something, you had to bring it yourself. *Leur maison, c'est la vraie auberge espagnole !* If you want to eat in their house, better take the food with you.

La presse fait ses choux gras de cette affaire : The press is feathering its nest with this case.

Rather like spinach, cabbage was also a poor man's dish - but with a little pork-rind in it, it becomes *gras* - and tempting. The *gras* used was usually someone else's however, so *faire ses choux gras* means to make profit, usually at someone else's expense.

Manger la soupe à la grimace : If a husband comes home late and his dinner is burned, all he will get are the sulks and bad temper of his wife - or so the story goes!

Tomber dans les pommes : to faint. To fall into the apples? But apples grow up trees! No, it comes from the verb we saw earlier,

12 Imaginez-vous que tout va mal, vous n'avez pas de travail, c'est la fin des haricots et les carottes sont cuites.

13 Vous n'êtes pas dans votre assiette, mais il ne faut pas s'en faire : on vous trouvera quelque chose pour mettre du beurre dans les épinards.

14 Mais ce qu'on vous propose n'est pas très net, vous n'êtes pas sûr : c'est du lard ou du cochon ? mais vous êtes certain que cette affaire-là va partir en brioche. **(9)**

15 Vous en discutez entre la poire (à moins qu'elle n'ait été coupée en deux) et le fromage et vous voilà reparti.

16 Vous n'êtes pas encore sorti de l'auberge (qu'elle soit espagnole ou autre) ; vous êtes certain que quelqu'un va faire ses choux gras de cette affaire

17 et il ne vous restera qu'à manger de la soupe à la grimace - et vous vous inquiétez tellement que vous finissez par tomber dans les pommes.

18 Nous espérons que vous n'avez pas une indigestion. Pour la faire passer, nous voulons vous raconter notre anecdote préférée à propos de la table.

19 Elle concerne Alexandre Dumas, gastronome avisé - et redoutable mangeur par-dessus le marché. **(10)**

20 On l'invita à un dîner où il ne put manger à sa faim.

21 Tout à coup un silence tomba autour de la table, et un invité dit, comme beaucoup en pareille circonstance : — Tiens, un ange passe.

NOTES (suite)

pâmer, to faint. However, the legend in Normany - where apples are used to make a powerful spirit called *calvados* - has it that, if one sniffs the brew before it has been properly distilled, the odour is so powerful that you will fall into (and because of) the apples. You choose which version you prefer!

12 Imagine that everything is going badly, you have no work, and things are at a bitter end.

13 You don't feel very happy, but you mustn't worry: someone will find you something that will give you that little bit extra.

14 But what you are offered is not very clear, you're not sure whether it's good or disastrous, but you're certain that the business in question will fold.

15 You talk about it at an opportune moment, and you're off again.

16 You're not yet out of the woods; you're certain that someone is going to feather his nest out of this affair

17 and you'll be left to sulk - and you worry so much about it that you pass out.

18 We hope you don't have indigestion. To help it pass, we want to relate our favourite anecdote about table matters.

19 It concerns Alexandre Dumas, a shrewd gastronome - and a redoubtable eater to boot.

20 He was invited to a dinner where he was unable to eat enough to satisfy his hunger.

21 Suddenly a silence fell around the table and a guest said, as do many in such circumstances. — Oh. An angel has passed.

NOTES (suite)

(9) *Net* (fem. *nette*): clear, not blurred.
J'ai la nette impression : I have the clear impression. But if something is not that clear, it is not above suspicion. *Cette histoire n'est pas très nette :* This story doesn't sound right. *Je vais vous dire la vérité ; je voudrais en avoir le cœur net :* I'm going to tell you the truth; I want to have this off my chest.
Net (adverb) by extension, means honestly, outright.
Je vous ai dit tout net que je ne voulais plus vous voir : I told you quite clearly that I didn't want to see you again.
Note the expression *La voiture s'est arrêtée net.*

(10) *Par-dessus le marché :* into the bargain, to boot.
Non seulement il est gourmand, mais c'est un fin cuisinier par-dessus le marché : Not only is he a gourmand (let's not translate this by greedy!), but he's a fine cook into the bargain.

22 Dumas leva sa belle tête léonine et, d'une voix lugubre, lança : — Qu'on le découpe !

23 Bon appétit !

Au lieu des exercices habituels, nous vous donnerons ici huit phrases en français "conventionnel" ; remplacez les mots en gras par des expressions prises dans le texte.

1. Son histoire n'est pas très nette ; je ne sais pas **si c'est honnête ou risqué.**
2. Elle a dansé jusqu'à cinq heures du matin puis elle **s'est évanouie.**
3. J'ai remboursé une partie, mais nous ne sommes pas **tirés d'affaire.**
4. Qu'est-ce qui lui arrive ? Il ne me semble pas être **à l'aise.**

****

SOIXANTE-DIXIEME (70e) LEÇON

Bon voyage !

1 Tout n'a qu'un temps - et nous voilà à la dernière leçon. Si nous pouvons nous permettre de remanier une phrase célèbre,

2 nous avons gagné la bataille, pas la guerre !

3 Effectivement, nous avons vaincu l'accord du participe passé et nous nous sommes tirés d'affaire avec le passé simple et le passé antérieur. **(1)**

NOTES

(1) *Il avait de gros problèmes de santé, mais il est hors d'affaire maintenant :* He had bad health problems, but he's out of danger now.

L'affaire here refers to a difficult situation. To get out of such a situation: se tirer d'affaire.

Cela allait assez mal il y a quelque temps, mais nous avons pu nous

22 Dumas lifted his handsome lion-like head and, in a
    lugubrious voice, said: Let it be carved up!
23 Bon appétit! (in French in the text).

---

5. Vous ne pouvez pas vous décider ? **Faites donc un
    compromis !**
6. Jean travaille beaucoup mais c'est son associé qui en
    tire profit.
7. Cela n'a pas marché et j'ai eu droit **aux reproches** de
    mes collègues.
8. L'exercice est amusant, et nous apprenons le français,
    qui plus est !

Réponses

1. si c'est du lard ou du cochon. 2. est tombée dans les pommes. 3.
sortis de l'auberge. 4. bien dans son assiette. 5. Coupez la poire en
deux ! 6. fait ses choux gras. 7. à la soupe à la grimace. 8. par-dessus le
marché !

****

70th LESSON

Bon voyage !

1 All good things come to end - and here we are at
   the last lesson. If we may allow ourselves to adapt a
   famous phrase
2 we have won the battle but not the war!
3 Indeed, we won against the agreement of the past
   participle, and we got out of difficulties with the
   passé simple and the *passé antérieur*.

NOTES (suite)

tirer d'affaire : Things were going badly some time ago, but we
were able to get out of our difficulties.
Note the idioms:
Ne vous inquiétez pas pour le directeur ; j'en fais mon affaire : Don't
worry about the manager; I'll take care of him
and *N'en faites pas toute une affaire :* Don't make an issue out of it.

4 La petite escarmouche avec le participe présent s'est bien passée (on peut passer sous silence la rixe avec les adjectifs),

5 et nous avons sagement contourné les embuscades tendues par l'imparfait du subjonctif.

6 Mais, sérieusement, apprendre une langue n'est point une série de batailles ; il y a des difficultés qu'il faut surmonter, certes,

7 mais cela ne fait qu'ajouter à notre plaisir quand nous pouvons lire des pages d'Hugo ou de Proust

8 en savourant les nuances, les finesses, les richesses de leur langage et de leur pensée.

9 Vous avez approfondi vos connaissances non seulement de la grammaire et de la syntaxe,

10 mais surtout de ce que représente une langue : le pays qui l'a bercée et les gens qui la parlent, (2)

11 et n'est-ce pas le but de toute étude linguistique

12 de pouvoir communiquer avec d'autres ? D'autant que les Français aiment à parler et admirent celui qui s'exprime bien. (3)

13 D'après l'avis d'un éminent Anglais, si Dieu redescendait sur terre, tous les peuples se mettraient à genoux,

14 excepté les Français, qui diraient : — Alors, vous êtes là ? Il était grand temps ! On va pouvoir discuter un peu !

15 Ne mettez pas ce livre de côté ; relisez-le un peu tous les jours,

16 mais nous espérons que vous vous sentez prêts à lire des romans, des journaux en français,

---

NOTES (suite)

(2) *Un berceau :* a cradle. It may be used metaphorically, meaning a place which nurtured - the French often say:

4 The little skirmish with the present participle went off well (we can ignore the scuffle with the adjectives)

5 and we wisely went around the ambushes laid by the imperfect subjunctive.

6 But, seriously, learning a language is not at all a series of battles; there are difficulties which must be overcome, of course,

7 but that only adds to our pleasure when we are able to read pages of Hugo or Proust,

8 savouring the shades of meaning, the fine points and the richness of their language and their thought.

9 You have not only deepened your knowledge of grammar and syntax

10 but above all, of what a language represents: the country that nurtured it and the people who speak it

11 and is that not the aim of any linguistic study,

12 to be able to communicate with others? Especially since the French like to talk, and admire the person who expresses himself well.

13 According to the opinion of an eminent Englishman, if God came back down to earth, all peoples would kneel down

14 except for the French who would say - So, there you are? It was high time! Now we can have a little chat!

15 Don't put this book aside; re-read it a little every day

16 but we hope you feel ready to read novels and newspapers in French

NOTES (suite)

Le Pays de Loire est le berceau de la langue française : The Loire region is the home of the French language.
The verb *bercer* (literally, to rock a cradle) means also to nurture.
Une berceuse : a lullaby.

(3) The verb *aimer* can be constructed in two ways when followed by the dependent infinitive. *Il aime parler* or *Il aime à parler.* The first form is the more usual, the second more literary. (The construction with *à* would never be used with an infinitive beginning with *a-,* to avoid a hiatus.)
Il aime agir : He likes to act.
It is very important to learn the postpositions, which is why we recommend that you re-read this book as often as possible so that you assimilate the whole construction of a verb naturally.

17 à écouter la radio, à aller voir des films, à voyager - et ce n'est pas uniquement en France que cette langue vous sera utile - elle est utilisée

18 en Suisse, en Belgique, au Québec et Montréal, dans certains pays d'Afrique,

19 ainsi que partout où se trouvent les gens qui aiment l'esprit, les discussions, la culture - même la cuisine -,

20 et dont vous faites désormais partie grâce à votre bonne pratique du français.

EXERCICES

1. Pour bien réussir, il faut savoir contourner les problèmes. **2.** Tu t'occupes des valises ; quant à la douane, j'en fais mon affaire. **3.** C'est le pays qui m'a bercé. **4.** Il faut surmonter quelques difficultés, mais ça ne fait qu'ajouter au plaisir. **5.** N'est-ce pas la raison pour laquelle vous étudiez ce livre ? **6.** D'après l'avis d'un collègue, je dirais que les Français aiment à parler.

Mettez les mots qui manquent.
Fill in the blanks.

1 *Il . . . . ce texte ; il est trop long.*

We would have to adapt this text; it is too long.

2 *. . . . . conduire . 'est . . . . . évident !*

Learning to drive is not at all obvious.

3 *Ils avaient de gros ennuis avec la police mais nous . . . . .*

. . les . . . . ' . . . .

They had bad problems with the police but we were able to get

them out of their difficulties.

17 to listen to the radio, to go and see films, to travel - and it's not just in France that this language will be useful to you - it is used

18 in Switzerland, in Belgium, in Quebec and Montreal, in certain countries in Africa

19 as well as everywhere you find people who like wit, discussions, art - even cooking

20 and whom you are henceforth a part of, thanks to your good 'pratique du français'.

IL FAUT SURMONTER QUELQUES DIFFICULTÉS. MAIS ÇA NE FAIT QU'AJOUTER AU PLAISIR

EXERCISES: 1. To succeed properly, you must know how to go round problems.   **2.** You take care of the cases; as for the Customs, I'll deal with them.   **3.** It's the region/country where I was born and bred.   **4.** You have to get over certain difficulties but that only adds to the pleasure.   **5.** Isn't that the reason for which you are studying this book?   **6.** According to the opinion of a colleague, I would say that the French like to talk.

4   J' . . . . .   lire cet auteur, ...   les

. . . .   et les   . . . .   de son style.

I like to read this author, savouring the shades of meaning and the

finer points of his style.

5   . . . . . ' . . . ' . . . . !

All good things come to an end!

Mots qui manquaient :

1. - faudrait remanier - **2.** Apprendre à - n - point - **3.** - avons pu - tirer d'affaire **4.** - aime à - en savourant - nuances - finesses - **5.** Tout n'a qu'un temps.

IRREGULAR VERBS

The tenses not indicated are regular. Ex.: *Imperfect,* j'allais, tu allais, etc.

The past tense is formed by using *avoir.*

I

Aller *(to go)*
Indicatif présent: je vais, tu vas, il va, nous allons, vous allez, ils vont.
Futur: j'irai, tu iras, il ira, nous irons, vous irez, ils iront.
Conditionnel: j'irais, tu irais, il irait, nous irions, vous iriez, ils iraient.
Subjonctif présent: que j'aille, que tu ailles, qu'il aille, que nous allions, que vous alliez, qu'ils aillent.
Impératif: va, allons, allez.
Part. passé: allé - *Part. prés.:* allant.

Envoyer *(to send)*
Ind. prés.: j'envoie, tu envoies, il envoie, nous envoyons, vous envoyez, ils envoient.
Futur: j'enverrai, tu enverras, il enverra, nous enverrons, vous enverrez, ils enverront.
Condit.: j'enverrais, tu enverrais, il enverrait, nous enverrions, vous enverriez, ils enverraient.
Subj. prés.: que j'envoie, que tu envoies, qu'il envoie, que nous envoyions, que vous envoyiez, qu'ils envoient.
Part. passé: envoyé - *Part. prés.:* envoyant.

II

Apprendre *(to learn) - voir prendre*

Atteindre *(to reach) - voir peindre*

Battre *(to beat)*
Ind. prés.: je bats, tu bats, il bat, nous battons, vous battez, ils battent.

Boire *(to drink)*
Ind. prés.: je bois, tu bois, il boit, nous buvons, vous buvez, ils boivent.
Imparfait: je buvais, tu buvais, il buvait, nous buvions, vous buviez, ils buvaient.
Futur: je boirai, tu boiras, il boira, nous boirons, vous boirez, ils boiront.

Condit.: je boirais, tu boirais, il boirait, nous boirions, vous boiriez, ils boiraient.
Subj. prés.: que je boive, que tu boives, qu'il boive, que nous buvions, que vous buviez, qu'ils boivent.
Impératif: bois, buvons, buvez.
Part. passé: bu - *Part. prés.:* buvant.

Comprendre *(to understand) - voir prendre*

Conduire *(to conduct, to drive, to lead)*
Ind. prés.: je conduis, tu conduis, il conduit, nous conduisons, vous conduisez, ils conduisent.
Imparf.: je conduisais, tu conduisais, il conduisait, nous conduisions, vous conduisiez, ils conduisaient.
Futur: je conduirai, tu conduiras, etc.
Condit.: je conduirais, tu conduirais, etc.
Subj. prés.: que je conduise, que tu conduises, etc.
Part. passé: conduit - *Part. prés.:* conduisant.

Connaître *(to know, be acquainted with)*
Ind. prés.: je connais, tu connais, il connaît, nous connaissons, vous connaissez, ils connaissent.
Imparf.: je connaissais, tu connaissais, il connaissait, nous connaissions, vous connaissiez, ils connaissaient.
Subj. prés.: que je connaisse, que tu connaisses, qu'il connaisse, que nous connaissions, que vous connaissiez, qu'ils connaissent.
Part. passé: connu - *Part. prés.:* connaissant.

Construire *(to construct, to build) - voir conduire*

Coudre *(to sew)*
Ind. prés.: je couds, tu couds, il coud, nous cousons, vous cousez, ils cousent.
Imparf.: je cousais, tu cousais, etc.
Subj. prés.: que je couse, que tu couses, etc.
Part. passé: cousu - *Part. prés.:* cousant.

Craindre *(to fear)*
Ind. prés.: je crains, tu crains, il craint, nous craignons vous craignez, ils craignent.
Imparf.: je craignais, tu craignais, etc.
Subj. prés.: que je craigne, que tu craignes, etc.
Part. passé: craint - *Part. prés.:* craignant.

Croire *(to believe)*
Ind. prés.: je crois, tu crois, il croit, nous croyons, vous croyez, ils croient.
Imparf.: je croyais, tu croyais, il croyait, nous croyions, vous croyiez, ils croyaient.
Futur: je croirai, tu croiras, il croira, etc.
Condit.: je croirais, tu croirais, etc.
Subj. prés.: que je croie, que tu croies, qu'il croie, que nous croyions, que vous croyiez, qu'ils croient.
Impératif: crois, croyons, croyez.
Part. passé: cru - *Part. prés.:* croyant.

Croître *(to grow)* [intransitive]
Ind. prés.: je croîs, tu croîs, il croît, nous croissons, vous croissez, ils croissent.
Imparf.: je croissais, tu croissais, etc.
Subj. prés.: que je croisse, etc.
Part. passé: crû - *Part. prés.:* croissant.

Détruire *(to destroy)* - *voir conduire*

Dire *(to say, to tell)*
Ind. prés.: je dis, tu dis, il dit, nous disons, vous dites, ils disent.
Imparf.: je disais, tu disais, il disait, nous disions, vous disiez, ils disaient.
Futur: je dirai, tu diras, il dira, nous dirons, vous direz, ils diront.
Condit.: je dirais, tu dirais, il dirait, nous dirions, vous diriez, ils diraient.
Subj. prés.: que je dise, que tu dises, qu'il dise, que nous disions, que vous disiez, qu'ils disent.
Impératif: dis, disons, dites.
Part. passé: dit - *Part. prés.:* disant.

Ecrire *(to write)*
Ind. prés.: j'écris, tu écris, il écrit, nous écrivons, vous écrivez, ils écrivent.
Imparf.: j'écrivais, tu écrivais, il écrivait, nous écrivions, vous écriviez, ils écrivaient.
Futur: j'écrirai, tu écriras, il écrira, nous écrirons, vous écrirez, ils écriront.
Condit.: j'écrirais, tu écrirais, il écrirait, nous écririons, vous écririez, ils écriraient.

Subj. prés.: que j'écrive, que tu écrives, qu'il écrive, que nous écrivions, que vous écriviez, qu'ils écrivent.
Impératif: écris, écrivons, écrivez.
Part. passé: écrit – *Part. prés.:* écrivant.

Eteindre *(to extinguish)* – *voir peindre*

Faire *(to do, to make)*
Ind. prés.: je fais, tu fais, il fait, nous faisons, vous faites, ils font.
Imparf.: je faisais, tu faisais, il faisait, nous faisions, vous faisiez, ils faisaient.
Futur: je ferai, tu feras, il fera, nous ferons, vous ferez, ils feront.
Condit.: je ferais, tu ferais, il ferait, nous ferions, vous feriez, ils feraient.
Subj. prés.: que je fasse, que tu fasses, qu'il fasse, que nous fassions, que vous fassiez, qu'ils fassent.
Impératif: fais, faisons, faites.
Part. passé: fait – *Part. prés.:* faisant.

Frire *(to fry) (used only in these forms)*
Ind. prés.: je fris, tu fris, il frit.
Futur: je frirai, tu friras, il frira, nous frirons, vous frirez, ils friront.
Part. passé: frit.
(in the other tenses, faire frire *is used instead of* frire*).*

Instruire *(to instruct)* – *voir conduire*

Joindre *(to join)*
Ind. prés.: je joins, tu joins, il joint, nous joignons, vous joignez, ils joignent.
Imparf.: je joignais, etc.
Futur: je joindrai, tu joindras, etc.
Condit.: je joindrais, tu joindrais, etc.
Subj. prés.: que je joigne, etc.
Part. passé: joint – *Part. prés.:* joignant.

Lire *(to read)*
Ind. prés.: je lis, tu lis, il lit, nous lisons, vous lisez, ils lisent.
Imparf.: je lisais, tu lisais, il lisait, nous lisions, vous lisiez, ils lisaient.
Futur: je lirai, tu liras, il lira, nous lirons, vous lirez, ils liront.

Condit.: je lirais, tu lirais, il lirait, nous lirions, vous liriez, ils liraient.
Subj. prés.: que je lise, que tu lises, qu'il lise, que nous lisions, que vous lisiez, qu'ils lisent.
Impératif: lis, lisons, lisez.
Part. passé: lu - *Part. prés.:* lisant.

Mettre *(to put)*
Ind. prés.: je mets, tu mets, il met, nous mettons, vous mettez, ils mettent.
Imparf.: je mettais, tu mettais, il mettait, nous mettions, vous mettiez, ils mettaient.
Futur: je mettrai, tu mettras, etc.
Condit.: je mettrais, tu mettrais, etc.
Subj. prés.: que je mette, que tu mettes, qu'il mette, que nous mettions, que vous mettiez, qu'ils mettent.
Impératif: mets, mettons, mettez.
Part. passé: mis - *Part. prés.:* mettant.

Naître *(to be born)*
Ind. prés.: je nais, tu nais, il naît, nous naissons, vous naissez, ils naissent.
Imparf.: je naissais, tu naissais, etc.
Subj. prés.: que je naisse, que tu naisses, etc.
Part. passé: né - *Part. prés.:* naissant.

Paraître *(to appear, to seem)* - *voir connaître*

Peindre *(to paint)*
Ind. prés.: je peins, tu peins, il peint, nous peignons, vous peignez, ils peignent.
Imparf.: je peignais, tu peignais, il peignait, nous peignions, vous peigniez, ils peignaient.
Subj. prés.: que je peigne, que tu peignes, etc.
Part. passé: peint - *Part. prés.:* peignant.

Permettre *(to allow)* - *voir mettre*

Pleindre *(to pity)* - **Se plaindre** *(to complain)*
- *voir craindre*
Plaire *(to please)*
Ind. prés.: je plais, tu plais, il plaît, nous plaisons, vous plaisez, ils plaisent.
Imparf.: je plaisais, tu plaisais, il plaisait, nous plaisions, vous plaisiez, ils plaisaient.

Subj. prés.: que je plaise, que tu plaises, qu'il plaise, que nous plaisions, que vous plaisiez, qu'ils plaisent;
Part. passé: plu - *Part. prés.:* plaisant.

Prendre *(to take)*
Ind. prés.: je prends, tu prends, il prend, nous prenons, vous prenez, ils prennent.
Imparf.: je prenais, tu prenais, il prenait, nous prenions, vous preniez, ils prenaient.
Subj. prés.: que je prenne, que tu prennes, qu'il prenne, que nous prenions, que vous preniez, qu'ils prennent.
Impératif: prends, prenons, prenez.
Part. passé: pris - *Part. prés.:* prenant.

Produire *(to produce) - voir conduire*

Promettre *(to promise) - voir mettre*

Remettre *(to put back or to hand over) - voir mettre*

Rire *(to laugh)*
Ind. prés.: je ris, tu ris, il rit, nous rions, vous riez, ils rient.
Imparf.: je riais, tu riais, il riait, nous riions, vous riiez, ils riaient.
Futur: je rirai, tu riras, etc.
Condit.: je rirais, tu rirais, etc.
Subj. prés.: que je rie, que tu ries, qu'il rie, que nous riions, que vous riiez, qu'ils rient.
Impératif: ris, rions, riez.
Part. passé: ri - *Part. prés.:* riant.

Suivre *(to follow)*
Ind. prés.: je suis, tu suis, il suit, nous suivons, vous suivez, ils suivent.
Imparf.: je suivais, tu suivais, il suivait, nous suivions, vous suiviez, ils suivaient.
Sub. prés.: que je suive, que tu suives, qu'il suive, que nous suivions, que vous suiviez, qu'ils suivent.
Impératif: suis, suivons, suivez.
Part. passé: suivi - *Part. prés.:* suivant.

Surprendre *(to surprise) - voir prendre*

Se taire *(to keep silent, to shut up) - voir plaire*

Vivre *(to live)*
Ind. prés.: je vis, tu vis, il vit, nous vivons, vous vivez, ils vivent.
Imparf.: je vivais, tu vivais, il vivait, nous vivions, vous viviez, ils vivaient.
Subj. prés.: que je vive, que tu vives, qu'il vive, que nous vivions, que vous viviez, qu'ils vivent.
Impératif: vis, vivons, vivez.
Part. passé: vécu - *Part. prés.:* vivant.

III

Acquérir *(to acquire)*
Ind. prés.: j'acquiers, tu acquiers, il acquiert, nous acquérons, vous acquérez, ils acquièrent.
Imparf.: j'acquérais, tu acquérais, il acquérait, nous acquérions, etc.
Futur: j'acquerrai, tu acquerras, il acquerra, nous acquerrons, etc.
Condit.: j'acquerrais, tu acquerrais, il acquerrait, nous acquerrions, etc.
Subj. prés.: que j'acquière, que tu acquières, qu'il acquière, que nous acquérions, etc.
Part. passé: acquis - *Part. prés.:* acquérant.

Bouillir *(to boil)*
Ind. prés.: je bous, tu bous, il bout, nous bouillons, vous bouillez, ils bouillent.
Imparf.: je bouillais, etc.
Subj. prés.: que je bouille, que tu bouilles, etc.
Part. prés.: bouillant.

Conquérir *(to conquer)* - *voir acquérir*

Courir *(to run)*
Ind. prés.: je cours, tu cours, il court, nous courons, vous courez, ils courent.
Imparf.: je courais, etc.
Futur: je courrai, tu courras, il courra, nous courrons, etc.
Condit.: je courrais, tu courrais, il courrait, nous courrions, etc.
Part. passé: couru.
Subj. prés.: que je coure, etc.
Part. prés.: courant.

Couvrir *(to cover)* - *voir ouvrir*

Cueillir *(to gather, to pluck)*
Ind. prés.: je cueille, etc.
Imparf.: je cueillais, etc.
Futur: je cueillerai, etc.
Condit.: je cueillerais, etc.
Subj. prés.: que je cueille, etc.
Part. prés.: cueillant.

Découvrir *(to discover)* - *voir couvrir*

Dormir *(to sleep)*
Ind. prés.: je dors, tu dors, il dort, nous dormons, vous dormez, ils dorment.
Imparf.: je dormais, etc.
Subj. prés.: que je dorme, etc.
Part. prés.: dormant.

Fuir *(to flee, to shun)*
Ind. prés.: je fuis, tu fuis, il fuit, nous fuyons, vous fuyez, ils fuient.
Imparf.: je fuyais, etc.
Subj. prés.: que je fuie, que tu fuies, qu'il fuie, que nous fuyions, que vous fuyiez, qu'ils fuient.
Part. passé: fui - *Part. prés.:* fuyant.

Mentir *(to lie, tell a lie)*
Ind. prés.: je mens, tu mens, il ment, nous mentons, vous mentez, ils mentent.
Imparf.: je mentais, etc.
Subj. prés.: que je mente, que tu mentes, qu'il mente, que nous mentions, que vous mentiez, qu'ils mentent.

Mourir *(to die)*
Ind. prés.: je meurs, tu meurs, il meurt, nous mourons, vous mourez, ils meurent.
Imparf.: je mourais, etc.
Futur: je mourrai, tu mourras, etc.
Condit.: je mourrais, tu mourrais, etc.
Subj. prés.: que je meure, que tu meures, qu'il meure, que nous mourions, que vous mouriez, qu'ils meurent.
Part. passé: mort - *Part. prés.:* mourant.

Offrir *(to offer)*
Ind. prés.: j'offre, etc.
Imparf.: j'offrais, etc.
Subj. prés.: que j'offre, etc.
Part. passé: offert - *Part. prés.:* offrant.

Ouvrir *(to open)* - *voir offrir*

Partir *(to leave, go away)* - *voir mentir*

Repentir (se) *(to repent)* - *voir mentir*

Secourir *(to succour)* - *voir courir*

Sentir *(to feel or to smell)* - *voir mentir*

Servir *(to serve)* .
Ind. prés.: je sers, tu sers, il sert, nous servons, vous servez, ils servent.
Imparf.: je servais, tu servais, etc.
Impératif: sers, servons, servez.
Part. passé: servi - *Part. prés.:* servant.

Souffrir *(to suffer)* - *voir offrir*

Tenir *(to hold)*
Ind. prés.: je tiens, tu tiens, il tient, nous tenons, vous tenez, ils tiennent.
Imparf.: je tenais, etc.
Futur: je tiendrai, tu tiendras, il tiendra, etc.
Condit.: je tiendrais, tu tiendrais, il tiendrait, etc.
Subj. prés.: que je tienne, que tu tiennes, qu'il tienne, que nous tenions, que vous teniez, qu'ils tiennent.
Impératif: tiens, tenons, tenez.
Part. passé: tenu - *Part. prés.:* tenant.

Venir *(to come)* - *voir tenir*

IV

Asseoir (s') *(to sit down)*
Ind. prés.: je m'assieds, tu t'assieds, il s'assied, nous nous asseyons, vous vous asseyez, ils s'asseyent.
Imparf.: je m'asseyais, etc.
Futur: je m'assiérai, etc.
Condit.: je m'assiérais, etc.
Subj. prés.: que je m'asseye, etc.

Impératif: assieds-toi, asseyons-nous, asseyez-vous.
Partic. passé: assis - *Part. prés.:* s'asseyant.

Devoir *(to owe, or to have to/must)*
Ind. prés.: je dois, tu dois, il doit, nous devons, vous devez, ils doivent.
Imparf.: je devais, tu devais, il devait, nous devions, etc.
Subj. prés.: que je doive, que tu doives, qu'il doive, que nous devions, que vous deviez, qu'ils doivent.
Part. passé: dû - *Part. prés.:* devant.

Falloir *(to be necessary, must) (impersonal)*
Ind. prés.: il faut.
Imparfait: il fallait.
Futur: il faudra.
Condit.: il faudrait.
Subj. prés.: qu'il faille.
Part. passé: il a fallu.

Pleuvoir *(to rain) (semi-impersonal)*
Ind. prés.: il pleut, ils pleuvent.
Imparf.: il pleuvait, ils pleuvaient.
Futur: il pleuvra, ils pleuvront.
Condit.: il pleuvrait, ils pleuvraient.
Subj. prés.: qu'il pleuve, qu'ils pleuvent.
Part. passé: plu. - *Part. prés.:* pleuvant.

Pouvoir *(to be able to, can or may)*
Ind. prés.: je peux, tu peux, il peut, nous pouvons, vous pouvez, ils peuvent.
Futur: je pourrai, tu pourras, il pourra, nous pourrons, vous pourrez, ils pourront.
Condit.: je pourrais, tu pourrais, il pourrait, nous pourrions, vous pourriez, ils pourraient.
Subj. prés.: que je puisse, que tu puisses, qu'il puisse, que nous puissions, que vous puissiez, qu'ils puissent.
Part. passé: pu - *Part. prés.:* pouvant.

Savoir *(to know)*
Ind. prés.: je sais, tu sais, il sait, nous savons, vous savez, ils savent.
Futur: je saurai, tu sauras, il saura, nous saurons, vous saurez, ils sauront.
Condit.: je saurais, tu saurais, il saurait, nous saurions, vous sauriez, ils sauraient.
Subj. prés.: que je sache, que tu saches, qu'il sache, que